MW01670933

Transfer Pricing Developments Around the World 2018

Transfer Pricing Developments Around the World 2018

Edited by

Michael Lang
Alfred Storck
Raffaele Petruzzi

Wolters Kluwer

Published by:
Kluwer Law International B.V.
PO Box 316
2400 AH Alphen aan den Rijn
The Netherlands
E-mail: international-sales@wolterskluwer.com
Website: lrus.wolterskluwer.com

Sold and distributed in North, Central and South America by:
Wolters Kluwer Legal & Regulatory U.S.
7201 McKinney Circle
Frederick, MD 21704
United States of America
Email: customer.service@wolterskluwer.com

Sold and distributed in all other countries by:
Air Business Subscriptions
Rockwood House
Haywards Heath
West Sussex
RH16 3DH
United Kingdom
Email: international-customerservice@wolterskluwer.com

Printed on acid-free paper.

ISBN 978-90-411-9564-7

e-Book: ISBN 978-90-411-9565-4
web-PDF: ISBN 978-90-411-9566-1

© 2018 Michael Lang, Alfred Storck & Raffaele Petruzzi

All rights reserved. No part of this publication may be reproduced, stored in a retrieval system, or transmitted in any form or by any means, electronic, mechanical, photocopying, recording, or otherwise, without written permission from the publisher.

Permission to use this content must be obtained from the copyright owner. More information can be found at: lrus.wolterskluwer.com/policies/permissions-reprints-and-licensing

Printed in the United Kingdom.

FSC
MIX
FSC® C103993

Editors

Prof. Dr. DDr. h.c. Michael Lang is the head of the Institute for Austrian and International Tax Law of WU (Vienna University of Economics and Business) and Academic Director of both the LLM Program in International Tax Law and the Doctoral Program in International Business Taxation (DIBT) of this university. He is the president of the Austrian Branch of the International Fiscal Association (IFA) and has been visiting professor at Georgetown University, New York University, Sorbonne, Bocconi, Peking University (PKU), University of New South Wales (Sydney), and others.

Prof. Dr. Alfred Storck is co-chair of the board of directors of the WU Transfer Pricing Center at the Institute for Austrian and International Tax Law at Vienna University of Economics and Business (WU) and, since April 2009, has been a visiting professor at the same Institute. The focus of his research and teaching activities are international business taxation and transfer pricing. From 2009 until January 2015, Alfred Storck was teaching as Honorary Professor for Company Taxation and Managerial Finance at the Institute of Accounting, Controlling and Auditing (ACA) at the University of St. Gallen, Switzerland. Before his activities at both universities, Alfred Storck held various executive positions in a large multinational company headquartered in Switzerland. Alfred Storck is acting as co-editor of the journal "Transfer Pricing International" and is appointed as arbitrator in transfer pricing disputes.

Dr. Raffaele Petruzzi, LLM, is managing director of the WU Transfer Pricing Center at the Institute for Austrian and International Tax Law at WU (Vienna University of Economics and Business) and an international tax advisor specializing in international corporate taxation and transfer pricing at L&P—Ludovici Piccone & Partners, Milan (Italy), as well as providing transfer pricing advisory at L&P Global, Vienna (Austria). Since 2007, Raffaele has gained extensive experience in dealing with topics related to international corporate taxation and transfer pricing from both a practical perspective (by working in different countries within international advisory firms and in the tax department of a multinational) and from an academic perspective.

Contributors

Giammarco Cottani heads the Transfer Pricing practice at the tax and law firm "Ludovici and Partners." In his role, Giammarco Cottani has gained substantial expertise in the area of dispute prevention and dispute resolution measures as well in providing assistance in complex audits of large MNE groups. Until August 2015, he acted as Advisor on International Tax to the Central Assessment Director of Italy Revenue Agency. In this role, he focused on international tax issues related to large multinational groups and SMEs with a specific focus on transfer pricing issues. He was one of the delegates for Italy involved in the BEPS project. From 2009 to 2011, he worked as a Transfer Pricing Advisor in the Transfer Pricing Unit of the OECD where he was involved in the introduction of the new Chapter IX of the OECD Transfer Pricing Guidelines concerning business restructurings. He led or co-led more than 20 events in the area of transfer pricing for a number of non-OECD countries. Giammarco Cottani currently serves as a Member of the UN Sub-Committee Group in charge of the Draft of the Practical Manual on Transfer Pricing for Developing Countries. He is also currently involved in providing technical assistance to developing countries on behalf of the UN and the World Bank. Giammarco Cottani is a member of the faculty of the International Tax Center of the University of Leiden for transfer pricing. He was the National Reporter for Italy during the 2011 IFA Congress on the topic of cross-border business restructurings. He teaches regularly in a number of graduate and post-graduate courses both in Italy and around the world in the field of transfer pricing. He received his degree in law from LUISS Rome University in 2003, an LLM in European and International Taxation from the European Tax College (Tilburg and Leuven) in 2005, and a PhD in Corporate Taxation from LUISS Rome University in 2009.

Stefaan De Baets has been a Senior Counsel Transfer Pricing with PwC since January 1, 2016, where he is responsible for avoiding and settlement of transfer pricing controversy, further development of the transfer pricing market, and promoting the key presence of PwC on that market as well as delivering contributions to the development of transfer pricing policies. From April 1, 2011 to December 31, 2015, he was a Transfer Pricing Advisor at the OECD in Paris, France. Until he joined the OECD, Stefaan worked for the Federal Public Service of Finances in Belgium, mostly on transfer pricing, for more than twenty years. He was a delegate for Belgium to the OECD Working Party 6 (transfer pricing) from March 1996 to March 2011 and to the Joint Transfer Pricing Forum from March 2003 to March 2011. Stefaan is a guest lecturer on international taxation at the University of Lausanne (Switzerland), the Catholic University of Leuven (Belgium), and the Ecole des Mines (France).

Pieter Deré joined PwC in 2006. He is a Director at PwC Tax Consultants and a member of PwC's International Tax and Transfer Pricing group in Belgium. He is a member of the PwC State Aid Working Group and a member of the PwC EU Direct Tax group. This group is PwC's pan-European network of EU direct tax and State aid experts. They specialize in all areas of direct tax including the fundamental freedoms, EU directives, and State-aid rules. Pieter has extensive experience in advising clients on the ongoing changes in the worldwide and European fiscal landscape.

Komal Dhall is the Head of KPMG's Global Transfer Pricing Services practice and is a member of KPMG's Global Tax Leadership team. She has worked extensively with large multinationals in establishing and defending their transfer pricing related to intellectual property and related valuations for over twenty years. She is based in New York and has spent over five years also practicing in the UK.

Junling Gao has been the Transfer Pricing manager at UCB since February 2018 where she assists the group in navigating the constantly evolving transfer pricing landscape around the world. Prior to joining UCB, Junling had gained more than ten years of professional experience in Big 4 firms. She has specialized in transfer pricing at PwC Belgium since 2014 and has obtained extensive experience in transfer pricing documentation, dispute avoidance (through unilateral and bilateral APAs), dispute resolution (MAP), and transfer pricing audit management. Junling holds an LLM in European Law and a Master's Degree in Advanced Accounting from Ghent University and an LLM in International Taxation from Tilburg University.

Sébastien Gonnet is Vice President of the Global Transfer Pricing Practice at NERA Economic Consulting. Based in Paris, he specializes in the areas of transfer pricing, intellectual property, and valuation. For a number of years, he has advised multinational companies in transfer pricing system design and implementation, business restructurings, and intellectual property and business valuation primarily in Europe, and also in China, in a range of industries including industrial and retail clients as well as financial institutions. He also acts as an expert economist in advance pricing agreements and tax audits in Europe and China. Sébastien is a frequent lecturer and has authored many publications on the economics of transfer pricing. He is also a frequent speaker at transfer pricing, intellectual property, and valuation conferences and training workshops and has presented to tax authorities in Europe and China. He is listed in International Tax Review's World's Leading Transfer Pricing Advisors by Expert Guide. Mr. Gonnet is the founder and president of Transfer Pricing Economists for Development (TPED—www.tped.eu), a Paris-based think-tank aimed at promoting the development and sharing of business economics knowledge in transfer pricing as an enabler of development of emerging economies and developing countries. Before joining NERA Economic Consulting, Sébastien Gonnet was an economist at KPMG. He holds a Master of Science in Management from HEC, Paris (Ecole des Hautes Etudes Commerciales) and a Master of Science in International Taxation from Paris II Law University.

Marcus Heyland is a manager in KPMG's Washington National Tax practice based in Philadelphia. Marcus is part of a core team focusing on US Tax Reform and fully understanding its implications on transfer pricing structures and transactions.

Sayee Prasanna is a Research and Teaching Associate in the WU Transfer Pricing Center at the Institute for Austrian and International Tax Law at WU (Vienna University of Economics and Business). Sayee has worked extensively as an international tax and transfer pricing consultant with EY India. His experiences include global transfer pricing documentation, transfer pricing audit defense at various appellate forums, advance pricing agreement processes, and advisory projects for multi-national companies. Sayee is a Doctoral Candidate in Economics and Social Sciences at the WU (Vienna University of Economics and Business).

Prita Subramanian is a Principal in KPMG's Washington National Tax Practice and is based in Boston. In addition to her focus on US Tax Reform, she also specializes in the transfer pricing of intangible property. She has worked with multinationals to set and defend their transfer pricing structures.

Paulina Szotek is a Senior Tax Consultant at PwC Belgium, Brussels. She joined PwC's Transfer Pricing Team in February, 2015, where she contributes to a wide range of the firm's tax advisory practice in the field of International Tax, Transfer Pricing, and EU Competition Law. She is also a PhD candidate at Maastricht University (the Netherlands) where she is currently writing her thesis on the topic of Group Taxation, Transfer Pricing, and State Aid. She obtained a Master's degree in International and European Tax Law from Maastricht University (2014).

Cameron Taheri is a Managing Director in KPMG's Transfer Pricing Dispute Resolution Practice and is based in Washington, D.C. Cameron works with multinationals primarily to resolve audit inquiries or to negotiate mutual agreement procedures or advance pricing agreements.

Isabel Verlinden is a Brussels-based International Tax Partner heading up PwC's Global Transfer Pricing practice with over 3,000 full time Transfer Pricing experts. In that capacity, she is a Member of PwC's Global Tax Leadership team. She has gathered first-hand knowledge of the TP challenges faced by companies operating across the globe from over twenty-five years of experience working for PwC (and its legacy firms) in Brussels and Washington, DC. For many years, Isabel has helped leading global companies to navigate in a vast array of industries through the pitfalls stemming from cross-border transacting where domestic rules may lack coherence and consistency, not to mention a lack of adaptation to the rapidly evolving world marked by technological advancement. This is typically an area where direct tax and the growing attention to indirect taxes come together in the analysis. Her work is often accompanied by ensuring upfront certainty through Advance Pricing Agreements. In the absence of upfront assurance, seeking effective means to alleviate double taxation is part of her day-to-day practice as well. She represents PwC vis-à-vis the OECD in all Transfer Pricing related matters. She is also PwC's representative at the European Commission's Joint Transfer Pricing Forum. She is an active writer for international tax and business periodicals. She has co-authored close to 100 articles and books to date. She is often solicited by academia and events' organizers to talk about transfer pricing. At the IFA Congress in Basel in 2015, she acted as a panelist on the topic 'State Aid review as a means to combat aggressive tax planning' and at the IFA Congress in Rio de Janeiro in 2017 on the topic 'The Future of Transfer Pricing'. Isabel has a degree in Applied Economics (University of Louvain)—major in International Business Affairs, a degree in Financial Economics (Brussels University)—major in Accountancy, and a degree in commercial and Financial Sciences (Brussels University)—Major in Fiscal Sciences.

Jasna Voje is a Tax Consultant at PwC Belgium, Brussels. She focusses on topics of European and International Corporate Taxation and Transfer Pricing. Before joining PwC Belgium in early 2017, she acquired experience as a trainee at the European Commission, DG TAXUD working on Corporate Tax Transparency. Besides her work, Jasna is an MSc Candidate at University of Oxford where she currently follows a part-time program, MSc in Taxation. She obtained a Double Master's degree in International and European Tax Law from KU Leuven (2015) and the University of Zürich (2016).

Oliver Wehnert is an international tax partner in the Düsseldorf office of EY and heads the international tax services practice in Germany, Switzerland, and Austria. He joined EY 1998 after working for PwC for six years. He was named by the International Tax Review numerous times as one of the "World's Leading Transfer Pricing Advisers." Oliver Wehnert has vast experience in client services on intercompany pricing, international tax planning, transfer pricing controversy services, and operating model effectiveness projects. Oliver's experiences include: global transfer pricing documentation projects, transfer pricing audit defense, and operating model effectiveness projects. He has significant experience in TP Controversy including supporting clients with their applications to tax authorities of various countries in Europe, the Americas, and Asia for mutual agreement procedures and Advance Pricing Agreements. Oliver has numerous years of experience in providing transfer pricing services to a wide variety of industry sectors, particularly, the pharmaceutical, automotive, and RCP sector. He is a German certified tax consultant and holds an MBA-degree from the University of Paderborn. He frequently speaks at German and international transfer pricing conferences and is a regular contributor to various tax journals including IStR and ISR and the International Tax Review.

Summary of Contents

Table of Contents

CHAPTER 4
Transfer Pricing Developments in Developing Countries and Emerging Economies
Giammarco Cottani 111

CHAPTER 5
Recent Developments on Transfer Pricing Documentation and Country-by-Country Reporting
Oliver Wehnert 141

Preface

Transfer pricing is currently one of the most relevant and challenging topics in the international tax environment. It is under constant development around the globe, and the years 2017–2018 have certainly been no different in this regard. The intense work of international organizations has provided new guidance on these topics with several projects.

Transfer pricing developments in 2017–2018 centered around three main areas such as documentation, comparability, and dispute avoidance and resolution. Organizations such as the OECD, EU, UN, World Bank, and IMF as well as key jurisdictions were busy providing their guidance on the above topics. In particular, the OECD, after releasing its new Transfer Pricing Guidelines in July 2017, is currently working, on the one hand, on implementing and monitoring the newly developed guidelines and, on the other hand, on drafting guidance related to topics such as profit attribution for permanent establishments, the profit split method, and intra-group financing. Further, the issue of digitalization of the economy poses tax challenges for many jurisdictions who have often taken a recourse to unilateral measures or are planning to do so since, thus far, no universal consensus has been reached in this area. Finally, we witnessed increasing litigious activities in transfer pricing during recent times on topics such as intra-group financing, services and intangibles, and CSA as well as cases dealing with the relationship between transfer pricing and customs.

The European Union and its Joint Transfer Pricing Forum are still performing a considerable amount of work on transfer pricing. This work is focusing on topics such as tax transparency and the potential use of public CbCR, taxation of the digitalization of the economy, CCTB and CCCTB, improving double taxation dispute resolution mechanisms with the use of the new directive as well as the still-unsolved problem of interplay between TP and customs. Moreover, the EU continues to work on State aid cases.

The United States (US) has been contending that the current domestic rules and regulations are, to a large extent, fully in accordance with the BEPS outcome. However, at the end of 2017, the US introduced a significant tax reform which embraced the territoriality principle, reduced tax rates (aiming to foster the growth of the national economy), and dealt with base erosion and profit shifting (via an expanded subpart F rule and limitations on certain intragroup payments). Furthermore, the reform brought changes in the approach towards intangibles and APAs. In addition, there are significant amounts of interesting case law from the US Courts.

Transfer pricing has also been an important topic in developing countries that have introduced transfer pricing rules into their domestic legislation. Many BRICS countries and other emerging economies are facing major economic changes that impact the assessment of their understanding of transfer pricing topics. Key developing markets such as China, India, Brazil, and Mexico are intensively working on their rules and are actively participating in the public debate. However, due to their particular economic situation, they quite often develop approaches on certain TP issues which are unique to their respective legislations.

In regard to more substantial issues, with the rise of the BEPS project, it has been widely accepted that the fight against 'aggressive tax planning' and tax avoidance also requires changes in the way companies report their business activities as part of the documentation for taxes. Action Plan 13 introduced revised standards of transfer pricing documentation incorporating a master file, local file, and a template for country-by-country reporting (CbCR) of revenues, profits, taxes paid, and certain measures of economic activity. Moreover, in this area, the OECD released the 2017 Transfer Pricing guidelines which adopted the results of the BEPS project as well as the Guidance on Implementation of CbCR.

Another hot topic in transfer pricing is the comparability analysis which still plays a key role in current practice. A common concern that pertains particularly to developing countries is related to the availability of data regarding transactions between independent parties, so-called "comparables," which are crucial when determining the arm's length level of prices in transactions between associated entities. With a view to the above, a number of international organizations and initiatives undertook advanced studies regarding the comparability analysis in order to derive solutions to the common issues. Among them, the recent guidance of the OECD and the UN as well as the works of the Platform for Collaboration on Tax and of the EU Joint Transfer Pricing Forum and World Bank Group are the most significant. In addition, the EC State aid proceedings brought a new perspective on the application of the comparability analysis in practice.

Further, financial transactions including corporate lending, cash concentration, and guarantee issues have been a matter of increased attention in the recent years with an increasing amount of case law. Various BEPS Action items have been relevant in this area (i.e., Actions 2, 4, 6, 8, 9, 10 and 13), and the progress made by the OECD in this respect is shifting its focus to transfer pricing issues in order to draft guidance concerning transfer pricing aspects of related party financial transactions. However, the OECD's work has not yet provided sufficient insights into these topics to the public. Hence, as a universal guidance at an international level is still not available, many challenges remain unsolved in the field of intra-group financing from a transfer pricing perspective.

Last, but not least, the Transactional Profit Split Method (TPSM) has been gaining relevance in recent years particularly due to the role of integrated value chains and significant intangibles developed by MNEs. This relevance has been supported by the work of the OECD on BEPS Action 10 and several public consultations that it held on transfer pricing matters related to this topic. The OECD released its revised initial discussion draft on 22 June 2017, which was very well welcomed, however, it did not represent the final consensus.

The WU Transfer Pricing Center at the Institute for Austrian and International Tax Law is conducting research projects to analyze the above-mentioned transfer pricing topics and their global impacts. The current research is based on eight topic-based papers which have been drafted by well renowned international experts on transfer pricing. The results of this work were presented and discussed at the third 'Global Transfer Pricing Conference: Transfer Pricing Developments around the World' in February 2018 at the premises of the WU (Vienna University of Economics and Business). This book is aimed at academics, practitioners (including the business community and advisory firms), international organizations, and government officials who are tax and transfer pricing experts as well as CEOs and CFOs who are interested in this topic. The book provides an in-depth analysis of the above-described topics as well as the global impacts and suggestions for future solutions to any issues that are raised.

The editors would like to express their sincere thanks to the authors who made it possible to provide this ambitious work. Many thanks are forwarded to Kluwer Law International BV for supporting and cooperating with this publication project. Last, but not least, the editors would like to thank Renée Pestuka, Karol Dziwiński, and Sayee Prasanna for their precious support, and Jenny Hill for providing linguistic support to the authors during the publishing process.

Prof. Dr. Dr. hc. Michael Lang
Prof. Dr. Alfred Storck
Dr. Raffaele Petruzzi, LL.M.

CHAPTER 1
Global Transfer Pricing Developments

*Raffaele Petruzzi & Sayee Prasanna**

* This chapter is based on information available as of Jan. 19, 2018. The authors would like to thank Prof. Dr. Alfred Storck (Co-Chair of the Board of Directors of the WU Transfer Pricing Center) and Prof. Dr. Jeffrey Owens (Director of the WU Global Tax Policy Center) for their valuable input and feedback to this chapter. The views expressed in this chapter are solely those of the authors.

1 INTRODUCTION

The transfer pricing global legislative framework has undergone several and relevant changes during the past year in the wake of continuing international guidelines. In 2017, international organizations have largely focused on providing additional guidance on the implementation of significant reforms that were introduced in past years. The Organisation for Economic Co-operation and Development (OECD) continued to provide several guidelines on specific transfer pricing issues which could be viewed as a follow-up to ensure effective implementation of the BEPS Action Plan.[1] While the OECD largely played an active monitoring role by overseeing the implementation of action plans, the United Nations (UN) published its revised Practical Manual on

1. OECD, *Aligning Transfer Pricing Outcomes with Value Creation, Actions 8–10—2015 Final Reports*, OECD/G20 Base Erosion and Profit Shifting Project (Paris: OECD Publishing, 2015).

Transfer Pricing for Developing Countries[2] (UN TPM) with updated country practices. The European Union (EU) undertook several measures mainly for ensuring tax transparency. Further, the European Commission (EC) continued investigations into illegal state aid in connection with transfer pricing rulings and, during the latter part of the calendar year, released a 'blacklist' of noncooperative tax jurisdictions for the first time. The World Customs Organization (WCO) issued its second case study[3] in light of its continued intent to align transfer pricing and customs valuation. The Platform for Collaboration on Tax (PCT)—a joint initiative of the International Monetary Fund (IMF), OECD, UN, and World Bank Group (WBG)—published the final toolkit[4] providing practical guidance to developing countries on issues related to the access of comparables data for transfer pricing analyses.

The above guidance, directives, and reports were aimed at complimenting the guidelines that have come into force as part of the legislative changes in several countries. The work of international organizations also provided further clarity and support to tax administrators and multinational enterprises (MNE) in understanding the evolution of transfer pricing provisions both locally and globally.

This chapter will examine the above developments in detail. While section 2 will describe the developments under the work of the international organizations, section 3 will look into the influence of these developments on country specific transfer pricing legislations and jurisprudence.

2 RECENT DEVELOPMENTS ON THE WORK OF INTERNATIONAL ORGANIZATIONS

Having released its BEPS Final Reports, the OECD published its revised Transfer Pricing Guidelines[5] (OECD TPG). This 2017 edition of the OECD TPG incorporates substantial changes reflecting the 2015 BEPS Final Reports on Actions 8–10, "Aligning Transfer pricing Outcomes with Value Creation" and on Action 13, "Transfer Pricing Documentation and Country-by-Country Reporting." The OECD TPG also includes revised guidance on safe harbor rules that were approved in 2013 which aims to promote certainty in tax positions. More about the work of the OECD is covered in section 2.1.

The 2017 UN TPM covered four key aspects: (1) transfer pricing in the current global context, (2) the arm's length principle; (3) policy implementation concerns; and (4) country specific transfer pricing practices, including those in India, Brazil, China, South Africa, and Mexico. section 2.2 captures these revisions in detail.

The EU's presence in international transfer pricing developments was significant during 2017. The EC continued its efforts into investigations to assess whether

2. United Nations, *Practical Manual on Transfer Pricing for Developing Countries* (April 2017).
3. World Customs Organization, *Customs Valuation and Transfer Pricing, Case Study 14.2* (October 30, 2017) *Source*: http://www.wcoomd.org/en/media/newsroom/2017/october/second-case-study-on-transfer-pricing-and-customs-valuation.aspx.
4. World Bank. *A toolkit for addressing difficulties in accessing comparables data for transfer pricing analyses*. Platform for Collaboration on Tax. Washington, D.C.: World Bank Group (June 2017).
5. OECD, OECD Transfer Pricing Guidelines for Multinational Enterprises and Tax Administrations 2017, Paris; OECD Publishing.

countries have granted MNEs undue incentives in formulating and delivering transfer pricing legislations or its interpretation of tax rulings resulting in illegal state aid. Moreover, intensive work has been conducted on enhancing transparency surrounding many issues including the exchange of tax rulings and County-by-Country Reports (CbC Reports). The EU Joint Transfer Pricing Forum (JTPF), as part of its ongoing work program for 2015–2019, agreed to the Final Report[6] on the "Use of Comparables" in the EU. The report establishes best practices and solutions by way of recommendations to improve comparable searches for transfer pricing in the EU. These developments are covered in section 2.3.

The toolkit on issues related to the access of comparables data for transfer pricing analyses, jointly published by the IMF, OECD, UN, and World Bank Group, was a response to the request by the Development Working Group of the G20 to provide guidance on transfer pricing matters for developing countries. Finally, the WCO's second case study illustrated the use of transfer pricing information in the course of verification of the customs value by tax officers in a practical situation. These developments are covered in section 2.4.

2.1 Transfer Pricing Developments at the OECD

Published on July 10, 2017, the revised OECD TPG substantially reflects the changes resulting from incorporating the 2015 BEPS Final Reports on Actions 8–10 and Action 13. These amendments to Chapters I, II, V, VI, VII and VIII were approved by the OECD Council and incorporated into the OECD TPG already in May 2016.[7] The key revisions are summarized below.

(i) Revisions to specific chapters[8]

- the current provisions of Chapter I, section D of the OECD TPG have been deleted in their entirety and replaced by new guidance;
- numerous paragraphs have been added to Chapter II of the OECD TPG immediately following paragraph 2.16;
- a new paragraph has been inserted following paragraph 2.9 of the OECD TPG;
- the current provisions of Chapter V of the OECD TPG have been deleted in their entirety and replaced by new guidance and annexes;
- the current provisions of Chapters VI, VII, and VIII of the OECD TPG and the annex to these chapters have been deleted in their entirety and replaced by new guidance and an annex.

6. *See* EU (2016), *Study on comparable data used for transfer pricing in the EU*, EU Publishing, Brussels (December 8, 2016). *Source*: https://ec.europa.eu/taxation_customs/business/company-tax/transfer-pricing-eu-context/joint-transfer-pricing-forum_en (last accessed January 8, 2017).
7. *See* OECD Press Release (June 15, 2016). *Source*: http://www.oecd.org/tax/transfer-pricing/oecd-council-approves-incorporation-of-beps-amendments-into-the-transfer-pricing-guidelines-for-multinational-enterprises-and-tax-administrations.htm.
8. *See* Petruzzi, R., *Global Transfer Pricing Developments*, in: Lang, M., Storck, A. & Petruzzi, R. (eds), *Transfer Pricing Developments Around the World* (Vienna: Kluwer, 2017), pp. 1–46.

(ii) Business restructuring[9]

Further, the revised OECD TPG and confirms to the guidance on business restructurings introduced by the reports on BEPS Actions 8–10 and 13. These changes were approved by the OECD Council in April 2017. The 2017 guidance provides that transactions owing to business restructuring are to be accurately delineated. This entails the identification of parties' commercial or financial relations and the conditions attached to those relations, which then helps in ascertaining the value of transfer within the MNE groups.

It is pertinent to note that specific emphasis has been placed on the delineation of transactions in two scenarios, i.e., in pre-restructuring and post-restructuring. It is observed in the guidelines that a comparative analysis influences arm's length compensation, risk assessment between the parties and, therefore, the selection of the appropriate transfer pricing method for the transaction. As a first step to delineation of the transactions, written contracts between contracting parties are to be analyzed, i.e., before and after undertaking the restructuring, in order to obtain evidence of the roles and responsibility of the MNEs involved and the compensation model that supports the determination of arm's length compensation. The revised OECD TPG also states that the accuracy of demarcation should be based on a valuation that is undertaken specifically for the restructuring from a transfer pricing perspective, and the arm's length price of each delineated transaction is to be obtained independently instead of a combined result for the MNE group as a whole.

Another key suggestion emanating from the revised OECD TPG is the emphasis on the identification of group synergies owing to business restructuring. The guidelines state that the factors that could result in synergies are to be identified. Such synergies act as an indicator of risk borne by parties to the restructuring process and would lead to determination of appropriate compensation for contributing to synergistic outcomes.

(iii) Safe harbor[10]

The revised guidance also includes amendments concerning the topic of safe harbors with respect to Chapter IV. These changes were approved by the OECD Council in May 2013. The primary aim has been to encourage the use of bilateral or multilateral safe harbors in order to reduce compliance burdens while ensuring that issues of double taxation or double nontaxation do not arise.

The publication of the revised OECD TPG incorporating the changes resulting from the 2015 BEPS Final Reports on Actions 8–10 and Action 13 has officially initiated a "new era" for the interpretation and application of transfer pricing rules around the world. Taxpayers and tax administrations can now count on guidance that is more detailed and are clearer on various topics. Nevertheless, the new guidance continues to develop the understanding of the arm's length principle based on an economic

9. *See* OECD (2017), OECD Transfer Pricing Guidelines for Multinational Enterprises and Tax Administrations 2017, OECD Publishing, Paris, at pp. 365–413.

10. *See* OECD (2013), *Revised Section E on Safe Harbours in Chapter IV of the Transfer Pricing Guidelines*, (May 16, 2013), Paris. *Source*: https://www.oecd.org/ctp/oecd-approves-revision-section-e-tp-guidelines.htm.

interpretation.[11] This interpretation, although better able to align transfer pricing outcomes with value creation, might potentially lead to increasing diverging views not only between taxpayers and tax administrations but also between tax administrations of different countries. Therefore, it will be of outmost importance in the future, on the one hand, to continually invest in training and resources dedicated to transfer pricing topics (both for taxpayers and tax administrations) and, on the other, to improve the efficiency and effectiveness of mechanisms of avoidance and resolution of transfer pricing disputes (e.g., rulings, APAs, MAPs, and arbitration).

Moreover, although the OECD TPG has been drafted in an OECD framework, 60 countries have been involved in the work leading to the finalization of BEPS Actions 8–10,[12] including emerging economies as well as developing countries. Therefore, it will need to be assessed whether non-OECD countries will also more systematically accept and apply the new OECD TPG in the future.

2.1.1 Transfer Pricing Documentation and Country-by-Country Reporting[13]

The BEPS Action 13 Final Report had suggested a standardized approach to three-tiered transfer pricing documentation[14] that includes a master file, local file, and CbC Report. After the incorporation of the above reports into Chapter V of the revised OECD TPG, the OECD provided additional guidance throughout the year in order to facilitate a smooth transition into the new compliance requirements for both MNEs and tax policy experts in countries.

Questions and clarification were raised by the MNE groups and tax administrators in the run up to implementation. More specifically, the year 2017 being the first year during in which the filing of the CbC Report is undertaken, the intense data collection and reporting in the form and manner prescribed by the OECD required continuous engagement between international bodies and complying jurisdictions. For this purpose, the OECD, as of December 2017, updated and published the following guidance:

---

11. For further information on this topic, *see* Petruzzi, *The Arm's Length Principle: Between Legal Fiction and Economic Reality*, in: Lang, M., Storck, A. & Petruzzi, R. (eds), *Transfer Pricing in a Post-BEPS World* (Vienna: Kluwer, 2016), pp. 1–27.
12. Albania, Argentina, Australia, Austria, Azerbaijan, Bangladesh, Belgium, Brazil, Canada, Chile, Colombia, Costa Rica, People's Republic of China, Croatia, Czech Republic, Denmark, Estonia, Finland, France, Georgia, Germany, Greece, Hungary, Iceland, India, Indonesia, Ireland, Israel, Italy, Jamaica, Japan, Kenya, Korea, Latvia, Lithuania, Luxembourg, Malaysia, Mexico, Morocco, Netherlands, New Zealand, Nigeria, Norway, Peru, Philippines, Poland, Portugal, Russian Federation, Saudi Arabia, Senegal, Singapore, Slovak Republic, Slovenia, South Africa, Spain, Sweden, Switzerland, Tunisia, Turkey, United Kingdom, United States, and Vietnam.
13. For further information on this topic, *see* Kaeser/Bremer, *Transfer Pricing and Documentation Requirements*, in: Lang, M., Storck, A. & Petruzzi, R. (eds), *Transfer Pricing in a Post-BEPS World* (Vienna: Kluwer, 2016), pp. 187–207.
14. *See* OECD, *Transfer Pricing Documentation and Country-by-Country Reporting, Action 13 - 2015 Final Report*, OECD/G20 Base Erosion and Profit Shifting Project (Paris: OECD Publishing, 2015), p. 9.

Last Updated	*Guidance*	*Purpose*
November 2017	Guidance on implementation of Country-by-country Reporting: BEPS Action 13[15]	Consistency in implementation and Resolving key questions from tax administrators and MNEs
September 2017	Guidance on the appropriate use of information contained in Country-by-Country reports[16]	Guidance on infrastructure necessary for maintaining critical information contained in CbC Reports
September 2017	Handbook on Effective Implementation[17]	Filing and use of CbC Reports, the exchange of CbC Reports, operational aspects of CbC Reporting and guidance, stakeholder engagement and training
September 2017	Handbook on Effective Tax Risk Assessment[18]	To support countries in the effective use of CbC Reports by incorporating them into a tax authority's risk assessment process and highlighting the challenges in using CbC Reports with potential solutions. Also, other data sources that should be used alongside CbC Reports in tax risk assessments

Key concerns of CbC Reports that were addressed are further elaborated below.

2.1.1.1 *Issues Relating to the Definition of Items Reported in the CbC Report*

During 2017, the definition of revenues was clarified to include extraordinary income and gain from investment activities and states that such income needs to be aggregated for reporting purposes. Regarding the definition of related parties, the associated enterprises defined in Action 13 are to be interpreted as 'Constituent Entities' for reporting purposes. Also, regarding the question on a specific situation when there is more than one constituent entity in a reporting jurisdiction, the guidance has clarified

15. *See* OECD (2017), Guidance on the Implementation of Country-by-Country Reporting–BEPS Action. 13, OECD, Paris (November 2017). Source: www.oecd.org/tax/guidance-on-the-implementation-of-country-by-country-reporting-beps-action-13.pdf.
16. OECD (2017), *BEPS Action 13 on Country-by-Country Reporting—Guidance on the appropriate use of information contained in Country-by-Country reports*, OECD/G20 Base Erosion and Profit Shifting Project, OECD, Paris. Source: www.oecd.org/tax/beps/beps-action-13-on-country-by-country-reporting-appropriate-use-of-information-in-CbC-reports.pdf.
17. OECD (2017), *Handbook on Effective Implementation*, OECD, Paris (September 2017). Source: www.oecd.org/tax/guidance-on-the-implementation-of-country-by-country-reporting-beps-action-13.pdf.
18. *See* OECD (2017), Country-by-Country Reporting: *Handbook on Effective Tax Risk Assessment*, OECD, Paris. Source: www.oecd.org/tax/beps/country-by-country-reporting-handbook-on-effective-tax-risk-assessment.pdf.

that an aggregation of intra-jurisdictional transactions is preferred from a reporting point of view. However, in a situation when a particular country's laws may require the Ultimate Parent Entity to undertake consolidated reporting for tax purposes and such a consolidation eliminates intra-group transactions at the level of individual line items, it is advised that the taxpayers be provided with the option of consolidated reporting and keeping in mind the consistency of reporting across the years. Further clarification on the treatment of income taxes accrued and paid for reporting purposes have been provided. The clarification also states that financial statements should be prepared using fair value accounting and how negative accumulated earnings are to be considered for reporting purposes.

2.1.1.2 *Issues Relating to the Entities to Be Reported in the CbC Report*

The guidance has clarified that investment entities are not exempt from the CbC Report requirements. The guidance discusses the possibility of a company that is a subsidiary of an investment holding company, incorporated with the purpose to control other entities could constitute an MNE group requiring compliance if the group revenue exceeds the threshold. The necessity of transacting companies of an MNE group to fulfill compliance requirements is driven by the accounting policies. The guidance provides clarity on situations when the IFRS[19] or the accounting standards followed by the jurisdiction of the ultimate parent entity need to be considered. Also, treatment of minority shareholders and guidance on pro-ration of such shareholders for consolidation and reporting purposes have been discussed.

2.1.1.3 *Issues Relating to the Filing Obligation for the CbC Report*

Since the CbC Report requirement is a threshold based compliance (i.e., it applies only to groups with consolidated revenues exceeding EUR 750 million), the definition of consolidated group revenue has been clarified to include all of the revenue that is (or would be) reflected in the consolidated financial statements. Further, in situations when the ultimate parent entity (or the surrogate entity) that is required to undertake the compliance follows a shorter accounting period, the guidance suggests that one of the below methodologies could be adopted to identify the consolidated group turnover, i.e.: (i) the actual total consolidated revenue; (ii) revenue of the shorter period extrapolated to a twelve-month accounting period; or (iii) pro-rated share of EUR 750 million for the relevant accounting period. It is also important to note that the options could lead to conflicting views on whether the reporting requirement threshold is breached. To avoid such conflicts, the guidance suggests that the ultimate parent entity or the surrogate entity can undertake a voluntary compliance.

19. *Source*: http://www.ifrs.org/about-us/.

2.1.1.4 *Issues Relating to Mergers/Acquisitions/Demergers*

As per the guidance that was issued, the consolidation of group revenue for reporting purposes should be undertaken regardless of the restructuring undergone during the fiscal year of reporting. Further guidance on specific fact patterns where ambiguities could arise is provided in the guidance.

Further, apart from the above guidance, the OECD has enabled activation of the automatic exchange relationships between the jurisdictions to enable seamless transfer of CbC Reports under the multilateral competent authority agreement on these reports. The automatic exchange commencing June 2018 is set to empower tax administrators with key information with an MNE group level view. Currently, 1,400 automatic exchange relationships are in place among jurisdictions committed to exchanging CbC Reports including those under EU Council Directive 2016/881/EU and bilateral competent authority agreements; this includes 31 countries with the United States (US).[20]

A key concern among the MNE groups ever since the inception of the CbC reporting (CbCR) rules has been the security and confidentiality of information made available to the tax administrators of multiple jurisdictions. In order to address potential challenges, in September 2017, the OECD published *Guidance on the appropriate use of information contained in Country-by-Country reports*.[21] The guidance refers to the Action 13 Report which restricts the use of the CbC Report to the purpose of: (i) high level transfer pricing risk assessment; (ii) assessment of other BEPS related risks; and (iii) economic and statistical analysis, whenever appropriate. From a transfer pricing perspective, the issue on how the data contained in the CbC Reports would influence transfer pricing audits has been the main concern for the MNE groups. Through this guidance, the OECD states that the information contained in CbC Reports could be used for high level transfer pricing risk assessment but should not form the fundamental basis on which transfer pricing audits are concluded. It is imperative that tax administrators consider the CbC Reports as an important tool in conducting audits. However, the risk of tax administrators using information to arrive at a formulary apportionment assessment cannot be ruled out. The guidance states jurisdictions involved in exchange of CbC information should undertake measures to restrict access to CbC Reports in order to avoid misuse and provides six control questions[22] that need to be considered for an internal check on the appropriate use of CbC Reports. This guidance is assumed to be significant due to the potential conflicts that could arise between two taxing States on the usage and interpretation of data available in the CbC Reports. It is expected that the OECD will provide further guidelines on best practices

20. *See* OECD Press Release (December 21, 2017). *Source*: http://www.oecd.org/ctp/exchange-of-tax-information/beps-action13-jurisdictions-implement-final-regulations-for-first-filings-of-cbc-reports.htm (last accessed December 27, 2017).
21. *See* OECD (2017), *BEPS Action 13 on Country-by-Country Reporting—Guidance on the appropriate use of information contained in Country-by-Country reports*, OECD/G20 Base Erosion and Profit Shifting Project, OECD, Paris. *Source*: www.oecd.org/tax/beps/beps-action-13-on-country-by-country-reporting-appropriate-use-of-information-in-CbC-reports.pdf.
22. *See Supra* n. 20, p. 10.

and possible case studies where CbC Reports are misused. Given that June 2018 marks the commencement of exchange of CbC Reports, more work by the OECD on this front is foreseen.

Further, from an operational perspective, the OECD provided updated and new Information Technology (IT) tools and supporting guidance[23] to undertake the technical implementation of the exchange of tax information under the Common Reporting Standard (CRS), on CbC Reports, and in relation to tax rulings (ETR). A dedicated XML Schema and User Guide have been developed to provide structured feedback on received CbC Reports. This portal is aimed at ensuring swift and uniform electronic transit of CbC Reports between jurisdictions.

In summary, while the OECD undertook several steps during 2017,[24] further clarification on how the CbC Report should be read in conjunction with the master file and local file are required. In this context, on the one hand, the OECD might need to analyze solutions that could limit the risk of any misuse by tax administrations of the information contained in the new documentation requirements. The OECD could further analyze issues in connection with data protection and loss of confidentiality while balancing the use of information that is obtained to assess if the TP policy is not in line with reality. Also, the topic of sharing the information provided by the new documentation requirements is a relevant one that could raise many issues. For example, once the new standards have been fulfilled by taxpayers, numerous questions would need to be assessed in order to guarantee that this information is not inappropriately shared.[25]

2.1.2 Hard-to-Value-Intangibles

The Final Report on Actions 8–10 of the BEPS Action Plan had suggested providing an implementation approach to pricing Hard-To-Value-Intangibles (HTVI) in the framework of Section D.4 of Chapter VI of the OECD TPG. Pursuant to this commitment, on May 23, 2017, the OECD invited comments on the discussion draft[26] on HTVI.

The key considerations in the discussion were the following:

- Basic principles for enabling the implementation of the HTVI approach
- Specific examples that clarify the implementation of the HTVI approach under specific scenarios

23. *See* OECD (2017), *Country-by-Country Reporting XML Schema: User Guide for Tax Administration*, OECD, *Source*: http://www.oecd.org/tax/beps/country-by-country-reporting-xml-schema-user-guide-for-tax-administrations.pdf.
24. For more information, refer to Chapter 5 of this book.
25. *See* Petruzzi, R., Navisotschnigg, F., *BEPS and EU requirements for Country-by-Country Reporting*, in: Lang, Haunold (eds.), *Transparenz und Informationsaustausch: Der gläserne Steuerpflichtige* (Vienna: Linde, 2017), pp. 51–78.
26. *See* OECD (2017), *BEPS Action 8: Implementation Guidance on Hard-to-Value Intangibles*, OECD/G20 Base Erosion and Profit Shifting Project, OECD, Paris. *Source*: http://www.oecd.org/tax/transfer-pricing/BEPS-implementation-guidance-on-hard-to-value-intangibles-discussion-draft.pdf.

- Finally, the suggestion to pursue the option of a Mutual Agreement Procedure (MAP) under the applicable treaty in resolving disputes arising out of valuing HTVI.

Various commentators have provided their views[27] on the outcome of the discussion draft. At this stage, the OECD is evaluating these comments, and further clarification or consultations can be expected. Key concerns raised by the stakeholders is the use of *ex-post* data that is available to tax authorities thereby granting the benefit of hindsight during the course of transfer pricing audits, an option that the taxpayers would not have simply owing to the timing difference and limited capabilities of estimating the value of HTVI at the time of reporting the transaction. For reducing the complexity of issues, the OECD has encouraged the use of a MAP for resolving potential disputes.

2.1.3 *Transactional Profit Split Method*[28]

In continuation with the work on the transactional profit split method (TPSM), the OECD has held public consultations on transfer pricing matters related to this topic. This consultation was a culmination of the long drafting exercise starting from the time of publishing the BEPS Actions 8–10 and leading to an initial discussion draft in 2016[29] which was subsequently revised on June 22, 2017.[30] The comments from different parties were made available to the public, and a corresponding public consultation was held on November 6–7, 2017 to discuss these comments.[31]

Under the revised draft, the OECD has provided greater clarity on its position on the TPSM by specifying conditions under which it is applicable along with a list of ten examples that illustrate its application. The 2017 draft sought to improve the short-comings of the 2016 draft in addressing the implementation aspects of the TPSM.

As a highlight and a change compared to the 2016 Discussion Draft, the 2017 Discussion Draft rightly left out the considerations on the form of integration, i.e., the sequential integration and the parallel integration, when deciding whether the TPSM is the most appropriate method. First of all, the reality of MNEs may reflect a more complex way of integration that falls outside the defined sequential and parallel

27. *See* OECD (2017), *Comments Received on Public Discussion Draft, BEPS Action 8: Implementation Guidance on Hard-to-Value Intangibles*, OECD/G20 Base Erosion and Profit Shifting Project, OECD, Paris. *Source*: http://www.oecd.org/ctp/transfer-pricing/Public-comments-received-on-the-Implementation-Guidance-on-Hard-to-Value-Intangibles-2017.pdf.
28. For further information on this topic, *see* Chapter 8 in this book.
29. OECD (2016), *BEPS Public Discussion Draft BEPS Actions 8–10: Guidance on Profit Splits*, OECD/G20 Base Erosion and Profit Shifting Project (Paris: OECD Publishing, 2016). *Source*: https://www.oecd.org/tax/transfer-pricing/BEPS-discussion-draft-on-the-revised-guidance-on-profit-splits.pdf.
30. OECD, *BEPS Public Discussion Draft BEPS Actions 8–10: Revised Guidance on Profit Splits*, OECD/G20 Base Erosion and Profit Shifting Project (Paris: OECD Publishing, 2017). *Source*: https://www.oecd.org/ctp/transfer-pricing/Revised-guidance-on-profit-splits-2017.pdf.
31. OECD, *BEPS Comments received on Public Discussion Draft BEPS Actions 8–10: Revised Guidance on Profit Splits Part I and Part II*, OECD/G20 Base Erosion and Profit Shifting Project (Paris: OECD Publishing, 2016).

integration in the 2016 Discussion Draft. Secondly, the highly integrated sequential operations in practice may indeed prove to be cases of when the TPSM is the most appropriate method. For example, the concerned entities in many arm's length joint ventures in which one entity performs the preliminary R&D work and the other is responsible for sale and marketing of the products in a sequential manner agree to share the joint profits generated in the end. Instead of focusing on sequential integration and parallel integration, the 2017 Discussion Draft introduced the very useful concept of inter-dependency together with interrelation as an indicator to picture the level of integration. The new considerations in the context of integration are very useful for indicating to what extent high integration may be evident in the application of the TPSM.[32]

While there has been commendable improvements to the work on TPSM, there are a few gaps that have been highlighted in the comments provided by stakeholders. It has been observed that the distinction between "actual" and "anticipated" profits seems artificial and, therefore, could lead to counterproductive outcomes in its current format.[33] It is expected that the OECD will clarify or modify the definition of these terminologies in order to avoid ambiguities. The question on adjustments to the purchasing power parity (PPP) made for profit splitting amounts has largely been answered by various stakeholders with concerns of the consistency of accounting and the cumbersome steps that would further be needed to make its application effective.

Further, it has been suggested that further guidance is to be provided on the splitting of losses under the specific scenarios. For the splitting of losses, focus may need to be primarily on the entity that controls the risks as it normally has a negative perception of the result or to look at the responsibilities that are perceived to give rise to risks realization.[34] Moreover, the RACI model and the bargaining analysis could generate reliable transfer pricing results if dealt with properly in the application of the TPSM.[35] Also, it is suggested that the OECD considers including more references to the value chain analysis as an important tool in a transfer pricing analysis that appears to be subsumed under the reference to functional analysis[36] in the 2017 guidance. The OECD is expected to finalize the drafts and issue the final version in 2018.

32. *See* Storck, A. Petruzzi, R & Peng, C. OECD, *BEPS Comments received on Public Discussion Draft BEPS Actions 8–10: Revised Guidance on Profit Splits Part II*, OECD/G20 Base Erosion and Profit Shifting Project (Paris: OECD Publishing, 2016) pp. 199–213.
33. *See* PWC, OECD, *BEPS Comments received on Public Discussion Draft BEPS Actions 8–10: Revised Guidance on Profit Splits Part II*, OECD/G20 Base Erosion and Profit Shifting Project (Paris: OECD Publishing, 2016) pp. 99–102.
34. Storck. A et al., Global Transfer Pricing Conference: Transfer Pricing Developments around the World, 24 International Transfer Pricing Journal 4 (2017), 270–279.
35. Petruzzi R. & Peng X., The Profit Split Method: Historical Evolution and BEPS Insights, Transfer Pricing International 1 (2/2017), 44–54 (peer reviewed).
36. *See* Storck, A. Petruzzi, R & Peng, C. OECD, *BEPS Comments received on Public Discussion Draft BEPS Actions 8–10: Revised Guidance on Profit Splits Part II*, OECD/G20 Base Erosion and Profit Shifting Project (Paris: OECD Publishing, 2016) pp. 199–213.

2.1.4 *Attribution of Profits to Dependent Agent Permanent Establishments and to Warehouses*[37]

The BEPS Action 7 "*Preventing the Artificial Avoidance of Permanent Establishment Status, Action 7*" Final Report[38] covered issues related to the existence of PEs in specific situations and recommended amendments to Article 5 of the OECD Model while it provided an indication that further work would follow. The *2017 PE Discussion Draft*[39] (2017 PE Draft) was built on the work undertaken earlier and comments received on the respective discussion drafts that dated July 4, 2016. Further consultation was undertaken on November 6–7, 2016 to discuss these comments with an aim to provide final guidelines by 2018.

The *2017 PE Draft* clarified that changes made to Article 5(5) and 5(6) of the Model Tax Convention (MTC) by the report on Action 7 have modified the threshold for the existence of a *deemed PE* under Article 5(5). However, they have not modified the nature of the *deemed PE*. Therefore, the attribution of profits to that PE is deemed to exist under the pre-BEPS version of Article 5(5) and will, therefore, be applicable to a PE that is considered as existing under the post-BEPS version of Article 5(5). Broadly, the profits to be attributed to a PE are to be determined in accordance with Article 7 of the relevant tax treaty, i.e., profits attributable to a PE are those that the PE would have derived if it were a separate and independent enterprise engaged in the same or similar activities under the same or similar conditions. The *2017 PE Draft* explained that the above principle applies regardless of whether a tax administration adopts the Authorized OECD Approach (AOA) contained in Article 7 of the 2010 version of the MTC or any other approach used to attribute profits under a previous version of Article 7 of the MTC.

The *2017 PE Draft* contains four examples illustrating the attribution of profits to PEs resulting either from the changed definition of a Dependent Agent Permanent Establishment (DAPE) or from the anti-fragmentation rule. The first two examples relate to the DAPE and illustrate that the profits of such a PE in the case of sales and marketing activities would generally be equal to the revenue from the sales of goods related to the intermediary's sales activities minus: (i) an arm's length purchase price of the goods from the DAPE's head office; (ii) other expenses attributable to the PE; and (iii) the arm's length remuneration of the dependent agent enterprise. In the third example in which the PE performs procurement activities, the profits of the PE would equal the arm's length sales price of the goods to the PE's head office minus: (i) the

37. *See* Cottani, C., *Commissionaire Arrangements/Low-Risk Distributors and Attribution of Profits to Permanent Establishments*, in: Lang, M., Storck, A. & Petruzzi, R. (eds.), *Transfer Pricing in a Post-BEPS World* (Vienna: Kluwer, 2016), pp. 159–186.

38. OECD (2015), *Preventing the Artificial Avoidance of Permanent Establishment Status, Action 7 - 2015 Final Report*, OECD/G20 Base Erosion and Profit Shifting Project (Paris: OECD Publishing). *Source:* http://www.oecd.org/tax/preventing-the-artificial-avoidance-of-permanent-establishment-status-action-7-2015-final-report-9789264241220-en.htm.

39. OECD, *Discussion Draft on Additional Guidance on the Attribution of Profits to Permanent Establishments* (June 22–September 15, 2017). *See* https://www.oecd.org/tax/transfer-pricing/beps-discussion-draft-additional-guidance-attribution-of-profits-to-permanent-establishments.pdf.

amounts paid by the intermediary to the unrelated suppliers; (ii) other expenses attributable to the PE; and (iii) the arm's length remuneration of the intermediary. In all of the three examples, the rights and obligations relating to the contracts that are concluded on behalf of the nonresident entity or in which it plays the principal role are attributed to the PE. The final example demonstrates what profits should be attributed to a PE that are recognized as a result of the anti-fragmentation rule (i.e., a warehouse PE providing storage and delivery services and an office PE providing merchandising and collection of information services).

In summary, to avoid conflicting outcomes, it would be ideal to consider merging Article 7 and Article 9 to jointly reflect the same understanding of the arm's length principle. However, as an immediate measure, further guidance on aligning different outcomes of both articles is necessary and, in such a process, the following aspects could be considered:[40]

- Clarification on the separate legal entity approach, without any deviation, is the core principle that has to be followed.
- Clarification on the substance-over-form approach to be adopted uniformly across the two articles with emphasis on the actual conduct of the parties over and above the details evident from the contract. If the actual conduct of the parties is strictly followed under Article 9, the potential for differences to the application of Article 7 tends to be close to nil since the actual conduct of parties and the performance of significant people functions show a close teleological similarity.
- Clarification on capital allocation between associated enterprises and in a PE context should follow considerations related to corporate finance methodology rather than inflexible rules.

2.1.5 Digitalization of the Economy

The OECD has long recognized the need for adaptive tax systems and has made fair attempts to address the challenges of digitalization of the economy as part of its BEPS Project within its Action 1 Final Report.[41] However, in light of the pace of changes, even before some of these recommendations are understood and translated into effect by different stakeholders including MNEs and tax administrations, the dynamic nature of digitalized businesses outpace the implementation time. A key feature of digitalized businesses has always been the lack of need for physical presence. The absence of physical presence reduces the applicability of traditional international tax principles. Apart from these business realities, key MNEs have used innovative means of tax planning to minimize tax charges. Google, for example, charges its affiliates with

40. *See* Storck, A. Petruzzi, R & Holzinger, R. OECD, *Comments received on Public Discussion Draft on Attribution of Profits to Permanent Establishments*, OECD/G20 Base Erosion and Profit Shifting Project (Paris: OECD Publishing, 2016) pp. 403–413.
41. *See* OECD (2015), Addressing the Tax Challenges of the Digital Economy, Action 1 - 2015 Final Report, OECD Publishing, Paris.

royalties for the use of its search engine. The income stream from these arrangements is paid to Bermuda using a so-called Double Irish Dutch sandwich structure. The lack of market comparables for intangibles poses a problem for tax authorities because it is difficult to determine what the arm's length nature is of some transactions.[42]

Notwithstanding the shortcomings of the existing tax systems, many countries have contemplated while some have implemented (or are in the process of implementing) legislations to tackle the digitalization of the economy during 2017. The ideas of modifying the existing PE concept or introducing an equalization levy was originally discussed in BEPS Action 1.[43]

On September 22, 2017,[44] stakeholders were invited by the Task Force on the Digital Economy (TFDE)[45] to provide comments on the tax challenges of the increasing digitization of the economy. This was followed by a public consultation on November 1, 2017. A final report should be prepared by the OECD that will be presented to the leaders of the G20 in April 2018.

The presence of a virtual PE has been a key focus of discussion and debate in considering the tax implications of the digitalized economy. A tax nexus based on "significant economic presence" would lead to the expansion of the scope under the existing definitions in the treaties. Highly digitalized business models are characterized by high mobility, reliance on data, use of networks synergies, etc. The assets that generate the most value for these businesses are brand, platform, know-how, data, etc.[46] While there has been an emerging consensus to view data as the key driver of value creation, the debate is expected to shift toward the means of valuing the relative contribution of data across the digital value chain.

To aid attribution, the use of a value chain analysis has been proposed as a key tool for identifying value creation.[47] Moreover, the use of Blockchain technology can potentially considerably improve the performance of this analysis. The VCA deploys terminologies such as "use value" and "exchange value" and/or "total value" that may be useful in establishing the nexus of a digital PE and the quantum in the attribution of profits to it.[48] This establishes the need to modify the way functional analyses are conducted and also the way data is considered in determining the functional profile of digital businesses. Customers who generate unconscious value to the business could be considered key value drivers.[49] With this aim, the concept of PE may be reinterpreted. "Data" can be perceived as "natural resources" under Art. 5(2)(f) or active customers might provide the sufficient nexus with the market jurisdiction. The transfer pricing

---

42. *See* Juranek S, Schindler D, Schjelderup G. *Transfer Pricing Regulation and Taxation of Royalty Payments*. J Public Econ. Theory (2017), 1–17.
43. *Supra* n. 40, pp. 165–166.
44. *See* OECD Press Release, *Source*: http://www.oecd.org/tax/beps/public-comments-received-on-the-tax-challenges-of-digitalisation.htm (last accessed December 27, 2017).
45. TFDE is a subsidiary body of the OECD Committee on Fiscal Affairs which includes non-OECD and non-G20 country participants.
46. Petruzzi, R. & Buriak, S., *Addressing the Tax Challenges of the Digitalization of the Economy: A Possible Answer from a Proper Application of Transfer Pricing Rules?* (forthcoming).
47. *Supra* n. 45, p. 34.
48. *Supra* n. 45, p. 34.
49. *Supra* n. 45, p. 34.

analysis will then attribute profits to such digital PEs. Also, another suggestion has been to attribute more value to the division(s) undertaking analytics and strategic functions using the data.[50] The concept of a virtual/digital PE, allocation rules, and use of technology continues to be of critical debate among academicians, practitioners, and MNEs.[51] Considering the above suggestions, the OECD is expected to undertake concerted efforts to move from theoretical frameworks for addressing digital transactions to practical guidance.[52]

In summary, the next OECD Report on the Digital Economy (an interim Action 1 report due in April 2018 and a final report due in 2020[53]) could provide more certainty on various proposals and legislations but, in the meantime, countries are expected to take additional unilateral measures in domestic tax laws which could also result in a potential breach of treaty obligations.[54] A collective work and consensus based approach, however, is encouraged.

2.1.6 *Dispute Resolution*

The BEPS Action 14 Final Report[55] outlined the minimum standards and best practices for resolving cross-border disputes under the MAP. All of the members of the inclusive framework on BEPS have committed to the implementation of the BEPS Action 14 minimum standard and to have their implementation reviewed pursuant to the agreed Terms of Reference and Assessment Methodology.[56]

On November 27, 2017, the OECD released the MAP statistics for the 2016 reporting interval.[57] From a transfer pricing perspective, it is pertinent to note that transfer pricing cases account for slightly more than half of the MAP cases that are pending resolution. Also, it has been observed that transfer pricing cases take more

50. OECD, *Tax Challenges of Digitalization, Comments Received on the Request for Input—Part I*, p. 77. *Source*: http://www.oecd.org/tax/beps/tax-challenges-digitalisation-part-1-comments-on-request-for-input-2017.pdf.
51. The WU Global Tax Policy Center (WU GTPC) at the Vienna University of Economics and Business, Singapore University of Social Sciences (SUSS), and New Economy Taxation (NET) launched in August 2017, the Digital Economy Tax Foundation (DET), a new multi-stakeholder initiative to provide a neutral global forum for discussions among government, business, international, and regional organizations and academia and undertake policy-relevant research ion taxation issues arising from the Digital Economy. The most recent conference on Digital Tax Transformation was held in Vienna (December 18–19, 2017).
52. *See* Olbert/Spengel, World Tax Journal, Vol. 9, Issue 1/2017, p. 3.
53. *Source*: https://www.oecd.org/tax/tax-policy/tax-challenges-digital-economy-request-for-input.pdf (last accessed January 8, 2018).
54. *See* section 3.1.
55. OECD, *Making Dispute Resolution Mechanisms More Effective, Action 14 - 2015 Final Report*, OECD/G20 Base Erosion and Profit Shifting Project (Paris: OECD Publishing, 2015).
56. OECD, *BEPS Action 14 on More Effective Dispute Resolution Mechanisms: Peer Review Documents*, OECD/G20 Base Erosion and Profit Shifting Project (Paris: OECD Publishing, 2016), pp. 7–31.
57. *Source*: https://home.kpmg.com/xx/en/home/insights/2017/11/tnf-oecd-mutual-agreement-procedure-statistics-for-2016.html (last accessed December 27, 2017).

time on average than other cases—approximately 30 months are needed for transfer pricing cases and 17 months for other cases. All of these signify the existing complexity of transfer pricing disputes.[58]

The OECD also released peer review documents from specific countries[59] during the year as part of implementation and monitoring activities. The peer review reports represent the first evaluation of how countries are implementing the new minimum standards that were agreed to in the OECD/G20 BEPS Project. In Stage 2 of the peer review process, each jurisdiction's efforts to address any shortcomings identified in its Stage 1 peer review report will be monitored.

As mentioned before[60] and confirmed by the numbers provided in the OECD statistics, efficient and effective mechanisms to resolve transfer pricing disputes will be increasingly needed in the future, and the work of OECD on BEPS Action 14 is very much welcome. Considering that transfer pricing disputes are perceived as being of higher complexity than other international tax disputes as well as requiring a different set of skills and understanding than other tax issues (i.e., a better understanding, e.g., of business administration, economics, corporate finance), it might be advisable to conceive different types of MAP mechanisms, i.e., one dedicated to general tax disputes and one dedicated to transfer pricing disputes.

Related to the exchange of information across countries with the goal of dispute resolution, The OECD published a peer reviewed analysis[61] on the legal framework of countries and its application as part of its Global Forum on Transparency and Exchange of Information for Tax Purposes (Global Forum). The Global Forum is charged with in-depth monitoring and peer review of the implementation of the standards of transparency and exchange of information for tax purposes. The Ratings[62] categorize jurisdictions as "Compliant," "Largely Compliant," "Provisionally Legally Compliant," "Partially Compliant," "Provisionally Partially Compliant," and "Non-Compliant."

The work of the OECD has always prioritized implementation of dispute resolution frameworks. It is relevant to recall propositions to implement "Baseball Arbitration" to resolve tax treaty disputes with the introduction of an arbitration clause in the OECD Model in 2008.[63] In this regard, the OECD's future work on baseball arbitration for transfer pricing disputes could provide a more uniform and certain procedure characterized by a lower number of hearings and lower administrative burden.[64] The

58. *See* OECD Press Release, *Source*: http://www.oecd.org/tax/dispute/mutual-agreement-procedure-statistics.htm (last accessed January 8, 2018).
59. September 2017—Belgium, Canada, the Netherlands, Switzerland, the United Kingdom and the United States; and, in November 2017—Austria, France, Germany, Italy, Liechtenstein, Luxembourg, and Sweden.
60. *See* section 2.1.
61. *Source*: http://www.oecd.org/tax/transparency/thepeerreviewreportsataglance.htm (last accessed January 18, 2018).
62. *Source*: http://www.oecd.org/tax/transparency/exchange-of-information-on-request/ratings/#d.en.342263.
63. More precisely, it was the introduction of a mandatory arbitration clause in the protocol to the US-Germany DTT in 2006; *see* Ault & Sasseville, id., p.209.
64. *See* Petruzzi, R., Koch, P., Turcan, L., "The Baseball Arbitration in Comparison to Other Types of Arbitration," in: Lang and Owens (eds.), International Arbitration in Tax Matters (Amsterdam: IBFD, 2015), pp. 139–158.

OECD along with the UN, World Bank, International Chamber of Commerce (ICC), and the EC have proposed to work in conjunction with each other to generate new approaches to tax dispute resolution.[65]

2.1.7 *Toolkit for Low-Income Countries*

Since 2016, the OECD along with the IMF, the UN, and the WBG have constituted the PCT[66] to intensify the cooperation between these organizations on tax issues. It frames and formalizes the periodical discussions in the international organizations on the implementation of standards for international tax matters, improves focus on guiding developing countries, and accordingly provides guidance. On January 24, 2017, the PCT issued a discussion draft for public consultation and later, on June 22, 2017, it released the comments received on the discussion draft.

Among various challenges existing in transfer pricing, the most recent toolkit[67] aims at "Addressing Difficulties in Accessing Comparables Data on Transfer Pricing Analyses." This guidance specifically addresses the ways that low-income countries can overcome the issue of the lack of comparables data or of market prices for goods and services transferred within MNEs.

The toolkit highlights the issue of the lack of data for undertaking comparability analyses[68] and proposes certain indicative steps to minimize or resolve the deficiency. The toolkit reiterates that an understanding of the taxpayer's circumstances and accurately delineating the actual transaction form the basis for comparability analyses. The toolkit relies on the methodology prescribed by the OECD in undertaking the analysis.[69]

Given the absence of adequate data in low-income countries, the toolkit suggests the use of optimal data. On some of the case studies on country specific practices, such as South Africa,[70] the guidance states that the analysis should be carried out based on the information readily disclosed by the MNEs. The toolkit suggests that the use of customs data could also assist in validating transfer prices. The toolkit also addresses the use of comparability adjustments in determining arm's length prices. Specific methods that could be applied to different fact patterns have been discussed. For instance, given the importance of natural resources in developing countries, specific

65. Vienna Multi-Stakeholder Group on Improving Cross-border Dispute Resolution (Vienna: January 24, 2018).
66. Established in April 2016, *see* http://www.worldbank.org/en/programs/platform-for-tax-collaboration (last accessed December 27, 2017).
67. *See* World Bank. 2017. *The Platform for collaboration on tax: comments received on public discussion draft—A toolkit for addressing difficulties in accessing comparables data for transfer pricing analyses (English)*. Washington, D.C.: World Bank Group. *Source*: http://documents.worldbank.org/curated/en/416681495637398223/The-Platform-for-collaboration-on-tax-comments-received-on-public-discussion-draft-a-toolkit-for-addressing-difficulties-in-accessing-comparables-data-for-transfer-pricing-analyses (last accessed December 27, 2017).
68. For more information on Comparability Analysis, refer to Chapter 6 of this book.
69. *See* The Platform for Collaboration on Tax: *A Toolkit for Addressing Difficulties in Accessing Comparables Data for Transfer Pricing Analyses*, p. 20. *Source*: http://www.oecd.org/tax/toolkit-on-comparability-and-mineral-pricing.pdf.
70. *See supra* n. 63, p. 50.

guidance on the use of quoted prices (e.g., commodity exchanges) of commodity transactions in the public domain are encouraged. While there is no settled position among tax administrators of the various jurisdictions regarding comparability adjustments, the toolkit suggests that comparability adjustments for working capital differences, accounting differences, and country risk adjustments could be commonly observed. In this process, the toolkit provides specific case studies for undertaking such adjustments. The work undertaken in this regard assumes relevance because, in practice, developing countries continue to question the need for such economic adjustments and continue to view these adjustments as supplementary means of defense during transfer pricing audits. Further, the toolkit suggests that the use of safe harbors, benefit tests, profit splits, and protective measures should be further encouraged in developing countries.

Besides the above core considerations on matters surrounding comparability issues in developing or low-income countries, the toolkit also includes a supplementary guidance note on extractive industries. The toolkit is expected to act as a reference for undertaking comparability analyses for transactions in the mining sector with increased focus on copper, gold, iron ore, and thermal coal. The case studies provided for each category of these mined products have been well received by the stakeholders.

In the coming times, the toolkit is expected to enhance its coverage and include several focus areas such as oil and gas industries, freight markets, trading and logistics entities, hedging transactions (risk management), and related areas.

The work of the PCT aimed at solving issues related to comparability analyses and the lack of comparable data is very much welcome as it provides useful insights on various practical methodologies and solutions. Going forward, it might be advisable to expand the scope of the work of the PCT to many other transfer pricing topics when internationally agreed practical solutions are required.

2.2 Transfer Pricing Developments at the European Union[71]

In 2017, the EC and the EU JTPF largely focussed their work on topics such as the use of economic valuation techniques for transfer pricing and improving double taxation dispute resolution mechanisms. The EC's measures on state aid control based on enquiry into the tax ruling practices of Member States (MS) and investigation into tax rulings and schemes that grant preferential tax treatment to some companies had implications from a transfer pricing perspective. Negotiations have advanced on the Common Consolidated Corporate Tax Base (CCCTB),[72] which was relaunched by the Commission in 2016. Once agreed, the CCCTB aims at providing a competitive, fair, and robust framework for taxing companies in the Single Market. Moreover, an amendment of the Anti-Tax Avoidance Directive (ATAD 2) that is aimed at curbing hybrid mismatches went into effect after the initial Anti-Tax Avoidance Directive in 2016 (ATAD). The European Parliament also voted in favor of public disclosure of

71. For further information on this topic, *see* Chapter 2 in this book.
72. COM(2016)683 and COM(2016)685.

certain information reported in the CbC Report maintained by EU countries under the OECD Action 13 requirements. In a significant move, the EC also published a "Blacklist"[73] of noncooperative jurisdictions[74] in implementing and maintaining tax transparency, fair taxation, OECD BEPS measures, and substance requirements for zero-tax countries.

Details on state aid and transfer pricing are provided in section 2.2.1 while ongoing work on tax transparency, specifically in the context of tax rulings and CbCR, is analyzed in section 2.2.2. Work undertaken by the EU JTPF is described in section 2.2.3, and other work on specific topics is covered under section 2.2.3.

2.2.1 Fiscal State Aid and Transfer Pricing

The year 2017 continued to feature heightened activity around EC investigations into specific country's practices on unlawful state aids. On October 4, 2017, the EC announced[75] that it would refer Ireland to the European Union Court of Justice (EUCJ) according to Article 108(2)[76] of the Treaty on the Functioning of the European Union (TFEU) for failing to recover the state aids granted to Apple[77] following its decision on August 31, 2016. The standard deadline for recovery was four months from the date of notification by the EC, i.e., January 3, 2017. The EC has stated that Apple continued to gain as the amount calculated by Ireland is considered as the undue state aid benefit.

Further, the EC also concluded that Luxembourg had granted illegal tax benefits of up to EUR 250 million to Amazon.[78] The EC's conclusions were based on the analysis and Luxembourgish ruling in 2003, which was extended to 2011, lowering the taxes paid by Amazon. Amazon EU and Amazon Europe Holding Technologies (AEHT), the holding company, were both incorporated in Luxemburg with their ultimate parent as Amazon Inc. (Amazon US). Amazon EU acted as an operating retail company throughout the EU and was responsible for contractual sales conclusions based on online sales. Therefore, the profits from such sales were recorded in Luxembourg. AEHT, having no employees as well as no office or business activities was an intermediary between Amazon US and Amazon EU and provided the license to use the intellectual property (IP) to Amazon EU. Based on a cost sharing agreement (CSA), AEHT made annual payments to Amazon US and contributed to the development of the IP. AEHT, being a fiscally transparent entity, was not subject to corporate taxes in Luxembourg. AEHT's partners in the USA deferred their tax liability. Profits recorded by the holding company were only taxed at the level of the partners and not at the level

73. *Source*: https://ec.europa.eu/taxation_customs/tax-common-eu-list_en.
74. American Samoa, Bahrain, Barbados, Grenada, Guam, Korea (Republic of), Macao SAR, Marshall Islands, Mongolia, Namibia, Palau, Panama, Saint Lucia, Samoa, Trinidad and Tobago, Tunisia, United Arab Emirates.
75. *See* EC Press Release, *Source*: http://europa.eu/rapid/press-release_IP-17-3702_en.htm (last accessed January 8, 2017).
76. *Source*: http://ec.europa.eu/competition/state_aid/legislation/provisions.html.
77. C(2016) 5605 final.
78. *See* EC Press Release, *Source*: http://europa.eu/rapid/press-release_IP-17-3701_en.htm (last accessed on January 8, 2017).

of the holding company itself. The holding company's partners were located in the US and have, so far, deferred their tax liability.

The EC assessed the following functional analysis:

(a) Amazon EU:
   (i) operates Amazon's retail business throughout Europe
   (ii) has over 500 employees
   (iii) selects the goods for sale on Amazon's websites in Europe
   (iv) buys the goods from the manufacturers
   (v) manages the online sale and the delivery of products to the customers
(b) AEHT:
   (i) has no employees, no offices, and no business activities
   (ii) acts as an intermediary between the operating company and Amazon in the US
   (iii) holds certain intellectual property rights for Europe under a CCA with Amazon in the US
   (iv) makes no active use of this intellectual property
   (v) merely grants an exclusive license to this intellectual property to the operating company that uses it to run Amazon's European retail business.

It was observed by the EC, based on its investigation, that over 90% of Amazon EU's profits were made as payments in lieu of the license received by Amazon EU from AEHT. It was also asserted by the EC that these payments were more than 1.5 times what AEHT had to pass on as consideration in the cost sharing arrangement to Amazon US. Based on this claim, the EC set the methodology for valuing the competitive benefit accrued to Amazon.

The Amazon and the Apple cases have been two of the many cases that the EC has pursued since June 2013. In October 2015, the EC decided that Luxembourg and the Netherlands had granted selective tax advantages to Fiat[79] and Starbucks,[80] respectively. Further, in January 2016, the Commission concluded that selective tax advantages were granted by Belgium to at least 35 MNEs by means of an "excess profit" tax scheme that was identified to be illegal under state aid rules. The Commission also has two ongoing in-depth investigations into concerns that tax rulings may give rise to state aid issues in Luxembourg regarding McDonald's and GDF Suez.[81]

While MNEs such as Apple have appealed against the decisions, the US Government applied to submit its views to the court as an intervener in the appeal proceedings. The primary contention of the US was that its intervention is necessary as its tax base would be affected, and the outcome of the state aid investigation in the case of

79. *See* Case T 759/15, Fiat Chrysler Finance Europe v Commission.
80. *See* Cases T 760/15, T 636/16, T 877/16, SA.38374: State aid implemented by the Netherlands to Starbucks. *Source*: http://ec.europa.eu/competition/elojade/isef/case_details.cfm?proc_code=3_SA_38374 (last accessed December 29, 2017).
81. *See* EC Press Release (October 4, 2017). *Source*: http://europa.eu/rapid/press-release_IP-17-3701_en.htm (last accessed December 29, 2017).

Apple could harm bilateral tax treaty negotiations with the EU MS as well as efforts to develop future transfer pricing rules within the OECD framework. However, the EU's General Court rejected the application made by the US Government, citing lack of establishment of interest by the US in the result of the case.

The EC decisions in the transfer pricing related State Aid cases might be criticized to a certain extent. One of the most relevant points of any transfer pricing analysis is the functional analysis (i.e., the analysis of functions performed, assets used, and risks assumed by the related parties in a transaction) that should be performed in the context of a complete global value chain analysis of the MNE group. In the Amazon case, for example, when focusing on the specific transaction under review (i.e., between Amazon Europe and AEHT), it seems that the value of the transaction is driven by Amazon Europe. However, as mentioned before, it is important to "frame" this specific transaction (and functional analysis) in the context of an analysis of the global value chain of the entire MNE group. Based on this, the members of the group who drive the value creation should be remunerated with the residual profits (or losses) of the business while those who perform only routine functions should gain a low (but stable) return.

When looking at Amazon's business model, the key value drivers have not been located in Luxembourg. The EC mentions that "the operating company was the only entity actively taking decisions and carrying out activities related to Amazon's European retail business. [...] its staff selected the goods for sale, bought them from manufacturers, and managed the online sale and the delivery of products to the customer." All of these functions sound quite routine in the context of Amazon's overall global value chain. Maybe the operating company could receive extra-remuneration (from a mere routine one) since it "also adapted the technology and software behind the Amazon e-commerce platform in Europe, and invested in marketing and gathered customer data." However, this extra-remuneration would not be constituting the entire residual profit. Rather, such a residual profit should be allocated to the company owning and developing the abovementioned key value drivers, i.e., the parent company of the group in the US.

In conclusion, the debate on fiscal State aid and transfer pricing has grown intensively with the many US headquartered companies facing challenges under the EU clampdown. While it is expected that the US would continue to balance tax fairness and competitiveness, the EU would also wish to balance both forces. The entire issue could have broader political-legal implications in times to come.

2.2.2 *Tax Transparency on Country-by-Country Reporting*

One of the most intriguing steps by the EC during 2017 has been the proposal for new transparency rules for intermediaries[82] that are involved in designing and/or selling

82. *See* EC (June 21, 2017). *Source*: http://europa.eu/rapid/press-release_IP-17-1663_en.htm.

harmful tax practices. As per the public release,[83] "intermediaries" are firms or persons—such as consulting firms, banks, lawyers, tax advisors, accountants, etc.—that can help their clients set up schemes to reduce their tax bills. This proposal gains utmost significance as it creates a compliance requirement for intermediaries to report cross-bordering advice of a specific nature indicated in the proposal and termed as "hallmarks" based on the EC's understanding of BEPS Action 12.[84] The EC has stated that the proposed rules rest on two pillars: "Fair and Effective Taxation" and "Global Tax Good Governance." One of the many examples provided by the EC of reportable arrangements are transactions that "*do not respect EU or international transfer pricing guidelines*." Since July 2017, tax authorities of the MS have commenced exchange of information and, from April 2018, exchange of CbC Reports will also come into force as part of the Council Directive amending Directive 2011/16/EU[85] regarding mandatory automatic exchange of information. With this exchange of information mechanism as the premise, the MS are also expected to exchange the reports on cross-border arrangements, forming a considerable amount of data at the tax authorities' disposal. With regard to intermediaries of non-EU countries, since the EU may not have jurisdiction over such intermediaries, the burden of compliance is proposed to be shifted to the corresponding taxpayer in the EU.

This proposal has been submitted to the European Parliament and the European Economic and Social Committee for consultation and to the Council for adoption. The EC estimates that the new rules would take effect from January 1, 2019, and the MS are expected to begin exchanging from thereon on a quarterly basis.

Further, in April 2016, the EC issued a proposal[86] that would require MNEs to disclose certain data of the CbC Report to the public. In February 2017, this proposal[87] was further crystallized as the Members of European Parliament (MEP) put forth certain amendments to the initial proposal. While the original proposal had been based on the turnover threshold of Euro 750 million, the amendments require all large undertakings as defined in the original Directive 2013/34/EU to publish their CbC Report information when a large undertaking is defined as exceeding at least two out of three of the following criteria: balance sheet total of Euro 20 million, net turnover of Euro 40 million, and 250 employees. The MEP has also proposed changes to the information to be disclosed.

The transparency and reporting requirements of the EU is expected to see intense developments in 2018 wherein more of these rules will become concrete. The EU is also

83. *Source*: https://ec.europa.eu/taxation_customs/business/company-tax/transparency-intermediaries_en (last accessed December 28, 2017).
84. OECD (2015), Mandatory Disclosure Rules, Action 12 - 2015 Final Report, OECD Publishing, Paris.
85. COM(2016) 26 final: Proposal for a Council Directive laying down rules against tax avoidance practices that directly affect the functioning of the internal market.
86. EC (2016), Proposal for a Directive of the European Parliament and of the Council amending Directive 2013/34/EU [Accounting Directive] as regards disclosure of income tax information by certain undertakings and branches,.
87. EC Press Release (June 2017). *Source*: http://europa.eu/rapid/press-release_MEMO-17-1677_en.htm (last accessed December 28, 2017).

expected to take into consideration concerns regarding the balancing of competitiveness in the region and ensuring that a fair share of taxes are subjected to taxation.

For some considerations on this topic, see section 2.1.1.

2.2.3 The Work of the EU JTPF

The work of the EU JTPF, by way of periodical meetings, broadly focused around three areas: (a) use of comparables in the EU, (2) economic valuation techniques in transfer pricing, and (3) dispute resolution mechanisms.

Firstly, on the report on economic valuation techniques for transfer pricing which has been under discussion since 2016, the JTPF concluded[88] in March 2017 that two aspects were critical, i.e., (a) whether there is a need for a "sanity check" in such valuation exercises for intangibles in TP and (b) how to apply the two-sided approach (i.e., valuing at the level of both parties and determining a price within the range of agreements). The respective recommendations are expected to be redrafted as an outcome of the various discussions. Discourses also reflected upon the documentation to be provided when using these techniques and how an appropriate balance between the need for information and the administrative burden can be achieved. The sections on building capacity and legislative proposal implications were not considered as being necessary for the report, and it was agreed to delete them. The EU JTPF also subsequently published the revised draft[89] attempt taking into account the above aspects and also attempted to avoid needless repetition of what has been provided in the OECD TPG. Further action on practical case studies along with incorporation of comments provided by stakeholders is expected in 2018.

Moreover, the EU JTPF finalized and approved the Report on Use of Comparables in the EU[90] with minor modifications. The report established best practices and pragmatic solutions by issuing various recommendations for both taxpayers and tax administrations in the EU and aimed at increasing the objectivity and transparency of comparable searches for transfer pricing analyses in practice.[91]

Furthermore, during a meeting in July 2017, the EU Directive on Dispute Resolution Mechanisms[92] was examined. The discussions focused on the basic expectations of the directive and its relevance for transfer pricing cases. In a public release[93]

---

88. EC (March 15, 2017) *Source*: https://ec.europa.eu/taxation_customs/sites/taxation/files/jtpf0052017ensummarymarch.pdf.
89. EC (May 2017), doc JTPF/003/2017/EN. *Source*: https://ec.europa.eu/taxation_customs/sites/taxation/files/jtpf003rev2017enecovaldraft_en.pdf.
90. EC (June 2016), doc. JTPF/007/FINAL/2016/EN. *Source*: https://ec.europa.eu/taxation_customs/sites/taxation/files/resources/documents/taxation/company_tax/transfer_pricing/forum/jtpf/2016/jtpf0072016_en.pdf.
91. *See* Petruzzi, R., *Global Transfer Pricing Developments*, in: Lang, M., Storck, A. & Petruzzi, R. (eds.), *Transfer Pricing Developments around the World* (Vienna: Kluwer, 2017).
92. EC (October 2016): Council Directive, Strasbourg - COM(2016) 686 final. *Source*: https://ec.europa.eu/taxation_customs/sites/taxation/files/com_2016_686_en.pdf.
93. *See* Press Release, *Source*: https://ec.europa.eu/taxation_customs/sites/taxation/files/jtpf_presentation_on_drm.pdf (last accessed December 29, 2017).

following the meeting, it was evident that the EU JTPF would view transfer pricing dispute resolution as one of its key focus areas in the coming times.

The work of the PCT and that of the EU JTPF is very much welcome and provides useful insights into various practical methodologies and solutions on relevant transfer pricing topics. Going forward, also in the case of the EU JTPF, it might be advisable to expand the scope of the work to many other transfer pricing topics where internationally agreed practical solutions are required.

2.2.4 Digitalization of the Economy

On September 21, 2017, the EC launched a new agenda[94] for ensuring a balance between fair-share and growth friendly taxation of the digitalization of the economy. The agenda discussed the challenges faced by the MS and the aim of the EC to provide solutions to them. Most importantly, the EC declared that the current framework of taxation is not in line with modern realities of the Digital Single Market. The EU placed on record that the effective tax rate of the digitalized economy is estimated to be half of that of physical companies. In this context, the EU also released a memo containing questions and answers that shed some light on the direction of taxing the digitalization of the economy. The EC stated that transfer pricing rules had previously been developed keeping in mind the "brick and mortar" business models. The challenge, the EC observed, remains to be the means to identify and value intangible assets in a digitalized economy and their contribution to value creation. This work requires alternative methods for attributing profit that better capture value creation in the new business models. based on the work of the OECD's, the two key counter measures to digital complexities that have been proposed by the EU include: (a) a "virtual PE" that would create local tax nexus for the overseas affiliate even without a sufficient physical presence in the source country; and (b) an "equalization levy" that would impose a flat rate of tax on gross turnover arising from the source country through specified transactions.

The proposal has been further confirmed by way of a Communication[95] from the EC to the European parliament and the Council in September 2017 presenting a French-led proposal that was supported by nine other MS, including Germany, Italy, and Spain. Unlike the BEPS Action 1 Final Report, the EC does not mention alternatives for equalization of tax bases; in other words, a levy proportional to the average number of monthly active users or the amount of data collected from "in-country customers

94. *See* EC Press Release (September 21, 2017). *Source*: http://europa.eu/rapid/press-release_IP-17-3305_en.htm.
95. COM(2017) 547 final, *A Fair and Efficient Tax System in the European Union for the Digital Single Market,* Brussels (September 21, 2017).

and users."[96] The debate is whether these bases that are identified as value drivers would stand the test of substance and whether, in reality, they would require further analysis.[97]

For some considerations on this topic, see section 2.1.5.

2.2.5 *Anti-avoidance*

On May 29, 2017,[98] the Council of the European Union (EU Council) adopted the Directive[99] amending the Anti-Tax Avoidance Directive (ATAD). This Directive, known as ATAD 2, aims to revise the scope of existing ATAD to hybrid mismatches involving non-EU countries. Additionally, ATAD 2 also includes forms of hybrid mismatches not addressed by ATAD. ATAD 2 was broadly agreed on by the ECOFIN earlier in February 2017. From a transfer pricing perspective, it is pertinent to note that the ATAD 2 is applicable in cases of a hybrid mismatch between "associated enterprises," between the head office and its PE, between two or more PEs of the same entity, or under a "structured arrangement." Based on Action 2 of the OECD BEPS Project, the ATAD was initially only applicable to hybrid instruments and hybrid entity mismatches between the EU MS with the aim of neutralizing them. However, with the recent consensus that is emerging extending the applicability to hybrid PE mismatches, the ATAD 2 may have far reaching impacts on taxpayers operating in the EU. Hybrid PEs are viewed as arrangements where the business activities in a jurisdiction are treated as being carried out through a PE by one jurisdiction while those activities are not treated as being carried out through a PE in another jurisdiction. As next steps, the MS will have until January 1, 2020 to transpose the Directive into national laws and regulations (January 1, 2022 for the implementation of reverse hybrid mismatches). The move increases the potential of growing transfer pricing implications arising from the OECD BEPS Action Plan beyond the Action 8–10 and Action 13.

2.2.6 *Dispute Resolution*

In May 2017, the EC issued a "Proposal for a Council Directive on Double Taxation Dispute Resolution in the European Union" addressing the need for harmonizing the approach to the interpretation of treaties between the MS. For this purpose, the EC stated that the existing Union Arbitration System that deals with transfer pricing and attribution of profits to PEs will play a larger role in tax treaty dispute resolution.[100]

96. *Source*: https://www.rte.ie/news/2017/0916/905202-donohoe-eu-tax-plan/ (last accessed January 3, 2017).
97. *Source*: https://www.loyensloeff.com/nl-nl/news-events/news/taxation-within-the-eu-of-digital-companies-options-and-implications (last accessed January 3, 2018).
98. EC Press Release (February 21, 2017). *Source*: http://www.consilium.europa.eu/en/press/press-releases/2017/02/21/corporate-tax-avoidance/ (last accessed January 2, 2017).
99. EC (May 12, 2017). *Source*: http://data.consilium.europa.eu/doc/document/ST-6661-2017-INIT/en/pdf (last accessed January 2, 2017).
100. EC (May 19, 2017), p. 5. *Source*: http://data.consilium.europa.eu/doc/document/ST-9420-2017-INIT/en/pdf. (last accessed January 2, 2017).

Mechanisms in the European Union Estimates show that there are currently around 900 double taxation disputes in the EU today that are estimated to be worth Euro 10.5 billion.[101] On October 10, 2017, the EC stated that the MS have agreed to resolve disputes related to tax treaties in a progressive manner. The decision that is based on a consensus between finance ministers in the EU aims at resolving disputes in connection with the interpretation of tax treaties with clear deadlines. The resolution provides the MS with a duty to time bound resolution and enforceable decisions.

For some considerations on this topic, see section 2.1.6.

2.2.7 VAT Implications of Transfer Pricing

Interplay between transfer pricing and Value Added Tax (VAT) has been an area of global focus. On February 28, 2017, the EC issued a working paper No. 923[102] on the possible VAT implications of transfer pricing. The EC concluded that transfer pricing adjustments might have VAT implications if there is a supply for consideration which can be linked directly to the supply. The working paper stated that a VAT implication owing to transfer pricing is evident in situations where transfer pricing adjustment could be seen as more or less a consideration given in exchange for a taxable supply of goods or services already made, i.e., as an adjustment to a price already paid leading to a modification of the taxable amount of that transaction for VAT purposes.[103] The delegations were requested to give their opinion on the issues raised. The paper provided the following guiding steps to identify the nexus between VAT and transfer pricing:

- Correlation between direct and indirect taxation
- Recognition of the arm's length principle in the VAT Directive;
- Viewing a transfer pricing adjustment as actual consideration given in exchange for supply;
- Allocation of the transfer pricing adjustment between bundled transactions in order to delineate the identified VAT implications transaction-wise;
- Establishing a linkage between supply and consideration.

Further opinions are being sought on this working paper and more activities around this topic are expected in coming times.

101. EC Press Release (October 10, 2017). *Source*: http://europa.eu/rapid/press-release_IP-17-3727_en.htm (last accessed January 2, 2017).
102. EC (February 28, 2017), *Value Added Tax Committee—Questions concerning the application of VAT Provisions*; European Commission, Brussels. *Source*: https://circabc.europa.eu/sd/a/55d34dce-faf8-42ba-8ec6-381a98540b9c/923%20-%20VAT%20Implications%20of%20Transfer%20Pricing.pdf (last accessed January 2, 2017).
103. taxud.c.1(2017) 1280928 Working paper No 923 VAT Committee Question, Pg.15.

2.2.8 *EU "Blacklist"*[104]

The EU "Blacklist" of noncooperative jurisdictions was conceived by the EC and subsequently taken forward by its MS. By means of releasing the list on December 5, 2017, the Commission placed the MS in a position to adhere to countermeasures against the identified jurisdictions. Seventeen countries have been identified as failing to meet agreed tax good governance standards. During 2018, the process is set to continue starting with a letter being sent to the blacklisted jurisdictions explaining the decision and what they can do to be de-listed. The EC and MS will continue to monitor all of the jurisdictions and update the list on an annual basis.

2.3 Transfer Pricing Developments at the United Nations

The work of the UN in 2017 addressed transfer pricing topics by means of its major update to the UN TPM. The 2017 UN TPM covers four key aspects: (1) transfer pricing in the current global context; (2) the arm's length principle; (3) policy implementation concerns; and (4) country specific transfer pricing practices including those in India, Brazil, China, South Africa, and Mexico. The UN also participated in the development of the abovementioned toolkit to address comparability issues for low-income countries.

2.3.1 *The 2017 UN Practical Manual on Transfer Pricing for Developing Countries*[105]

On April 7, 2017, the UN published the second edition of its "Practical Manual on Transfer Pricing for Developing Countries."[106] Further, the "Fifteenth Session of UN Committee of Experts on International Cooperation in Tax Matters: other issues" was held in October 2017 wherein several insights on the direction of the UN's upcoming work was discussed.

The 2013 "Practical Manual on Transfer Pricing for Developing Countries"[107] (2013 UN TPM) has been updated to reflect the recent developments in transfer pricing including the OECD recommendations under BEPS Actions 8–10 and 13.

Following the detailing of structural and content changes[108] to the 2013 UN TPM that was discussed in 2016, the revisions to the final UN TPM now majorly include the new chapters on intra-group services, cost contribution arrangements (Part B), and treatment of intangibles (Part B) corresponding to changes to the OECD TPG following BEPS Actions 8–10. With regard to issues impacting developing countries (Part B),

---

104. EC Press Release (December 5, 2017), *Source*: http://europa.eu/rapid/press-release_IP-17-5121_en.htm (last accessed December 28, 2017).
105. For more information, refer Chapter 4 of this book.
106. United Nations, *Practical Manual for Transfer Pricing for Developing Countries* (2017).
107. United Nations, *Practical Manual on Transfer Pricing for Developing Countries* (2013).
108. *See* Petruzzi, R., *Global Transfer Pricing Developments*, in: Lang, M., Storck, A. & Petruzzi, R. (eds), *Transfer Pricing Developments around the World* (Vienna: Kluwer, 2017).

issues surrounding use of secret comparables, application of the Transactional Net Margin Method (TNMM) when foreign comparables are used, and the so-called sixth method, referring to commodity pricing rules as applied in countries such as Brazil and Argentina, were discussed.

With regard to implementation aspects (Part C), the UN TPM emphasizes the need for capacity building within tax authorities apart from strengthening tax systems to ensure administrative effectiveness. Finally, on the country specific practices (Part D), Brazil, South Africa, India, and China along with the addition of Mexico have been covered. The UN Subcommittee aims at explaining transfer pricing topics by means of a very clear and consistent approach. Moreover, the usefulness of the UN TPM will most probably be confirmed not only for users interpreting transfer pricing topics but also for the ones in charge of policy decisions.[109]

Topics that require further clarification would be situations of when the OECD TPG and UN TPM may differ. Examples of such deviations include the list of low-value adding services[110] provided in the OECD TPG being absent in the UN TPM. Also, the detailed different ways to undertake comparable searches[111] have not been provided in the UN TPM. Another observable deviation could be the consideration of acquisitions in the UN TPM in discussing DEMPE that made it DAEMPE. With regard to updates on intra-group services, cost contribution arrangements, and treatment of intangibles as well as on the updates on the comparability analysis, on country-by-country reporting, and on the "sixth method," it will be interesting to assess how the guidance provided in these chapters will be aligned to the corresponding chapters of the OECD TPG. The differences between the documents, if any, would need careful consideration, particularly in situations involving OECD and non-OECD countries.[112]

Ultimately, the UN TPM should complement the OECD TPG whenever the latter is not able to support developing countries' tax administrations in enforcing their transfer pricing rules.[113] Indeed, the arm's length principle should apply in the same way in developing and nondeveloping countries. In continuation with its work to address the challenges, the UN Subcommittee met between October 17 and 20, 2017 to discuss several aspects. With regard to matters concerning the Subcommittee for Article 9 (Associated Enterprises), transfer pricing, having formed a new Subcommittee, i.e., the Committee of Experts, mandated that the Subcommittee reviews and once again updates the UN TPM in line with Article 9 OECD MTC and also considers the needs and realities of developing countries. This next update on the UN TPM is mandated to be ready for release and adoption by 2020-21.

109. Petruzzi, R., *Update of the United Nations Practical Manual on Transfer Pricing for Developing Countries*, Transfer Pricing International (2017), pp. 108–110.
110. *See* OECD (2017), OECD Transfer Pricing Guidelines for Multinational Enterprises and Tax Administrations 2017, OECD Publishing, Paris. pp 333–343.
111. *See* OECD TPG, pp. 147–169.
112. *See supra* n. 102.
113. *See* Cottani, *Transfer Pricing Developments at the United Nations*, Lang/Storck/Petruzzi (eds), *Transfer Pricing Developments around the World* (Vienna 2017) pp. 101–124.

2.3.2 *Digitalization of the Economy*

During its meeting in Geneva between October 17 and 20, 2017, the UN Committee of Experts on International Cooperation in Tax Matters formulated subcommittee assignments regarding digitization of the economy.[114] The subcommittee is mandated to analyze technical, economic, and other relevant issues and describe difficulties and opportunities that are especially of interest to the various affected agencies of developing countries and monitor international developments. The subcommittee will also suggest measures and draft provisions related to the digitalization of the economy with regard to income taxes, double tax treaty issues, and VAT as well as other indirect taxes and tax administration issues.[115]

Moreover, the UN published a detailed paper[116] on the tax challenges of the digitalization of the economy and discussed the global leadership role of the UN subcommittee to address the need for a consensus based approach in developed and developing countries. The paper states that a starting point to this exercise could be to analyze the definitions of digitalization and value creation and, secondly, strengthen the efficiency and operation capacity of the PE in the digital era. The paper also discussed the need for a specific subcommittee on the digital economy to examine relevant issues and undertake necessary action considering the concerns of developing countries. The paper notes that developing countries have already started creating milestones in the taxation of the digital economy. In summary, the starting point of the subcommittee's work is to analyze the definitions of digitalization and value creation and, subsequently, strengthen the efficiency and operation capacity of the PE in the digital era.[117]

For some considerations on this topic, see section 2.1.5.

2.3.3 *Extractive Industries*

The past efforts of the UN on extractive industries[118] will be continued as the new subcommittee will conduct further work on the update of the Extractive Industries Handbook to identify and consider the most pressing issues for developing countries.

---

114. *See* UN, *Challenges of the Digital Economy: An Overview, Committee of Experts on International Cooperation on Tax Matters*, Fifteenth Session, (E/C.18/2017/CRP.21), (Geneva: 2017). *Source*: http://www.un.org/esa/ffd/wpcontent/uploads/2017/10/15STM_CRP21_Overview-Digital-Economy.pdf.
115. Anghileri. D, *Key UN international tax committee elects leaders, sets new agenda,* MNE News (October 24, 2017). *Source*: https://mnetax.com/key-un-international-tax-committee-elects-leaders-sets-new-agenda-24152 (last accessed January 19, 2018).
116. UN (October 2017), *Tax Challenges in Digital Economy, Source*: http://www.un.org/esa/ffd/wp-content/uploads/2017/10/15STM_CRP22_-Digital-Economy.pdf.
117. *See supra* n. 107, pp. 34–35.
118. UN (March 31, 2017), *Transfer Pricing issues in Extractive Industries. Source*: http://www.un.org/esa/ffd/wp-content/uploads/2017/02/14STM_CRP9_TP-and-Extractive-Industries.pdf and http://www.un.org/esa/ffd/wp-content/uploads/2017/11/2017TB_14_Extractive_D4_3_Handbook.pdf (last accessed January 8, 2018).

2.3.4 Dispute Avoidance and Resolution

Additionally, a new subcommittee on dispute avoidance and resolution[119] has been mandated to draft a UN handbook on dispute resolution and avoidance carrying an update to the UN's Guide to the Mutual Agreement Procedure under Tax Treaties and drafts of possible changes to the UN model convention and/or commentaries. The UN has recommended more emphasis on issues affecting developing economies.

For some considerations on this topic, see section 2.1.6.

2.3.5 Toolkit for Low-Income Countries

The UN also participated in the development of the toolkit[120] to address comparability issues for low-income countries. For some considerations on this topic, see section 2.1.7.

2.4 Transfer Pricing Developments at Other International Organizations

The role of other international organizations in continuing to contribute to transfer pricing policy making during 2017 included the work of the WBG/IMF (see section 2.4.1) and WCO (see section 2.4.2).

2.4.1 Recent Developments at the World Bank Group and at the International Monetary Fund

For further information on the role of World Bank Group and International Monetary Fund on the Toolkit for Low-Income Countries, see section 2.1.7.

2.4.2 Recent Developments at the World Custom Organization

The WCO continued its work on its ambitious guidance on aligning customs outcomes with transfer pricing. In 2015, the WCO published its "Guide to Customs Valuation and Transfer Pricing" (the WCO Guide)[121] detailing the interplay between transfer pricing and customs and the information that could be used by administrators for audit purposes. Further, in 2016, the WCO continued its work on the interplay between transfer pricing and custom valuation as well as the strengthening of cooperation and exchange of information between customs and tax authorities. In this context, the

119. UN (October 11, 2017), *Mutual Agreement Procedure—Dispute Avoidance and Resolution. Source*: http://www.un.org/esa/ffd/wp-content/uploads/2017/10/15STM_CRP26_Mutual-Agreement-Procedure.pdf.
120. *See* section 2.1.7, above.
121. WCO, *Guide to Customs Valuations and Transfer Pricing* (2015).

WCO also released a case study in 2016 (Case Study 14.1[122]) that dealt with customs valuation taking into account the information provided in a company's transfer pricing study based on the TNMM when examining whether or not the price of imported goods had been influenced by the relationship between buyer and seller.

During 2017, the WCO issued a second case study (Case Study 14.2)[123] based on a request by China. The case deals with an importer of luxury handbags purchased from a related party, both operating under the same MNE group. The price is determined based on the Resale Price Method in which the profit margin of the importer is compared to the profit margin of a group of benchmarked companies that have similar functions and risks to the importer but who transact with unrelated parties. The gross margin of the importer in the case was 64%. The benchmarked range of margins of the comparable companies was within the range of 35% to 46%. The transfer pricing report maintained by the taxpayer in accordance with the OECD TPG is used in this valuation process. In this case, the importer earned a higher gross profit on the sale of the goods than the comparable companies considering, i.e., the intercompany transfer price (resulting customs value) should have been higher. During the audit process, it is made evident that the payment reported to customs does not factor a compensating adjustment to adjust for excess profits in the transaction value. Therefore, the transaction value method cannot be used in the given fact pattern and, instead, the taxpayer is suggested to use an alternative method (in sequential order of preference) for customs valuation purposes.

A popular argument that has been mooted by MNEs and tax practitioners has been the inherent anomaly in the treatment of import prices by the tax administration. In the case of a situation (in the circumstances described in the above case study) where the importer's profits are slightly in excess of the arm's length range, the direct taxes authorities in the country of importation may not disturb the status of the audit as the taxes have already been overpaid. However, the customs authorities may demand that the compensating effect on the import prices would increase a dutiable value base. Therefore, the above case study gives clear guidance that the compensating adjustment must be made for the transfer pricing to be used for customs purposes and, in fact, not making the adjustment is strong evidence that prices are not at arm's length.

In another scenario whereby currency controls exist (such as in China), supplemental payments out of the currency in lieu of compensating adjustments are difficult. While taxpayers prepare the transfer pricing documentation in good faith, establishing the arm's length nature of the import transaction with the assumption that a compensating adjustment will be made and, accordingly, taxes remain overpaid in the importing country. However, in reality, this may not be entirely possible due to the fact that the direct tax authorities may not question the excess taxes while customs authorities would seek to increase the import prices thereby resulting in overall excess outflow of taxes for MNEs.

122. *See* WCO, Case Study 14.1. *Source*: http://www.wcoomd.org/~/media/wco/public/global/pdf/topics/valuation/instruments-and-tools/case-study/case-study-14_1-en.pdf?db=web.
123. *See* WCO, Case Study 14.2. *Source*: http://www.wcoomd.org/-/media/wco/public/global/pdf/media/press-release/2017/case-study-14_2_en-release-version.pdf?la=en.

In summary, the resolution of this conflict begins with the recognition of compensating the adjustment on the actual import prices. Accounting policies for disclosing such adjustments also become extremely critical as they act as the starting point during audit processes.

3 RECENT DEVELOPMENTS IN COUNTRIES SPECIFIC TRANSFER PRICING LEGISLATION, GUIDELINES AND JURISPRUDENCE[124]

During the past year, many countries have continued to intensify their efforts in framing implementation rules in order to align them with the international guidelines presented in the previous sections. Adopting the three-tiered documentation structure including the CbC Report based on the *OECD recommendations* out of BEPS Actions 13 has been a key feature in amending country specific transfer pricing provisions across several tax jurisdictions. Furthermore, several judicial precedents and guidelines were laid down to reflect the *OECD recommendations* from BEPS Actions 8–10.

This section provides a collective synopsis of key developments in country specific legislative changes,[125] amendments to the administrative guidance, local laws, and some selected court cases.

These developments have been broadly identified in relation to the following topics:

- Digitalization of the economy and related attribution of profits to permanent establishments
- Intra-group financing arrangements
- Intra-group services, intangibles, and cost sharing arrangements
- Documentation
- Dispute resolution
- Customs valuation and transfer pricing
- Other notable developments.

3.1 Digitalization of the Economy

It is now widely acknowledged that the evolution of new technologies has reshaped the way business models and global MNE structures are built and, consequently, the readiness of tax systems to keep pace with these increasingly complex digitalized business models is under trial. Italy has taken a step forward and has adopted its

124. The information in this chapter is derived from various public tax portals such as the tax alerts provided by the IBFD and by tax consulting firms. The authors have selected the most relevant countries' developments on transfer pricing related topics. Apart from a few exceptions, details on laws and administrative guidelines that have not been approved when drafting this section (e.g., draft legislation and draft guidelines) have not been included.

125. For more information on developments in the EU and the US, refer to Chapters 2 and 3 of this book.

budget proposal for 2018 to implement "digital tax"[126] while smaller countries such as Malta and Luxembourg have expressed their apprehensions about these unilateral short-term fixes to the long drawn out process of resolving the problems of digital transactions.

The United Kingdom implemented "diverted profits taxes" (DPT) to counter the use of aggressive tax planning techniques by MNEs to divert profits using tax planning. A blanket rate of 25% is applicable on the identified diverted profits from the UK. While France proposed the implementation of a similar tax, the Constitutional Council of France observed the levy to be unconstitutional.

In March 2017, the Australian Parliament passed legislation[127] to implement DPT in order to allow the Australian Taxation Office (ATO) to impose a penalty of 40% on Australian and foreign owned Significant Global Entities (SGE).[128] The ATO proposed to deploy DPT in tandem with TP provisions which would necessitate MNEs to ensure appropriate evidence of their value chains and that profit attribution with respect to IP is in line with the OECD and documentation substantiating substance of foreign entities. The use of DPT as a tool to tackle tax structures has become increasingly considered due to implementation by the United Kingdom (UK). The UK, after a gap of three years, once again published transfer pricing statistics[129] in 2017 which included data on yield from DPT collections.

Contrary to the popular trend of introducing unilateral tax measures, New Zealand, which had initially provided a proposal[130] to DPT, has now turned its focus to developing a comprehensive package[131] of anti-avoidance measures to counter digital economy challenges.

With regard to the acceptance and recognition of an expanded defection or modification of PEs, Italy[132] seeks to amend the domestic definition of a PE as part of its budget proposal which could indirectly address the digital presence of large tech MNEs. The proposal states that there will be a mandatory discussion with the competent tax office about the possible presence of an Italian PE for nonresidents that have implemented more than 1,500 transactions with an overall value of Euro 1.5 million in a six-month period. While Saudi Arabia and Kuwait implemented a virtual PE concept as early as 2015 and 2016, the Israeli tax authorities issued their final

126. *Source*: https://www.reuters.com/article/italy-tax-digital/italian-budget-commission-approves-web-tax-on-digital-services-idUSL8N1OJ1EY (last accessed January 3, 2018).
127. ATO Press Release. *Source*: https://www.ato.gov.au/general/new-legislation/in-detail/direct-taxes/income-tax-for-businesses/diverted-profits-tax/?=redirected (last accessed January 3, 2018).
128. SGEs are companies which are members of groups with global revenue of AU$1 billion or more whether they operate domestically or have multinational activities.
129. *Source*: https://www.gov.uk/government/publications/transfer-pricing-and-diverted-profits-tax-statistics-to-201617 (last accessed January 3, 2018).
130. *Source*: http://taxpolicy.ird.govt.nz/sites/default/files/2016-other-cabinet-paper-transfer-pricing.pdf (last accessed January 18, 2017).
131. *Source*: https://www2.deloitte.com/nz/en/pages/tax-alerts/articles/why-nz-is-unlikely-to-introduce-a-diverted-profits-tax.html (Lase accessed January 18, 2018).
132. *Source*: http://www.ey.com/gl/en/services/tax/international-tax/alert--italy-considers-web-tax-and-other-measures-for-digital-economy (last accessed January 3, 2018).

Circular 04/2016 on internet activities that deemed a foreign company as having an Israeli PE if it has premises or representation in Israel and a "significant digital presence" involving Israeli users.[133]

India introduced an equalization levy in its Finance Bill 2016.[134] Based on the new rules, a 6% equalization levy is applied on business-to-business payments for digital services to nonresident service providers. Digital transactions include online advertisement, digital advertising space, and other similar transactions.

Israel, Italy, and China are also considering introducing VAT for digital services.[135]

Divergence in judicial precedence has also been a key feature of treating digital challenges. Judicial precedents in the case of Google in France[136] and India[137] in 2017 indicate differences in the judicial points of view The French court viewed the entire business model through the perspective of a PE whereby it observed that Google France did not enjoy de facto powers to conclude contracts on behalf on the nonresident entity based on contractual arrangements. The Indian Tribunal (a lower court), however, concluded that there was a significant transfer of technical services based on similar scrutiny of intercompany contracts and, hence, the transaction was in the nature of royalty subject to withholding taxes.[138]

3.2 Intra-group Financing Arrangements

Intra-group financing arrangements continued to be a focus area in transfer pricing legislation and policymaking in several countries. Intercompany loans, credit guarantees, and cash pooling are issues that are still faced with litigation across various tax jurisdictions. Australia and the UK provided several guidelines and amendments to existing legislation and jurisprudence on this topic.

The main highlight on this topic in 2017 was the decision on the Australian Chevron case[139] dealing with the question of the interest rate on intercompany loans meeting the arm's length criteria. The case emphasized that providing security for intra-group loans requires to meeting the arm's length criteria and also ruled that an "implicit" guarantee might not have a significant value which might not appear fully in

---

133. OECD (2017), *Tax Challenges of Digital Economy: Comments Received for Input: Part II*, p. 17 *Source*: https://www.oecd.org/tax/beps/tax-challenges-digitalisation-part-2-comments-on-request-for-input-2017.pdf
134. "To avoid some of the difficulties arising from creating new profit attribution rules for purposes of a nexus based on significant economic presence, an "equalization levy" could be considered as an alternative way to address the broader direct tax challenges of the digital economy." OECD (2014), Addressing the Tax Challenges of the Digital Economy, *supra* n. 9, 115.
135. *See supra* n. 107.
136. No. 15051 13 - French Republic v. Google Ireland Company Limited (July 12, 2017).
137. Google India Private Limited v. ACIT, IT (TP).
138. *See* Storck, A, Prasanna, S, *Indian Tribunal Decision on Google*, Transfer Pricing International, 6/2017.
139. Federal Court of Australia, *Chevron Australia Holdings Pty Ltd v. Commissioner of Taxation (2017)*, (April 21, 2017). *Source*: https://www.ato.gov.au/law/view/pdf/misc-case/rdr_2017 fcafc62.pdf.

line with the OECD TPG.[140] The court held that the question of the borrower's credit rating should be considered from the perspective of a lender and that a commercial lender would not approach this question in the same way as would a credit rating agency.[141] While Chevron appealed against the decision before the High Court, the case was withdrawn making the April 2017 decision now final. The Chevron case was followed by a public release of a guidance note by the ATO[142] making it clear that there will be heightened focus on cross-border related party financing arrangements. The guidance sets out a detailed framework for how the ATO differentiates risk based on zones and how the assessments would be customized to the risk profile of the arrangements in question, i.e., the higher the risk rating as per the matrix provided by the ATO, the more likely the arrangement will be reviewed. This guidance has also provided fresh impetus to questions surrounding intra-group financing arrangements in a transfer pricing construct across the world and is not restricted to being an implication to Australian transfer pricing provisions.

On the related issue of corporate guarantee being subjected to an arm's length analysis, the case of *Hornbach-Baumarkt AG v. Finanzamt Landau*[143] (C-382/16) analyzed the situation whereby a German private limited company, Hornbach-Baumarkt AG, provided comfort letters to banks and creditors to guarantee its Dutch subsidiaries and did not receive any compensation for these guarantees. The German tax officer concluded that the grant of comfort letters was not carried out on an arm's length basis and accordingly imputed an adjustment to the taxes to give effect to the income under independent circumstances. The taxpayer challenged this position in front of the German court that subsequently referred it to the EUCJ for a preliminary ruling whereby it was held by the Advocate General (AG) that the German legislation did not result in a restriction on the freedom of establishment. The views of the AG were based on the premise that financial guarantees always give rise to advantages that need to be compensated while alternatives of guarantee are perceived as a capital contribution. In India,[144] the debate of whether the provision of corporate guarantees is an international transaction and whether it constitutes a shareholder activity or not, as discussed in the OECD TPG,[145] was also analyzed. Another view is that the guarantee, in some circumstances, could be viewed as a capital contribution arrangement.

---

140. *See* paras. 1.164–1.167.
141. Storck, A, *Intra-Group Loan Financing and the Arm's Length Principle*, Transfer Pricing International, 1/2017.
142. *See* draft guidance - Practical Compliance Guideline PCG 2017/D4: ATO compliance approach to taxation issues associated with cross-border related party financing arrangements and related transactions.
143. *Source*: http://curia.europa.eu/juris/document/document.jsf?text=&docid=197855&pageIndex=0&doclang=EN&mode=req&dir=&occ=first&part=1&cid=1107258 (last accessed January 3, 2018).
144. *See* Indian Supreme Court admission of SLP in the case of Adani Enterprises Ltd [TS-408-SC-2017-TP], and Indian High-court ruling in the case of Glenmark Pharmaceuticals Ltd [TS-61-HC-2017(BOM)-TP].
145. *See* TPG (2017), p. 321.

Further, on the view of loan arrangements being treated as a capital contribution, an Argentinian[146] tax court published a ruling on a specific dispute on intercompany loan transactions being treated as "integrated capital contributions" against the taxpayer's claims that an arm's length borrower-lender relationship existed. The court stated that the loan represented a capital contribution due to the intensity of tax deductions (e.g., interest and foreign exchange losses in connection with the loan) not being aligned with the arm's length principle. Further, the economic relationship between the parties and nature of handling of funds indicated that the transaction was in the nature of capital contributions.

Another key area of legislative change in countries has been surrounding thin capitalization rules following the BEPS Action 4 Final Report wherein countries such as India[147] introduced thin capitalization rules. Australia released updated Frequently Asked Questions (FAQs)[148] on the topic which was viewed as tightening of the restrictions regarding the level of debt to equity by increasing the minimum threshold while leaving out small and medium enterprises (SMEs) from the compliance burden. The UK[149] also published new corporate interest restriction rules that have consequences on transfer pricing issues. Based on the new update, any transfer pricing adjustment imputed under the UK transfer pricing rules will be taken into account when calculating the corporate interest restriction of the group's "tax-interest" and "tax-EBITDA" while no equivalent transfer pricing adjustments will be made for the purposes of calculating the group's "group-interest" and "group-EBITDA." This results in favorable or unfavorable group ratios that are subjected to restriction.[150] China issued a circular[151] revising its thin capitalization rules. Also, in a decision published in July 2017, the French[152] Administrative Supreme Court ruled that transfer pricing rules should comply with thin capitalization rules. Norway[153] also issued a draft paper proposing changes to the definition of what constitutes the related party "group" under the provisions. Finally, in its 2017 tax reform bill, the US included provisions which limit the interest deduction for corporations to 30 percent of adjusted taxable income (initially EBITDA later EBIT) along with an interest barrier rule which limits the deduction to the extent that a US corporation's share of its group's global net interest expense exceeds 110 percent of the US tax payer's proportion in the group's global

146. *Source*: https://home.kpmg.com/be/en/home/insights/2017/02/tnf-argentina-court-characterizes-intercompany-loan-as-capital-contribution.html (last accessed January 2, 2018).
147. Indian Finance Act 2017.
148. ATO (2017). *Source*: https://www.ato.gov.au/Forms/International-dealings-schedule-instructions-2017/?page=5 (last accessed January 4, 2018).
149. UK(2017) *Source*: https://www.gov.uk/government/uploads/system/uploads/attachment_data/file/635972/corporate-interest-restriction-draft-guidance.pdf (last accessed January 4, 2018).
150. The new rules came into effect from April 1, 2017.
151. *Source*: http://www.internationaltaxreview.com/Article/3665432/China-Tax-implications-of-Chinas-regulatory-rules-on-cross-border-leverage.html (last accessed January 4, 2018).
152. *Source*: https://online.ibfd.org/kbase/#topic=doc&url=/data/tns/docs/html/tns_2017-08-23_fr_1.html&WT.z_nav=Pagination (last accessed January 4, 2018).
153. *Source*: https://home.kpmg.com/xx/en/home/insights/2017/05/tnf-norway-proposed-earnings-stripping-rule-changes.html (last accessed January 4, 2018).

EBITDA.[154] Consequent to the above, the reform also pointed to the requirement that MNEs with related party debt interests will still need to perform the same foundational analyses (i.e., debt capacity and repayment analyses) when facing scrutiny.

On the other hand, countries such as Poland[155] introduced the Advance Pricing Agreement (APA) provisions to ease the increasing burden of compliance with interest deductibility rules.

Lastly, the UK published a guidance note[156] on transfer pricing aspects of cash pooling arrangements that specifies the need for choosing the correct interest rates as a base for allocation of cash pooling benefits along with specific examples. The guidance also discusses the consequences of netting balances, the need for transactions reflecting substance in the case of long-term borrowing, and withholding tax issues associated with cash pools.

3.3 Intra-group Services, Intangibles, and Cost Sharing Arrangements

The valuation of intangibles for transfer pricing purposes has been a challenge in both digital and traditional business models. An early indicator of the emerging complexities behind valuation issues could be the US ruling in the case of Amazon[157] in early 2017 wherein the tax court rejected the IRS's use of the discounted cash flow method to recalculate a buy-in payment for Amazon's transfer under a cost sharing agreement (CSA) of preexisting intangibles to a Luxembourgish subsidiary of the Amazon group. The IRS has currently appealed against this decision. It is also pertinent to note that the IRS publicly released "practice unit"[158] training materials that intended to describe leading practices for specific international and transfer pricing issues and transactions in connection with CSAs. The practice unit observes that the US taxpayer could have a platform contribution (intangibles developed prior to a CSA being the base for subsequent research) provided to a Controlled Financial Corporation (CFC) in a low tax jurisdiction for tax efficiency purposes. For providing such a platform, the CFC is required to make an arm's length compensation to the US parent for the platform contribution, i.e., a "platform contribution transaction." The IRS noted that this transaction is separate from the transfer of the primary IP and, though the IP and platform may be combined for usage, the transactions require separate arm's length compensations. In the finalized guidance, the US also introduced revised patent box

154. *Source*: https://mnetax.com/us-republican-tax-reform-would-rewrite-international-tax-system-24358 (last accessed January 4, 2018).
155. *Source*: http://www.ey.com/gl/en/services/tax/international-tax/alert--poland---advanced-pricing-agreement-to-remove-new-limitation-on-tax-deductibility-of-intra-group-charges (last accessed January 4, 2018).
156. *Source*: https://www.gov.uk/hmrc-internal-manuals/international-manual/intm503100 (last accessed January 4, 2018).
157. US: Amazon.com, Inc. & Subsidiaries v. Commissioner of Internal Revenue (No 31197-12) [2017] 148 T.C. No. 8. *See also* Storck A, Miladinovic A, *US Tax ruled in Favor of Amazon US Addressing a Cost-Sharing Arrangement and the Related Transfer of Intangible Assets*, Transfer Pricing International, 5/2017.
158. US (2017): Transaction Unit, *Source*: https://www.irs.gov/pub/int_practice_units/iso_t_01_01_01-04.pdf (last accessed January 4, 2018).

rules on situations when R&D fractions to CSAs are applicable. Further, the US Treasury Department and the IRS issued a notice requesting comments on the existing regulations for modifying transfer pricing rules under section 482 of the US Internal Revenue Code with regard to CSAs.[159]

In May 2017, the Brazilian Federal Revenue Service concluded in a private and nonbinding ruling that the remuneration paid by a Brazilian company to a foreign related party under a CSA was considered as remuneration for technical services that are subject to the taxes applicable on the importation of services and to transfer pricing control.[160] Finnish tax administrations published their policy on intra-group services and how to determine the arm's length markup for various categories of intra-group services as follow-up to provide certainty after a key Supreme Court ruling[161] on CSAs where participants charged their services on a cost-to-cost basis without any markup. The Finnish tax administration alleged that the CSA was, in fact, a bunch of intra-group services that were not in line with arm's length principle and upheld the views of the tax authorities while discarding the markup claimed by the Finnish authorities to be unacceptable (7%) and revised it downwards (3%). Vietnam[162] introduced a specific law on intra-group technology transfers that mandated auditing of such transactions. Regarding intra-group service structures that result in possible "location savings," an Indian[163] lower court ruled that the mere existence of "location savings" and quantum of difference identified cannot be the basis for determining an arm's length price and, instead, the comparability analysis should capture the functional similarities between the taxpayer and comparable companies considered for testing the arm's length nature of transactions.

3.4 Documentation

The implementation of changes recommended in BEPS Action 13 for maintenance of documentation has now moved beyond mere legislation as MNEs are in the process of fulfilling the compliance requirement. As of December 20, 2017, sixty-two countries[164]

159. *Source*: https://www.gpo.gov/fdsys/pkg/FR-2017-10-17/pdf/2017-22406.pdf (last accessed January 4, 2018).
160. *Source*: https://gettingthedealthrough.com/area/69/jurisdiction/6/transfer-pricing-brazil/ (last accessed January 4, 2018).
161. *Source*: http://www.kho.fi/fi/index/paatoksia/vuosikirjapaatokset/vuosikirjapaatos/1505119873984.html (last accessed January 4, 2018).
162. Law No. 07/2017/QH14 effective July 1, 2018.
163. Parexel International Clinical Research Pvt. Ltd. v. DCIT.
164. Argentina, Australia, Austria, Belgium, Bermuda, Brazil, Canada, Chile, Cayman Islands, Colombia, Croatia, Costa Rica, Cyprus, Czech Republic, Denmark, Estonia, Finland, France, Gabon, Germany, Greece, Guernsey, Hungary, Iceland, India, Indonesia, Ireland, Isle of Man, Israel, Italy, Japan, Jersey, Korea, Latvia, Liechtenstein, Lithuania, Luxembourg, Malaysia, Malta, Mauritius, Mexico, Monaco, Netherlands, New Zealand, Nigeria, Norway, China, Poland, Portugal, Russia, Romania, Slovak Republic, Slovenia, South Africa, Spain, Sweden, Switzerland, Turkey, the UK, Uruguay. *Source*: http://www.oecd.org/tax/automatic-exchange/country-specific-information-on-country-by-country-reporting-implementation.htm (last accessed January 4, 2018).

have a CbCR law in place. Further, as of December 2017, over 1,400[165] bilateral exchange relationships have been concluded for exchanging CbC Reports with the first exchanges scheduled to take place in 2018. The full list[166] of available exchange relationships were also made accessible by the OECD in December 2017.

Further, on June 7, 2017, several countries[167] became signatories to the Multilateral Convention to Implement Tax Treaty Related Measures (MLI) to prevent BEPS, enabling the translation of proposals from the OECD BEPS Project to bilateral tax treaties. The signatories included non-OECD countries such as China and India thereby increasing the scope of application of MLIs.

In order to facilitate the seamless transition to modified documentation requirements, countries such as Australia extended the timelines for local filing of documentation comprising of the master file, local file, and CbC Report from December 31, 2017 to February 15, 2018. Further, the ATO published specific guidance on international related party agreements to be furnished in Part B of the local file for all controlled transactions reported in Part A and, subsequently, clarifications on reporting requirements of Part A and Part B of the local file.[168] The ATO published FAQs on simplified record keeping for transfer pricing purposes with an aim at reducing the compliance burden for SMEs.[169] Further, in a measure to promote robust documentation and a risk based audit, the ATO provided guidance on "offshore hubs"[170] undertaking activities that are commonly centralized such as marketing, sales, and distribution functions.

3.5 Dispute Resolution

In the wake of increasing uncertainties in tax positions, countries have taken steps to resolve disputes by way of alternative dispute resolution mechanisms such as the APA and the MAP. The US,[171] the UK,[172] Australia,[173]

165. OECD, *Source*: http://www.oecd.org/ctp/beps/beps-action13-jurisdictions-implement-final-regulations-for-first-filings-of-cbc-reports.htm (last accessed January 4, 2018).
166. *Source*: http://www.oecd.org/tax/automatic-exchange/country-by-country-exchange-relation ships.htm (last accessed January 4, 2018).
167. OECD (2017), Signatories and Parties to the Multilateral Convention to Implement Tax Treaty Related Measures to Prevent Base Erosion and Profit Shifting, Status as on 20 December 2017. *Source*: http://www.oecd.org/tax/treaties/beps-mli-signatories-and-parties.pdf
168. *Source*: https://www.ato.gov.au/Business/International-tax-for-business/In-detail/Transfer-pricing/Country-by-Country-reporting/Local-file-instructions--Part-A-and-Part-B/ (last accessed December 25, 2017).
169. *Source*: https://www.ato.gov.au/Business/International-tax-for-business/In-detail/Transfer-pricing/Simplifying-transfer-pricing-record-keeping---Frequently-asked-questions/ (last accessed December 25, 2017).
170. *Source*: https://www.ato.gov.au/Business/Large-business/In-detail/Business-bulletins/Articl es/Practical-compliance-guideline-for-offshore-hubs/ (last accessed December 25, 2017).
171. US, *Announcement and Report Concerning Advance Pricing Agreements, March 2017. Source*: https://www.irs.gov/pub/irs-utl/2016_apma_statutory_report.pdf (last accessed January 4, 2018).
172. *Source*: https://www.gov.uk/government/publications/transfer-pricing-and-diverted-profits-tax-statistics-to-201617 (last accessed January 4, 2018).
173. *Source*: https://www.ato.gov.au/Business/International-tax-for-business/In-detail/Advance-pricing-arrangements/?page=13 (last accessed January 4, 2018).

India,[174] China,[175] and Canada[176] issued APA statistics. The UK also released specific guidance preventing transfer pricing discussions in advance in situations when an APA may not be suitable for the dispute.[177] Safe harbor rules have been amended in countries such as Mexico[178] and India[179] in an attempt to provide greater certainty. Further, India also made amendments[180] to existing tax provisions by waiving the requirement of Article 9(2) in tax treaties to conclude an APA/MAP. In a relevant ruling,[181] the US tax court concluded that cancellation of APAs by the US IRS was abuse of discretion. Japan's National Tax Agency published a Transfer Pricing Guidebook[182] that detailed the approach that taxpayers could adopt to resolve potential disputes and guidelines that could be followed for maintenance of contemporaneous documentation.

3.6 Customs and Transfer Pricing

With regard to the alignment of transfer pricing and customs valuation, there has been a divergence of judicial precedents in specific jurisdictions during the year. The EUCJ issued its decision[183] that the customs "Transaction Value" cannot be based on transfer prices that are subject to "flat-rate" retrospective adjustments, making transactions that are subject to year-end adjustments ineligible for customs purposes. Japan instead issued specific guidance concerning how retroactive transfer pricing adjustments are to be addressed from a customs valuation perspective and stated that year-end adjustments would be considered to be part of customs value.

3.7 Other Notable Developments

Various countries[184] continued to implement documentation requirements proposed by the OECD by means of amendments and additional local guidance on CbCR.

---

174. *Source*: http://www.taxindiainternational.com/pdfdocs/APA_Annual_Report-01-05-2017.pdf (last accessed January 2, 2018).
175. *Source*: http://www.ey.com/Publication/vwLUAssets/China_issues_2016_Advance_Pricing_Agreement_Annual_Report/$FILE/2017G_06540-171Gbl_TP_China%20issues%202016%20APA%20Annual%20Report.pdf (last accessed January 2, 2018).
176. *Source*: https://www.canada.ca/en/revenue-agency/services/tax/international-non-residents/competent-authority-services/advance-pricing-arrangements/2016-apa-program-report.html?wbdisable=true (last accessed January 2, 2018).
177. OECD (2017), *United Kingdom Dispute Resolution Profile, 6 June 2017*. *Source*: *Source*: https://www.oecd.org/tax/dispute/United-Kingdom-Dispute-Resolution-Profile.pdf.
178. *Source*: https://home.kpmg.com/xx/en/home/insights/2017/07/tnf-mexico-negotiating-apas-fast-track-for-maquila-companies.html (last accessed January 5, 2018).
179. India, CBDT, Press Release (June 8, 2017). *Source*: http://incometaxindia.gov.in/Lists/Press%20Releases/Attachments/632/Press-Release-SAFE-HARBOUR-8-06-2017.pdf.
180. *Source*: http://pib.nic.in/newsite/PrintRelease.aspx?relid=173885 (last accessed January 5, 2018).
181. *Source*: https://home.kpmg.com/xx/en/home/insights/2017/07/tnf-united-states-cancellation-of-apas-by-irs-abuse-of-discretion.html (last accessed January 3, 2018).
182. Maintaining and Improving Voluntary Tax Compliance.
183. Hamamatsu case (C-529/16), December 20, 2017.
184. Belgium, Canada, Chile, Czech Republic, Finland.

Angola[185] established a new transfer pricing unit in its tax administration while Azerbaijan,[186] Botswana,[187] and Mozambique[188] introduced transfer pricing provisions during the year. Colombia[189] issued proposals to introduce TP regulations. Kosovo's[190] administrative instruction implementing TP regulations came into effect. Zambia[191] and Peru[192] also revised its TP regulations to align more with OECD TPG.

Danish tax authorities published an annual report[193]on transfer pricing adjustments. Germany issued official guidance on the tax consequences of related parties' use of similar company names. The guidance discussed the use of a company name providing economic benefits and its impact on the deductibility of license fees.[194]

The Dominican Republic[195] published revised TP information return requirements, modifying the timing for filing of information.

An analysis of other notable judicial precedence (apart from the rulings in the aforementioned sections) during the year includes Israel's Court[196] which ruled on a TP Case concerning sale of intellectual property (IP) post-acquisition to a US parent by an Israeli company. The main dispute between taxpayers and the tax authorities was on differences in the valuation of shares and the price paid for the IP. The Israel Court ruled that a segregation of various value components of *business restructuring* including synergies, workforce, and customer contracts is necessary for valuation purposes. Ongoing issues surrounding advertising, marketing, and promotion (AMP) expenses constituting *marketing intangibles* in India[197] saw the introduction of an "intensity test" in the absence of the "Bright-line test." India[198] also dealt with the issue of *pass-through costs* and computation of the *profit-level indicator* in undertaking a TP

185. *Source*: http://www.ey.com/gl/en/services/tax/international-tax/alert--angola-establishes-transfer-pricing-unit (last accessed January 3, 2018).
186. *Source*: https://home.kpmg.com/be/en/home/insights/2017/06/tnf-azerbaijan-transfer-pricing-rules-introduced-effective-for-2017.html (last accessed January 3, 2018).
187. *Source*: https://home.kpmg.com/xx/en/home/insights/2017/02/tnf-botswana-introduction-of-transfer-pricing-legislation-under-consideration.html (last accessed January 3, 2018).
188. *Source*: http://www.ey.com/gl/en/services/tax/international-tax/alert--mozambique-approves-transfer-pricing-regulations (last accessed January 3, 2018).
189. *Source*: http://www.ey.com/gl/en/services/tax/international-tax/alert--colombia-issues-proposed-transfer-pricing-regulations (last accessed January 18, 2018).
190. *Source*: http://www.ey.com/gl/en/services/tax/international-tax/alert--kosovo-s-transfer-pricing-administrative-instruction-is-in-force (last accessed January 18, 2018).
191. *Source*: http://www.ey.com/gl/en/services/tax/international-tax/alert--zambia-to-issue-revised-transfer-pricing-regulations (last accessed January 18, 2017).
192. *Source*: http://www.ey.com/gl/en/services/tax/international-tax/alert--peru-amends-transfer-pricing-rules (last accessed January 18, 2017).
193. *Source*: http://www.ft.dk/samling/20161/almdel/SAU/bilag/266/1784341.pdf (last accessed January 18, 2018).
194. *See* Perdelwitz, Ministry of Finance issues guidance on transfer pricing consequences of use of company names within group of companies, IBFD News (April 13, 2017).
195. *Source*: http://www.ey.com/gl/en/services/tax/international-tax/alert--dominican-republic-publishes-new-version-of-transfer-pricing-information-return (last accessed January 18, 2017).
196. *See* Azam, R, *Israeli court uses flawed logic in key transfer pricing decision*, MNE Tax News, (Gteko Ltd v. Kfar Saba Assessing Officer), 2017.
197. *See Louis Vuitton India Retail Pvt Ltd [TS-794-ITAT-2017(DEL)-TP] & Luxottica India Eyewear Pvt Ltd (ITA No. 344/Del/2017).*
198. Cushman and Wakefield (India) Pvt Ltd(TS-766-SC-2017-TP).

analysis. The Finnish court provided two rulings on *cost-sharing agreements*[199] and *intra-group services*[200] while the US[201] Court ruled against cancellation of APAs by the IRS. The Italian[202] court also ruled on *financial capacity* to assume risk and *allocation of financial risk* among transacting entities. New Zealand[203] ruled on the deductibility of management services that had no evidence of actual conduct of services.

4 CONCLUSIONS AND INSIGHTS

The year 2017 witnessed numerous developments on transfer pricing topics around the world. One of the most developed topics in 2017 that will continue to be developed in 2018 is transfer pricing documentation and the CbCR. The OECD has provided considerable clarifications on questions related to the implementation of the CbCR while the EU has more intensively worked on issues related to transparency (including proposals for public disclosure of some CbCR data). Consequently, sixty-two countries have implemented legislations introducing CbCR requirements, and 1,400 bilateral exchange relationships have been concluded for exchanging those reports with the first exchange scheduled for 2018.

Another important topic analyzed by many international organizations as well as countries' regulations has been the one of dispute avoidance and resolution. The OECD, in the framework of BEPS Action 14, has published peer review analyses as well as relevant statistics that show that TP cases are characterized by high complexity. The EU is working on a Directive on Dispute Resolution Mechanisms aimed at introducing a European arbitration system while the UN has created a specific subcommittee with the aim of drafting proposals addressing issues peculiar for developing countries. At the country level, Australia, Canada, China, India, Japan, Mexico, the UK, and the US have worked on these topics.

Comparability issues in a transfer pricing analysis have also been high on the agenda of international organizations with the PCT focusing work on proposals aimed at helping low-income countries and the EU JTPF working on solutions at the European level.

Moreover, many other topics (e.g., HTVI, TPSM, attribution of profits to PEs, intra-group financing, services, intangibles and CSA, use of economic valuation techniques, and issues related to the extractive industries) have been developed. Additionally, further work on the interrelation between, on the one hand, customs valuation and transfer pricing (see the work of WCO, EUCJ, and Japan) and, on the other hand, VAT and transfer pricing (see the work of the EU) have been conducted and will continue to be developed. Meanwhile, the EC has continued developing its views on fiscal state aid and transfer pricing in the EU. Finally, many countries

199. KHO 2017:146.
200. KHO:2017:145.
201. US v. Eaton-Corporation, US Tax Court, TC memo 2017-147 (July 2017).
202. Norway v. Hess Norge AS, Court of Appeal (May 2017).
203. New Zealand v. Honk Land Trustee Limited, Court of Appeal (March 10, 2017).

(Angola, Azerbaijan, Botswana, Colombia, Kosovo, Mozambique, Peru, and Zambia) have either introduced or amended their TP legislations and regulations.

However, the key topic that many international organizations and countries have been working on (and will keep doing so in the years to come) concerns the digitalization of the economy. At the international organizational level, the OECD held a public consultation in November 2017 and will present a paper in April 2018; the EU launched a new agenda in September 2017; and the UN published a paper in October 2017 and created a specific subcommittee that will deal with these topics. At the country level, the UK and Australia have introduced DPT; Israel, Italy, Kuwait, and Saudi Arabia have implemented concepts of a virtual or digital PE; India has implemented an equalization levy while France, Germany, Italy, and Spain have proposed similar measures at the EU level. Italy has also suggested a digital tax. Finally, Israel, Italy, and China are considering introducing VAT for digital services.

In conclusion, during 2018, the international organizations will once again be on the forefront of leading the transfer pricing developments and policy making. As far as the OECD is concerned, the work is expected to be largely focused on the pillars of the existing BEPS framework. What would be interesting is the interplay of transfer pricing with other Action reports of BEPS beyond Actions 8–10 and Action 13 which are conventionally transfer pricing focussed. For instance, the role of transfer pricing in Action 1 and Action 7 is expected to increase manifold as the importance of identification of value creation in the digital economy, attribution of profits, and consequent determination of the arm's length compensation will invariably be a transfer pricing question to answer. The Action 1 Report is also due for revision in 2018 as per the timelines proposed by the OECD. Also, the role of thin capitalization and the identification of substance (centered on Action 4) are expected to evolve with transfer pricing interactions. The year 2018 is also the first year that the CbCR will be open for exchange between tax administrations of different countries. The use of information contained in a CbCR by tax administrators will be tested for its effectiveness which could ultimately result in additional guidance.

At the EU level, along with the efforts of the EC to investigate illegal State aid and transfer pricing, the implementation of quick-fix taxes such as an equalization tax and adoption of longer term solutions such as redefining the scope of PEs would continue to drive tax legislative changes. Additionally, the further work on C(C)CTB and dispute resolution mechanisms is expected to increase, more specifically in light of the concerns expressed by non-EU jurisdictions, MNEs, and some of the MS that depend on a tax-competitive environment to attract investments. In this regard, it is also worth noting that the impact of the US tax reform in reducing corporate tax rates could have various implications on the way that the EU MS and the rest of the world (such as Canada) view tax and transfer pricing policies in 2018.

With regard to the developing countries, the UN will seek to provide further technical assistance and capacity building for strengthening member countries' practices. The ongoing conflict between customs valuation and transfer pricing, despite the efforts from the WCO, could trigger further guidance or recommendations from the WCO in the form of an update to its 2015 publication on aligning the same.

As highlighted by the UN report on Prospects for Global Macroeconomic Development[204], the global economic growth as of 2017 is estimated to have reached 3%, a significant acceleration compared to growth of just 2.4% in 2016 and the highest rate of global growth recorded since 2011. The responsibility of international organizations, governments, MNEs, and other stakeholders in handling the current economic growth with utmost assiduousness is paramount. Therefore, a coordinated and consistent approach to balance policy making, governments' expectation of the fair share of taxes, and enabling ease of conducting business would define the forthcoming tax legislative landscape.

204. UN, World Economic Situation and Prospects 2018, New York 2018; *Source*: https://www.un.org/development/desa/dpad/wp-content/uploads/sites/45/publication/WESP2018_Full_Web-1.pdf.

CHAPTER 2

Transfer Pricing Developments in the European Union

Isabel Verlinden, Stefaan De Baets, Pieter Deré, Paulina Szotek & Jasna Voje

It has been a busy and challenging year for those setting the Transfer Pricing (TP) rules, the ones having to apply them, and those writing about it in whichever capacity and serving whatever aim. The recent communication by, a global player, which is part of the so-called GAFAs[1] or FAANGs,[2] to move to a local sales organization in countries where it only has an office that currently supports sales to local advertisers,[3] has triggered quite some attention. It illustrates how keen many are to grasp (or speculate about) the impact of the broader tax and TP debate on business models in Europe and how business is preparing for others to come. "Fair taxation" of the digital economy is at the core of each tax debate, and the "fight against digital giants"[4] is becoming a common catch phrase in (social) media. While fairness is undoubtedly a noble cause, there seems to be less ado about the need for legal certainty. This is what was eloquently mentioned by Prof. Schoueri at the August 2017 IFA Conference in Brazil when sharing his valuable insights on the "Future of Transfer Pricing." As many know, companies, and public ones in particular, simply dislike surprises, even positive ones, however, the public deserves to know how well they are doing in a way that is as predictive as is reasonably possible. The changes in business model that technology giants are implementing or contemplating come, not coincidently, at a time when

1. Google, Apple, Facebook, Apple.
2. Facebook, Apple, Amazon, Netflix, Google.
3. S. Soong Johnston, *Facebook Restructures Amid Digital Economy Tax Debate*, Tax Notes International, December 18, 2017.
4. *See*, e.g., C. Stupp, *Tax fight draws divisions at EU digital summit*, Euractiv, September 29, 2017, available at http://www.euractiv.com/section/economy-jobs/news/tax-fight-draws-divisions-at-eu-digital-summit/; J. Garside, *From Google to Amazon: EU goes to war against power of US digital giants*, The Observer, July 6, 2014, available at https://www.theguardian.com/technology/2014/jul/06/google-amazon-europe-goes-to-war-power-digital-giants; M. Scott & N. Hirst, Commission ratchets up pressure in digital tax fight, Politico, April 10, 2017, available at https://www.politico.eu/article/vestager-apple-amazon-tax-luxembourg-ireland-margrethe/.

proposals are calling for a virtual permanent establishment (PE) and/or gross sales thresholds to levy taxes "at destination" which will undoubtedly result in double taxation and significant TP challenges.[5]

In the European Union (EU), probably more than anywhere else, the continuous stream of new developments makes it genuinely challenging to keep up to speed with things. This is especially the case as "tax policy" and "tax politics" are blurring into a mere amorphous can of worms that not a single legislator, public servant, or taxpayers dare to touch without fear for mental or bodily harm. Expectations are that it is likely an even bigger challenge to look forward to what is coming toward us in the next six to twelve months and prepare for that. In an attempt to shed some light, this chapter provides an overview of the main TP developments in the EU and gives insight into what is expected to come.

1 THE CALL FOR TRANSPARENCY

While many were still digesting the OECD Action 13 BEPS deliverables, the debate to make Country-by-Country Reporting (CbCR) public was sparked in the wake of public disclosures of sensitive taxpayer information related to jurisdictions often known for their benign weather and tax climate. The release of what was named publicly as the "Panama Papers" and the "Paradise Papers" triggered specific political attention from Mr. Pierre Moscovici, the EU Commissioner on taxation and the "transparency champion" of the EU.[6] Indeed, the papers come at a time when significant proposals to increase transparency on taxation are on the Council's table, and Mr. Moscovici's agenda is clear—to bring tax transparency to the EU.[7] The currently proposed additional transparency measures in the EU go well beyond the BEPS Action 13 standard and include a proposal to bring the CbCR into the public (so-called public CbCR), a proposal for mandatory disclosure rules for intermediaries or taxpayers that perform certain cross-border transactions (so-called DAC6), and the publication of an EU list of noncooperative tax jurisdictions that—according to the defined standards—are considered as not sufficiently transparent or cooperative and should be put on the naughty step.

The proposals add new provisions to the already existing framework for the administrative cooperation in the field of direct taxation that was introduced in 2011 with the Council Directive 2011/16/EU and provided for strong administrative cooperation in the field of taxation.[8] This initial directive was called "DAC1" and established exchanges of information on request; spontaneous exchanges; automatic exchanges; participation in administrative enquiries; simultaneous audits; and mutual notifications of tax decisions in the EU. It also provided for the necessary practical tools such

5. *Supra* n. 3.
6. Cover of Tax Notes International, December 18, 2017.
7. T. Sprackland, Pierre Moscovici: The Man with a Plan to Bring Tax Transparency to the EU, Tax Notes International, December 18, 2017, pp. 1105–1110.
8. Council Directive 2011/16/EU of 15 February 2011 on administrative cooperation in the field of taxation and repealing Directive 77/799/EEC, OJ L 64, 11.3.2011.

as a secure electronic system for the information exchange. In the past few years, in the post-BEPS era, it has been amended many times (each amendment receiving another "DAC" number) and further enhanced in light of the tax transparency agenda. DAC2[9] extended the scope to financial account information, DAC3[10] to information on cross-border tax rulings and advance pricing arrangements, DAC4[11] introduced the CbCR, and DAC5[12] further amended the Directive by providing tax authorities with access to anti-money laundering information.

While certain transparency measures are still at the stage of a proposal, it is demonstrated that they already have significant impact on a company's behavior. The proposals are discussed in more detail below.

1.1 A Status Update on Public CbCR

The CbCR standard has already been adopted through the Fourth Directive on Administrative Cooperation (DAC4).[13] It requires multinationals to report, among other things, their revenues, profits, taxes paid, and the number of employees in every country where they operate. DAC4 is bringing a significant level of information to the tax authorities allowing them to perform audits that are more tailored.

Compared to the OECD, the European Commission (EC), supported by the European Parliament (EU Parliament), wishes to take the reporting standards to a next level. It contemplates the introduction of a requirement for multinational groups and, when relevant, certain nonaffiliated stand-alone undertakings to provide the public with a report on income tax information when they exceed a certain size over a period of the last two consecutive financial years depending on the group's consolidated revenue or revenue of the nonaffiliated stand-alone undertaking. This transparency debate with the focus on public CbCR has already been discussed in the paper on TP developments in the EU that was published last year.[14] On July 4, 2017, the EU Parliament adopted a legislative Resolution on the EC's public CbCR proposal for a directive of the EU Parliament and of the Council, amending Directive 2013/34/EU. The adopted legislative resolution by the EU Parliament does not imply the adoption of public CbCR but was only the Parliament's formal negotiating mandate for entering into the so-called Trilogue negotiations with the Council of the EU and the EC for a final

9. Council Directive 2014/107/EU of 9 December 2014 amending Directive 2011/16/EU as regards mandatory automatic exchange of information in the field of taxation, OJ L 359/1, 16.12.2014.
10. Council Directive (EU) 2015/2376 of 8 December 2015 amending Directive 2011/16/EU as regards mandatory automatic exchange of information in the field of taxation, OJ L 332, 18.12.2015.
11. Council Directive (EU) 2016/881 of 25 May 2016 amending Directive 2011/16/EU as regards mandatory automatic exchange of information in the field of taxation, OJ L 146, 3.6.2016.
12. Council Directive (EU) 2016/2258 of 6 December 2016 amending Directive 2011/16/EU as regards access to anti-money-laundering information by tax authorities, OJ L 342, 16.12.2016.
13. Council Directive (EU) 2016/881 of 25 May 2016 amending Directive 2011/16/EU as regards mandatory automatic exchange of information in the field of taxation, OJ L 146, (2016).
14. For a detailed analysis and comparison with BEPS Action 13, please *see* Verlinden et al. Transfer Pricing Developments in the European Union, pp. 61–70.

compromise text.[15] Today, the EC's draft is still being discussed in Council by the 28 EU Member States at a technical level. There is a new Presidency compromise proposal that was agreed upon and later released on December 19, 2017.[16] A number of Member States oppose the legal basis of the EU draft Directive on public CbCR (allegedly at least seven, including at least one big Member State) and are believed to be ready to block this proposal if it were to come to a qualified majority vote in the Council. Therefore, the proposal is expected to require unanimity in the Council to be adopted.

The CbC Reports may be helpful for high-level TP risk assessment purposes. The information in the CbC Report in itself does not constitute conclusive evidence that transfer prices are or are not appropriate and that the information should not be used as a substitute for a detailed TP analysis of individual transactions and prices based on a comprehensive functional analysis and comparability analysis.[17] CbCR should not ordinarily serve as a blueprint for a TP audit.

The impact of public tax information is not new. Already, since 2010, raids on (shops of) technology companies happen to well serve the purpose of vulgarizing allegations around "tax dodging."[18] In accordance with DAC4, the tax authorities have access to the CbC Reports and can decide to perform a tailored audit. Under public CbCR, the contents are made public. As already explained, the information in the CbCR needs interpretation and analysis, but a business can be confronted with media scrutiny effects as oversimplified information on revenue, functions, and location of profits that are booked would be public. The impact is expected to be even more significant for companies in the Business-to-Consumer segment.

1.2 Disclosure Rules for Intermediaries

There is apparent concern of so-called information asymmetry, i.e., hinting that taxpayers have access to (an abundance of) information that tax authorities are deprived of. In an effort to reduce such an information gap, on June 21, 2017, the EC adopted a proposal for a Council Directive amending Directive 2011/16/EU requiring mandatory automatic exchange of information in the field of taxation in relation to

15. Trilogue is an informal tripartite meeting attended by representatives of the European Parliament, the Council and the Commission. The purpose of these contacts is to get agreement on a package of amendments acceptable to the Council and the European Parliament. The Commission's endorsement is particularly important, in view of the fact that, if it opposes an amendment which the European Parliament wants to adopt, the Council will have to act unanimously to accept that amendment. Any agreement in Trilogue is informal and "ad referendum" and will have to be approved by the formal procedures applicable within each of the three institutions. Based on European Commission, Codecision step by step, Glossary, available at http://ec.europa.eu/codecision/stepbystep/glossary_en.htm (last accessed January 4, 2018).
16. 13685/1/17 REV 1, Proposal for Directive of the European Parliament and the Council amending Directive 2013/34/EU as regards disclosure of income tax information by certain undertakings and branches (CBCR)—*Presidency compromise proposal—State of play.*
17. *Ibid.*, para. 6b.
18. *See* http://metro.co.uk/2010/10/27/protestors-shut-down-vodafone-store-over-tax-dodging-claims-563894/.

what are called "reportable cross-border arrangements."[19] The underlying idea is that, if certain reportable arrangements are put in place, the intermediary (or the taxpayer, in certain cases) is required to report this arrangement to the tax authorities in its Member State. Following the exchange of information, the tax authorities of all Member States would have access to this information and take this into account when performing tax audits. The aim is that such reporting and exchange of information would close the existing information gap.

The proposal by the EC may, to some extent, be inspired by the recommendations by the TAXE I and II and PANA special committees of the EU Parliament to discourage what they regard as aggressive tax planning arrangements and the intermediaries that advise taxpayers. The proposal has attributes of what BEPS Action 12 of the OECD BEPS initiative aimed for which is heavily inspired by existing mandatory disclosure regimes in the United States and the United Kingdom.

In the EU, Member States with already existing disclosure rules are the United Kingdom, Ireland, and Portugal. However, none of the national disclosure rules appear to apply to cross-border arrangements. The stated objective of this proposal, which provides for mandatory disclosure of cross-border arrangements by intermediaries or taxpayers to the tax authorities and mandates automatic exchange of this information among Member States, is to enhance transparency, reduce uncertainty over beneficial ownership, and dissuade intermediaries from designing, marketing, and implementing harmful tax structures. This will be explored below if this objective can be met.

1.2.1 Who Needs to Disclose?

The definition of an intermediary points to a person who carries the responsibility vis-à-vis the relevant taxpayer for *designing, marketing, organizing, or managing* the implementation of a reportable cross-border arrangement. Providing advice with regard to these activities, even if indirectly, would fall under the personal scope of the proposal.[20] In order to fall under the personal scope, the intermediary should also have a taxable presence in one of the Member States. The proposal primarily obliges the intermediary (such as professional services firms, lawyers) to disclose the reportable cross-border arrangement to the tax authority of the relevant Member State. As mentioned, the tax authorities can then exchange the information amongst each other.

The reporting obligation, however, can also be shifted to the taxpayer. This is the case where the intermediary does not have any taxable presence in the EU, where the intermediary has the right to a waiver from disclosing when case disclosing would constitute a breach under the legal professional privilege according to the relevant national law, or in the absence of an intermediary as the taxpayer would implement the arrangement without external support.

19. Proposal for a Council Directive amending Directive 2011/16/EU regarding mandatory automatic exchange of information in the field of taxation in relation to reportable cross-border arrangements, June 21, 2017. This contribution was written in February 2018 and it is based on the text of the proposal as relevant at that time.
20. Article 1(1)(21) of the Proposal (second compromise).

1.2.2 *What Needs to Be Disclosed?*

The EC does not define the term "aggressive tax planning" as, in their words, "*An endeavour to define the concept of aggressive tax planning would risk being an exercise in vain.*"[21] The proposal rather resorts to a number of predetermined hallmarks that are features rendering a cross-border arrangement to be reportable. As a result, an obligation to report does not imply that the arrangement is, as such, effectively considered as aggressive tax planning. That is up to the national tax authorities to determine based on the information they receive.

The proposed measure applies to a cross-border arrangement which is defined as an arrangement or series of arrangements in either more than one Member State or a Member State and a third country. A cross-border arrangement also covers dual resident taxpayers and taxpayers carrying out business through a PE in another jurisdiction insofar as the cross-border arrangement forms part or the whole of the business of that PE. Alternatively, the proposed measure may also apply to cross-border arrangements with a tax-related impact in at least two jurisdictions. Arrangements that are not cross-border are not in scope of the reporting.

For such arrangements to require being reported to the tax authorities, at least one of the hallmarks must be met. An annex to the proposal lists generic hallmarks that include, for example, an arrangement or series thereof whereby the taxpayer is under the obligation to not disclose how such an arrangement can secure a tax advantage vis-à-vis other intermediaries or the tax authorities or when the intermediary receives a fee for its services proportionate to the amount of the tax advantage. Specific hallmarks include (but are not limited to) the use of losses to reduce tax liability, conversion of income into lower-taxed revenue streams, and circular transactions. These specific identified features will serve as indicators rendering a cross-border arrangement reportable insofar as they meet the main benefits test which states that the main benefit for setting up a structure is to obtain a tax advantage.

Additionally, specific hallmarks related to cross-border transactions, TP, and automatic exchange of information, which do not need to comply with the main benefits test, are included in the proposal. It is apparent that the hallmarks are very broad and, hence, will likely capture a large number of (genuine) cross-border arrangements which can potentially result in an information overflow for tax authorities when all of them are reported and exchanged within the EU. There is a debate requiring further specification of the scope of requirements captured by these hallmarks.

A specific hallmark concerning TP as determined in Part E of Annex IV attracts attention. At the time of the first proposal, the wording used was "*An arrangement or series of arrangements which does not conform with the arm's length principle or with the OECD transfer pricing guidelines, including the allocation of profit between different members of the same corporate group.*" After a meeting of the High Level Working

21. Proposal for a Council Directive amending Directive 2011/16/EU as regards mandatory automatic exchange of information in the field of taxation in relation to reportable cross-border arrangements, June 21, 2017, p. 12.

Party, a second Presidency compromise was achieved.[22] The wording is now redrafted into "*An arrangement which benefits from simplified determination of arm's length price.*" The amended wording is not expected to significantly reduce the number of reportable arrangements. Indeed, the current wording of the hallmark risks impacting the TP practice to an even greater extent. Referring to the arm's length principle under the OECD and BEPS, there seems to be an impact on low-value adding services and safe harbor provisions that aim at simplifying procedures. This may impose additional documentation requirements, and the current wording leaves the door open for a potential EU arm's length principle as advocated in what are now called the "State aid cases" in mainstream jargon among tax and TP practitioners. In case the EU arm's length principle would indeed be recognized by the CJEU and, as such, be applicable in the case at hand or all other EU Directives, this would open the door to another level of scrutiny for TP purposes imposed by the EU.[23] The Presidency's comment below states:

> Based on the discussion held at the last meeting, a new wording has been inserted to describe the aim of the hallmark more precisely. The wording is based on BEPS Action 8-10 final report (sub-heading D2).[24]

As the wording is based on BEPS Actions 8-10, this would probably mean a simplified approach under the report. In this comment, the Presidency also confirms that this new wording has been inserted to more precisely describe the aim of the hallmark, which poses the question of what the actual aim is of this provision. It may theoretically mean disclosing all structures that include low-value adding services. The authors doubt how such an aim can be legitimate, let alone the provision itself being proportional, in light of EU law.

1.2.3 When Does the Scheme Have to Be Disclosed and What Are the Consequences of Nondisclosure?

The intermediaries (or the taxpayer in certain situations as described above) are obliged to disclose the reportable arrangements within five days beginning on the day after such arrangements become available to a taxpayer for implementation. When the disclosure is shifted to taxpayers in the absence of a liable intermediary, the timing for disclosure is placed slightly later; that is, within five days beginning on the day after the reportable cross-border arrangement or the first step in a series of such arrangements has been implemented. Reporting within five days will undoubtedly be a compliance

22. Proposal for a Council Directive amending Directive 2011/16/EU as regards mandatory automatic exchange of information in the field of taxation in relation to reportable cross-border arrangements—Presidency compromise, WK 12400/2017 INIT, October 31, 2017.
23. P. Szotek, *Is the Council about to confirm the existence of an EU arm's length principle?* Kluwer International Tax Blog, July 6, 2017, available at http://kluwertaxblog.com/2017/07/06/council-confirm-existence-eu-arms-length-principle/.
24. Proposal for a Council Directive amending Directive 2011/16/EU as regards mandatory automatic exchange of information in the field of taxation in relation to reportable cross-border arrangements—Presidency compromise, WK 12400/2017 INIT, October 31, 2017, point E.

challenge for intermediaries and also businesses directly. This is particularly true as the consequences of not reporting in a timely manner can be material in nature. The proposal allows the Member States to lay down penalties and take all measures necessary to ensure that the common framework is implemented. The penalties should be effective, proportionate, and dissuasive.

1.3 The EU List of Noncooperative Jurisdictions for Tax Purposes

After over a year of negotiations and discussion, the EU has adopted an EU list of noncooperative tax jurisdictions as part of the external taxation strategy. The list contains only non-EU Member States as the Member States are considered to be fully compliant when assessed against the EU list. The objectives of the list are to support increased transparency, fair taxation, and implementation of anti-BEPS standards. The work has been done in the context of the Code of Conduct Group, but the Council took the decision on which countries would eventually be listed. The list has no direct impact today, but it is expected that Member States will (and are strongly encouraged to) use and refer to the list when drafting tax legislation and anti-abuse provisions.

1.3.1 The Countries Listed

The so-called black list contains nine countries[25] that have failed to comply with international and EU good tax governance standards. Annex II of the proposal also provides a "grey list" that contains forty-seven countries that have committed to implement changes by 2018 or 2019. The countries on the grey list will be monitored and, based on that, either be removed from the list or put on the blacklist.

Eye-catching content lies in the Annex II where the countries with harmful tax regimes are listed under "Fair taxation." The list will be updated once a year with the possibility of including more countries in the screening and providing stricter rules with new elements.

1.3.2 The Criteria

The criteria under which the countries are being assessed are set out in Annex V of the proposal. The criteria that are outlined are:

- **Tax transparency**: The country should comply with international standards on automatic exchange of information and information exchange on request. It should also have ratified the OECD's multilateral convention or signed bilateral agreements with all Member States in order to facilitate this information exchange. Until June 2019, the EU only requires two out of three of the

25. The list as on January 23, 2018: American Samoa, Bahrain, Guam, Marshall Islands, Namibia, Palau, Saint Lucia, Samoa, Trinidad and Tobago. Further reviews and amendments are expected.

transparency criteria. After that, countries will have to meet all three transparency requirements to avoid being listed.
- **Fair taxation**: The country should not have harmful tax regimes that go against the principles of the EU's Code of Conduct or OECD's Forum on Harmful Tax Practices. Those that choose to have a zero-rate corporate taxation should ensure that this does not encourage artificial offshore structures without real economic activity. The zero-rate corporate taxation, however, is not a hard element in the assessment.
- **Implementation of anti-BEPS measures**: The country must have committed to implement the OECD's Base Erosion and Profit Shifting (BEPS) minimum standards.

Looking at the criteria and the countries on the list raises some questions on how this evaluation can be done practically in an objective way. Some countries in the list have a large number of companies that are present for genuine business reasons with operational activities. It seems that the list does not differentiate between genuine activities or not and, if a company has activities in the "black-listed countries," it can be exposed and subject to scrutiny.

Despite some uncertainties and potential lack of objectiveness, the list enhances the transparency and, in parallel, increases the risk of scrutiny, which can be damaging for a company. The criteria will be subject to change, as necessary, reflecting the international standards and the progress by all relevant jurisdictions.

2 TAXATION OF THE DIGITAL ECONOMY

The international efforts with regard to the tax challenges of the digitalization of the economy have been addressed in BEPS Action 1 which identified these as "broader tax challenges" and set a timeline to monitor the impact of the BEPS recommendations and other changes to the economy. It was agreed by all participating countries at that time that any unilateral action to address such challenges must respect existing treaty obligations.

The OECD has committed to reviewing the implementation phase of BEPS in 2020 and, at that point, it will be necessary to determine whether sufficient time has passed to identify a clear picture of the impact of these changes. BEPS Action 1 was included in this agreed review, and additional work is being undertaken for an interim report to be released in March 2018. The publication of a second interim report is anticipated for 2019 with the delivery of a final report in 2020. When sufficient time has been provided for implementation of the direct tax measures and any indirect tax (VAT/GST) measures have been reviewed and introduced, it will only then be possible to truly determine what additional measures (if any) are necessary to tackle the challenges of the new economy.

Addressing the challenges that the digital economy poses is high on the EU tax policy agenda. The EC has launched a public consultation with a few specific solutions in mind such as a withholding tax, a modified Common Consolidated Corporate Tax

Base (CCCTB), the concept of a virtual PE, etc. At this point in time, the virtual PE seems to be the least damaging option, however, commentators nevertheless have fundamental concerns about this concept.

Not only are the OECD and the EC acting on it, but also unilateral actions from individual countries are witnessed. For example, the UK has proposed a royalty withholding tax that would take effect in April 2019. The tax would be levied when a non-UK multinational group selling products and services in the UK transfers profits from those sales to an entity in a low-tax or no-tax jurisdiction that owns the group's intangible assets.[26]

2.1 Digitalization of the Economy

Global profits of multinational companies are generated through many activities by many legal entities in many countries. At the same time, synergy-related profits are also realized by such companies. Allocating profits based on functions, assets, and risks in the various countries has become an extremely complicated matter. The TP rules are increasing exponentially in number and complexity and have resulted in high compliance and enforcement costs as well as increased risk of double taxation.

Digitalization, both through a host of new products/services and through its impact on more traditional functions, materially affects value chains within multinational companies and sparks the conundrum about where value is generated. How these new value chains will run through different legal entities and countries will change the tax analysis. In short, business models and value chains are changing fundamentally and value creation is becoming increasingly independent of (physical) activities and physical presence in a market.

In the authors' submission to the public consultation, the Network of PwC Member Firms used an example of a French wine grower to illustrate the point. Even 30 years ago, it was possible for French wine growers to send boxes of wine to Dutch customers without being physically present in the Netherlands. This type of trade tends not to give rise to a PE in the Netherlands. The surge in speed with which information and communication technology is developing and proliferating implies that the same French wine grower can upscale its activities in the Dutch market without being physically present there and may even allow engaging more easily with consumers rather than intermediaries. However, all marketing, sales, distribution, and after-sales activities may still take place in France; in that sense, the location of where the value has been created has not changed, and digitalization has merely reduced barriers to growth. It is hard to understand why the French wine grower's digital access to the Dutch customer should be considered as yielding a different tax result than the result with the customer access of decades past.

26. HM Treasury, Autumn Budget 2017, point 4.9 Corporate tax, published on November 22, 2017, available at: https://www.gov.uk/government/publications/autumn-budget-2017-documents/autumn-budget-2017 (last accessed on January 2, 2017).

2.2 Toward a Sustainable Solution Embedded in International Tax Rules?

It can be recalled that the Estonian Deputy General for Tax & Customs policy, Mr. Dmitri Jegorov, said in late summer that "the test of a physical presence applied to something non-physical goes against logic. But where is that value created? We don't have an agreement on that."[27] This is understandable in the current political climate around "legitimate" tax planning. This does not take away that legal certainty should prevail over sticking plaster solutions. The burning question is how a virtual PE option can be married with the Authorized OECD Approach (AOA). In case it does not, (and limited technical ground is seen to say it does) it should be considered whether direct tax is the solution at all. Indeed, if we look at the OECD guidance under BEPS Actions 8–10 (Transfer Pricing outcomes where value is created), the application becomes troublesome as, for example, making a sale in a foreign country does not, as a matter of principle, lead to saying that the country of residency of the buyer is the source of the income.[28]

It can very well be that the "functional value creation" is where the R&D and/or manufacturing or creation of the product or service took place. If you talk to a "technology guru," (s)he will say that innovation and the speed by which it is brought to the market is the single most creator of "economic rent." It can be questioned how this can be captured properly under the existing rules or how a virtual PE would come to the rescue. The current tax law is clear, and there is no such thing as a treaty threshold in the absence of a fixed place of business. A virtual PE would probably be the preferred option over gross sales thresholds like the ones seen in India, the UK, and Australia, but they would multiply double taxation issues if they cannot be married with the AOA.

If legislators want to tax the proceeds of remote economic activity by remote sellers, then much more work is needed with residency versus source-based taxation in the middle of it. There is a significant amount of academic work on where economic rent sits.[29] Some are of the opinion that it is the network of users that creates the economic rent. As a result, the country of the buyers should be able to levy taxes. Others claim that one needs to start from the identification of the sources of competitive advantages relative to a taxpayer's peers. Another issue is that smart users of digital platforms gather vast amounts of user information, often free of charge, and take advantage of relatively low-cost infrastructure. One could ask, "Where is the value created: user information gathering (free of charge), the infrastructure (use of the algorithm), the development of the algorithm, or the sale of advertising space as a

27. E. Lamer, Estonian Presidency Sees Potential in CCCTB for Digital Economy Challenges, Tax Analysts, available at: https://www.taxnotes.com/worldwide-tax-daily/corporate-taxation/estonian-presidency-sees-potential-ccctb-digital-economy-challenges/2017/06/29/1vs25.
28. P. F. Kaka, "Source Taxation: Do we really know what we mean?," Tax Notes International. June 26, 2017, Vol. 86 Issue 13, p. 1221.
29. *See*, e.g., Stephen E. Shay, J. Clifton Fleming, Jr. & Robert J. Peroni, Getting Serious About Cross-Border Earnings Stripping: Establishing an Analytical Framework, 93 N.C. L. Rev. 673 (2015); R. J. Vann, Current Trends in Balancing Residence and Source Taxation, Sydney Law School Research Paper No. 14/107 (2014).

result of use of the algorithm and the data collected?" Some authors propose a radical solution to address these questions. They see data creation as a product of the users, therefore, data should be treated as labor—and, more specifically, regarded as the property of those who generate such information. In exchange for providing the information to companies, the users should be remunerated, and these payments would help distribute the wealth generated by AI.[30] This can go as far as questioning where the economic rent sits in the context of robots which raises multidimensional questions.[31] These examples demonstrate potential issues originating from the very basic concepts of international taxation (e.g., ability to pay, source versus residence, tax liability) which is a discussion from which one should not shy away.

The sole advantage of a virtual PE that we see is that it may be less undesirable than equalization levies, etc. However, the biggest disadvantage is that, in the absence of a decent treaty solution (with AOA) and given the shortcomings in double taxation remediation (and particularly that only a limited number of countries signed the MLI provision on mandatory arbitration), it might miss its goals. Indeed, if this would make the international tax rules more "fair," it would come at a high cost as legislators could only do so by compromising legal certainty.

2.3 Ring-Fencing Digital Economy?

With regard to the allocation of profits to a PE and considering the AOA, a virtual PE would exist exclusively for purposes of taxation of the digitized economy. One could raise the question of why virtual PEs need to be created in the case of the digitized economy while other types of business would remain subject to the classic rules of taxation (*see also* the neutrality aspect in the 2004 report below). In other words, the digital economy would be ring-fenced. Many "bricks-and-mortar" companies, i.e., groups other than the aforementioned FAANGs or GAFAs tap from digital disruption for parts of their activities such as increasing efficiencies in the supply chain or internal administrative processes, enhancing customer experience, and the like.

2.4 The Conundrum of Profit Allocation

A burning question is how to apply the authorized OECD approach to such virtual PEs, in particular when hypothesizing the PE as a separate entity on the basis of a factual (=real) and functional (=real) analysis in combination with the absence of (real) significant people functions. The virtual tax world would be miles apart from the actual business structure and would ordinarily violate the paradigm of taxation where value is created.

30. I. Arrieta Ibarra, L. Goff, D. Jiménez Hernández and J. Lanier and E. G. Weyl, Should We Treat Data as Labor? Moving Beyond "Free" (December 27, 2017). American Economic Association Papers & Proceedings, Vol. 1, No. 1,. Available at SSRN: https://ssrn.com/abstract=3093683.
31. *See* X. Oberson, Taxing Robots? From the Emergence of an Electronic Ability to Pay to a Tax on Robots or the Use of Robots, World Tax Journal, 2017 (Volume 9), No 2.

Already in the 2004 OECD Report on "Are the current treaty rules for taxing business profits appropriate for e-commerce," the Technical Advisory Group indicated some points against the development of the virtual PE which we believe are still valid after fourteen years.

2.5 Final Thoughts on Potential Changes in Regard to Taxation of the Digital Economy

Tax rules should help taxpayers allocate system profits in a consistent, coherent, and sustainable way. Tax authorities should be able to draw from rules that are easy to apply in a way that tax collection is final rather than a first step in time-consuming fights over double taxation issues. This is a potential waste of valuable management time for both taxpayers and public servants.

As for *neutrality*, a virtual PE is not a real PE and, in the absence of a place of business, one could wonder whether a PE should exist. The neutrality principle would be violated when there is a difference in outcome between a virtual PE and a real PE. This cannot be solved through fiction such as "virtual dependent agent PEs" as it departs from economic reality. In regard to *efficiency*, the reporting obligation may increase significantly, adding loads of red tape for taxpayers to prepare and tax authorities to digest. *Certainty and simplicity* would be at stake with a virtual PE increasing the uncertainty of MNEs in their tax positions (where they may not be even aware that a virtual PE exists in a certain jurisdiction). It would seem that not all countries are aligned on adopting the virtual PE concept. This would even increase the uncertainty of the MNE that is concerned.

3 STATE AID: LINE OF FIRE ON TRANSFER PRICING

Grappling with the interaction between TP and EU State aid rules is probably the last thing that TP practitioners have on their bucket list. At the bottom of said list is trying to survive while not caring at all. As State aid "attacks" tend to keep coming from behind, it is probably unwise not to stay agile in this domain where tax policy and politics appear to interfere at an unprecedented pace. Although formally in the basket of Mr. Moscovici, it is Ms. Vestager, political leader of the Directorate General Competition[32] regulating and monitoring competition in the EU (DG COMP), who likes to be in the ring with some very well-known MNEs. Mr. Moscovici describes this as working "in tandem": he prepares, she repairs.[33]

The interplay between TP and State aid is not new. The EC and, more in particular, the DG COMP, have been investigating national tax regimes and certain TP

32. *See* https://ec.europa.eu/commission/commissioners/2014-2019/vestager_en.
33. T. Sprackland, Pierre Moscovici: The Man With a Plan To Bring Tax Transparency to the EU, Tax Notes International, December 18, 2017, pp. 1106.

provisions on their compatibility with State aid rules for many years.[34] Already in 2001, the Competition Commissioner, Mr. Monti, initiated investigations into so-called coordination centers—involving 12 Member States.[35] The Commission did not accept the use of default methods and fixed rates without verifying whether they reflected the underlying economic reality and, as a consequence, Member States were requested to abandon those measures. The EC's decisions in these cases were based on the wording of the OECD TP Guidelines. It turned out that the methods as applied by the Member States compromised internationally recognized principles. To illustrate this, in the *Forum 187*[36] case, Belgium recalled that the Belgian tax administration was bound by the OECD TP Guidelines as a proper standard for reference. This is why the EC decided that the application of a notional cost-plus method where a fixed margin was set and certain value-added costs (such as personnel expenses) stayed out of the cost base departed from the OECD TP Guidelines and constituted State aid.[37] Hence, this case was assessed on the basis of the OECD TP Guidelines as an appropriate reference framework to which Belgium adheres in its national law and from which a deviation was proven.

However, in the aftermath of austerity measures that resulted from the financial and economic downturn and that required large efforts from citizens, the EC's attention has been drawn to tax planning strategies of MNEs, and only since five years or so ago did the EC begin to specifically look into the TP provisions and TP tax rulings.[38] The EC expressed its special interest in tax rulings and TP arrangements after the US Senate and the British Parliament looked deeper into how some large companies organized their tax affairs. The public discussion on what were traditionally called "loopholes" in tax systems that individuals and businesses have been using to escape from paying tax has later intensified due to various "papers" and "leaks" that were spread out in the press at length. The EC has an optimistic plan to launch and adopt the CCCTB, create and adopt new transparency rules for tax planning intermediaries, and establish rules at the EU level allowing taxation of profits generated by multinationals through the digital economy.[39] Therefore, it is not surprising that the topic of (deemed) aggressive tax planning has also grown on the fertile ground of the EU competition policy.

34. The EC's competence also covers the area of direct business taxation when measures mitigate the charges that an undertaking would normally bear. For further reference, please consult Case 173/73 *Italy v. Commission* [1974] ECR 709.
35. *See*, for example, Commission Decision of 22 August 2002 in Case C 48/2001 (ex NN 43/2000) on the aid scheme implemented by Spain in favor of coordination centers in Vizcaya, OJ L 31, 6.2.2003, p. 26; Commission Decision of 5 September 2002 on the aid scheme implemented by Germany for control and coordination centers, OJ L 177, 16.7.2003, p. 17; Commission decision of 16 October 2002 on the State aid scheme C 49/2001 (ex NN 46/2000)—Coordination Centers—implemented by Luxembourg, OJ L 170, 9.7.2003, p. 20, paragraph 53; and Commission Decision of 17 February 2003 on the aid scheme implemented by Belgium for coordination centers established in Belgium, OJ L 282, 30.10.2003, p. 25.
36. CJEU Joined Cases C-182/03 and C-217/03 of 22 June 2006, *Belgium and Forum 187 v. Commission*, ECLI:EU:C:2005:266, paras. 90–97.
37. Commission Decision on Belgian Coordination Centres (2003), at paras. 43 and 95.
38. *See* Verlinden et al. Transfer Pricing Developments in the European Union, pp. 49–61, where the State aid Framework and recent developments in State aid and Transfer Pricing have been analyzed in detail.
39. Speech of Jean-Claude Juncker on the State of the European Union, September 13, 2017.

It is against this background that the EC opened several formal State aid investigations into Advance Pricing Agreements[40] (APAs) granted by Ireland to Apple,[41] Luxembourg to Fiat[42] and Amazon,[43] the Netherlands to Starbucks[44] and, most recently, to Inter IKEA.[45] In addition to (unilateral) APAs, it has also analyzed "confirmatory tax rulings" by which national tax authorities confirm the (non-)application of a certain national legal provision to a specific situation and decided to open formal investigations into rulings granted by Luxembourg to McDonald's.[46] Furthermore, in September 2016, the EC opened a formal State aid inquiry into Luxembourg's tax treatment of GDF Suez (Engie)[47] which concerns the application of national legal provisions that had led to (internal accounting) mismatches, creating the alleged advantage. In parallel to this, it scrutinized the Belgian Excess Profit Ruling regime[48] and has opened a new investigation into the UK's Controlled Foreign Company (CFC)[49] law[50] that gives certain financing companies an exemption from anti-avoidance rules. So far, these investigations have resulted in five decisions in Starbucks, Fiat, Belgian Excess Profit regime, Apple, and Amazon concluding that illicit State aid was granted.

3.1 What to Expect on the EC's Approach to TP in the Months to Come?

State aid assessment in these cases boils down to the notion of an arm's length principle and the interpretation of the TP rules under the State aid framework enshrined in the EU Treaty. The recent approach of the EC in this field suggests that the OECD TP Guidelines cannot be seen as providing an authoritative opinion on TP issues as they

40. Advance Pricing Agreements are arrangements that determine, in advance of intra-group transactions, an appropriate set of criteria (e.g., method, comparables, and appropriate adjustments thereto, critical assumptions as to future events) for the determination of the transfer pricing for those transactions over a fixed period of time.
41. EC Decision SA.38373 State aid implemented by Ireland to Apple (August 30, 2016), not published on OJ.
42. EC Decision SA.38375 State aid which Luxembourg granted to Fiat (October 21, 2015), OJ L 351, 1–67 (December 22, 2016).
43. EC Decision SA.38944 State aid which Luxembourg granted to Amazon (October 4, 2017), not published on OJ.
44. EC Decision SA.38374 State aid implemented by the Netherlands to Starbucks (October 21, 2015), not published on OJ.
45. EC Opening Decision SA.46470 Alleged aid implemented by the Netherlands to Inter IKEA (December 18, 2017), not published on OJ.
46. EC Opening Decision SA.38945 Alleged aid by Luxembourg to Mc Donald's (December 3, 2015), OJ C 258, 11–49 (July 15, 2016), not published on OJ.
47. EC Opening Decision SA.44888 Alleged aid to GDF Suez (September 19, 2016), OJ C 36, 13–50 (February 3, 2017).
48. EC Decision SA.37667 Excess profit exemption in Belgium—Art. 185§2 b) CIR92 (January 11, 2016), OJ L 260, 61–103 (September 27, 2016).
49. The UK CFC rules aim to protect the UK corporate tax base by bringing into charge those profits which are artificially diverted from the UK into non-resident associated entities.
50. EC Opening Decision SA.44896 UK's Controlled Foreign Company (CFC) rules/tax scheme for multinationals (October 26, 2017), not published on OJ.

are not binding on the Member States.[51] Thus, in that case, the EC proposed a notion of the arm's length principle within State aid rules to which many stakeholders object and remind the EC that it should not act as a mere European tax police officer in the absence of fiscal harmonization at the European level.[52] Others have been arguing that investigations into national tax rulings have caused legal uncertainty and demand more clarification from the EC.[53] Criticism of this approach also reaches the previous EC's and the Court of Justice of the European Union's (CJEU) approach to TP. According to the CJEU, States should apply an arm's length principle as embedded in their national tax system to resemble prices that would have been charged "*in conditions of free competition*."[54]

In response to this criticism, on June 3, 2016, the DG COMP presented its approach to issues relating to direct business taxation and tax rulings in the Internal Working Paper on State aid and tax rulings (Working Paper). It was accompanied by the new Commission Notice on the notion of State aid as referred to in Article 107(1) of the Treaty on the Functioning of the European Union[55] prepared by the Commission in the context of modernization of State aid rules.

The basic premise of the Working Paper is that the EC has exclusive competence to enforce State aid rules upon the Member States (Article 105 of the Treaty on the Functioning of the European Union (TFEU)). This competence also covers the area of direct business taxation when measures mitigate the charges that an undertaking would normally bear.[56] Thus, direct benefits as well as other measures granting a financial advantage to an undertaking for free or on noncommercial terms fall under Article 107(1) TFEU. As Article 107(1) TFEU enjoys primacy over national fiscal autonomy[57] so does the arm's length principle developed by the EC under Article 107(1) TFEU providing that the EU courts will approve this approach to State aid and TP.

The special focus of DG COMP is on cases in which there is a manifest breach of the arm's length principle through a deviation from a reliable approximation of a market-based outcome in the ruling. In this respect, the Commission has a

51. Commission Notice on the Notion of State aid as referred to in Article 107(1) TFEU, adopted on May 19, 2016, paras. 172–173.
52. Gutachten des Wissenschaftlichen Beirats beim Bundesministerium der Finanzen, Steuervergünstigungen und EU-Beihilfenaufsicht: Problematik und Ansätze zur Lösung des Kompetenzkonflikts mit der Steuerautonomie, November 16, 2017.
53. *See*, for example, Report from the Commission to the European Parliament, the Council, the European Economic and Social Committee and the Committee of the Regions: Report on Competition Policy 2015 (COM(2016)) 393 final, 15.06.2016; U.S. Department of the Treasury White Paper: The European Commission's Recent State Aid Investigations of Transfer Pricing Rulings, August 24, 2016.
54. CJEU Joined Cases C-182/03 and C-217/03 of 22 June 2006, *Belgium and Forum 187 v. Commission*, ECLI:EU:C:2005:266.
55. COM (2016/C 262/01), OJ C 262, 19.7.2016, pp. 1–50, hereafter cited as the "Commission Notice."
56. Case 173/73 *Italy v. Commission* EU:C:1974:71.
57. Commission Decision of 17 February 2003 on the aid scheme implemented by Belgium for coordination centers established in Belgium, OJ L 282, 30.10.2003; Joined Cases C-182/03 and C-217/03 Belgium and Forum 187 *ASBL v. Commission* EU:C:2006:416.

particular concern over tax rulings confirming the taxable profits and remuneration of the company being part of the group of companies determined in a uniform manner and without a clear economic analysis. This should boil down to the question of robustness of a TP study, i.e., the selection of the TP method(s), the determination of the profit level indicator(s), the selection of the comparables, the selection of the tested party or parties, and the determination of a range within the final results that might not have led to an approximation of a market outcome.

Finally, in the Commission Notice, the EC proposed specific guidance.[58] According to the EC, the basic thrust of tax rulings embarking on TP methodologies is to comply with the arm's length principle under Article 107(1) TFEU independently of whether States have incorporated it into their national legal systems and in what form. This arm's length principle applied to a tax ruling endorsing a TP study would ensure that a company that is part of a corporate group of undertakings is not treated more favorably under a normal application of the ordinary corporate tax system in the Member State concerned compared to stand-alone companies taxed on actually recorded accounting profits. Thus, according to the EC, a tax ruling will not lead to problems of Article 107(1) TFEU in so far as there is no "selective advantage" as a result of lowering the addressee's tax liability in the Member State compared to companies in a similar factual and legal situation. This proposed assessment of the arm's length principle is based on the equality principle in taxation where all companies, big and small, integrated and stand-alone, should be taxed in a similar manner as they are considered as being objectively comparable.

However, neither the EC nor the CJEU have ever compared multinational companies with stand-alone entities. In the TP cases on coordination centers, the EC found a distinction in treatment of companies belonging to multinational groups, i.e., the coordination centers. In recent TP Decisions, the EC departs from this assessment and appears to compare all types of companies with one another. This approach does not bring much clarity to the matter of the TP under State aid rules.

3.2 The EC's Hunt for TP Rulings Continues: Amazon and Inter IKEA

The recently concluded State aid decisions confirm the approach taken by the EC in the first bulk of investigations (i.e., Fiat, Starbucks, Belgian Excess Profit regime, Apple).[59] For instance, in the press release on the Amazon Decision,[60] the EC was not, as such, concerned with the operational structure applied by Amazon. Also, the EC did not challenge the fact that Amazon group companies in Luxembourg are organized under a holding that is a transparent partnership not subject to tax in Luxembourg. It was also not considered that the operating entity in Luxembourg uses Intellectual Property (IP)

58. Commission Notice on the Notion of State aid as referred to in Article 107(1) TFEU, adopted on May 19, 2016.
59. *See* Verlinden et al. Transfer Pricing Developments in the European Union, pp. 49–61, where these cases have been analyzed in detail.
60. At the moment when this chapter was written, only a short press release on the final EC's Decision in Amazon was available.

to run its business in Europe while this IP is developed in the US and licensed by a holding company for exclusive use by the operating entity. The EC was also not troubled by the fact that the Amazon holding entity passed part of its proceeds from royalty payments it received from the operating entity to Amazon in the US as an annual contribution to the development costs of the IP. The EC also accepted the level of remuneration established by the US tax courts (and recently appealed by the IRS).[61]

What was challenged by the EC in the Amazon case was the ruling that endorsed a method used to calculate the amount of royalties paid by the operating company to the holding company which was not subject to tax in Luxembourg (i.e., the royalty that was paid). Similarly, in the recently opened State aid investigation into Inter IKEA's tax rulings, the EC questioned an annual license fee paid by the Inter IKEA operating entity in the Netherlands to the holding company in Luxembourg. The fee paid was in exchange for the use of IP rights relating to the franchise business (2006 ruling) as well as an interest payment from the operating entity in the Netherlands to its parent company in Liechtenstein (the 2011 ruling).[62] The main question that the EC asked in both cases was whether these payments reflected market conditions as tax rulings cannot endorse payments between companies within the same group that do not reflect economic reality. If that was the case, it would disadvantage local/stand-alone companies that are taxed on their actual profits and pay market prices for goods and services.

From a TP perspective, this is essentially a matter of determining the tested party and thus performing a functional analysis in order to establish which entity executes the least complex functions.[63] From a practical perspective, it involves performing a detailed functional analysis of the parties involved and their business under the tested transactions. This part of the comparability study aims at analyzing the tested transaction and the surrounding facts including the functions performed, assets used, and risks borne by the respective parties. Following the functional analysis and applying the benchmarking parameters to look for comparables, one of the TP methods must be selected and applied. The 2017 OECD TP Guidelines state that the arm's length principle "*(…) provides the closest approximation of the workings of the open market in cases where property (such goods, other types of tangible assets, or intangible assets) is transferred or services are rendered between associated enterprises*" (para. 1.14).

61. 148 T.C. No 8, *Amazon.com, Inc. v. Commissioner*, Docket No. 31197-12 (March 23, 2017).
62. At the moment when this chapter was written, only a short press release on the opening EC's Decision in Inter IKEA was available.
63. OECD Guidelines (para. 1.51): "In transactions between two independent enterprises, compensation usually will reflect the functions that each enterprise performs (taking into account assets used and risks assumed). Therefore, in delineating the controlled transaction and determining comparability between controlled and uncontrolled transactions or entities, a functional analysis is necessary. This functional analysis seeks to identify the economically significant activities and responsibilities undertaken, assets used or contributed, and risks assumed by the parties to the transactions. The analysis focuses on what the parties actually do and the capabilities they provide. Such activities and capabilities will include decision-making, including decisions about business strategy and risks (…). While one party may provide a large number of functions relative to that of the other party to the transaction, it is the economic significance of those functions in terms of their frequency, nature, and value to the respective parties to the transactions that is important."

Furthermore, they go on stating that the application of the arm's length principle "*(...) is based on a comparison of the conditions in a controlled transaction with the conditions that would have been made had the parties been independent and undertaking a comparable transaction under comparable circumstances*" (para. 1.33). Thus, in order for such a comparison to be useful, the economic relevant characteristics of the situation that is being compared must be sufficiently comparable, and a taxpayer must select the most appropriate TP method for establishing and testing its transactions with related parties.

Contrary to the above, the EC does not refer to the full benchmarking exercise in its decisions. It seems to take a broader view on the transactions involved to establish whether they are priced in a way that reflects economic reality and is in line with the arm's length principle under Article 107(1) TFEU. The EC's findings indicate that it is the Amazon holding and IP license owning entity that should be considered as the less complex entity and not the Amazon operating company owning the EU retail business, as determined in the ruling. Moreover, according to the EC, treating the operating company as the less complex leads to a shift in profits to a company where they remained untaxed. The EC apparently did not find any justification for this arrangement because it is considered that the holding company is an "empty shell" and only passed IP rights to the operating company. According to the (disputed) view of the EC, it has no business activities and is not actively involved in management, development, and use of the IP. According to the EC, the operating company is the company making decisions, carrying out activities related to Amazon's EU retail business as well as adapting technologies and software behind the Amazon IT platform in Europe, investing in marketing, and gathering data. The EC claims that this means that it managed and added value to the IP. The same approach is taken in the preliminary decision on the Inter IKEA case whereby the EC asks whether a Dutch company can be considered the less complex entity to the transactions at stake. In the EC's view, all of these tax rulings are based on the wrong presumption that the mere legal ownership of an IP makes the IP holder the more complex party while, according to the evidence gathered by the EC, holding companies actually assumed passive functions in relation to IP.

The EC thus concluded that Amazon generates the same amount of profits as a local company subject to Luxembourg's tax rules. According to the EC, any local company would have to pay four times more in taxes than did Amazon. Therefore, it concluded that the method used in the ruling inflated the royalty payment by the operating company and exceeded on average 90% of the company's profits. This is significantly more than what the holding company needed to pay Amazon in the US for the IP development. Likewise, in the Inter IKEA investigation, the EC preliminarily concluded that the two rulings granted to Inter IKEA by the Dutch tax authorities significantly reduced the operating company's profits that should be taxed in the Netherlands.

It is particularly regretful that the EC appears to draw firm conclusions in its press releases while it would be most beneficial to publish the full texts more swiftly in order to help tax practitioners to meaningfully comment. The conclusion that can be derived from the EC press releases on these cases is that, for State aid purposes, the EC continues to adopt a strictly legalistic transactional approach for assessing transfer prices by identifying whether there is any double non-taxation of profits and looking for the "weakest point" in the intra-group transactions from a State aid perspective. It does not, however, look behind the IP itself and services that parties to the transaction are receiving or giving. The OECD TP Guidelines state to the contrary that, when performing a functional analysis, "*it is important to understand how value is generated by the group as a whole, the interdependencies of the functions performed by the associated enterprises with the rest of the group, and the contribution that the associated enterprises make to that value creation*" (para. 1.51). It is, therefore, a missed opportunity that the General Court of the European Union rejected the application for leave to intervene in the Apple case lodged by the US.[64] According to the Court, the US failed to establish a direct interest in the State aid case, and there is "*no apparent link between the contested decision and the development of rules relating to transfer pricing within the framework of the OECD (...).*"[65] In those cases that involve US entities of investigated group companies,[66] the US could perhaps shed some more light on the value creation aspect in relation to the IP development and management functions within the multinational groups of companies.

3.3 An Era of Uncertainty?

With the emergence of those new investigations, it is probably accurate to state that "*there is one thing certain, namely, that we can have nothing certain (...).*"[67] This approach by the EC with the European State aid rules is certainly a further new development in the EC's assessments of national tax regimes and the TP provisions on their compatibility with State aid rules which calls into question such a broad interpretation of the equality principle within the arm's length assessment. Some Member States have openly expressed their views, stating that the EC applies the open-ended legal standard for assessing selectivity, and it should abandon recovery to leave it to legislators to change the tax law for the future.[68] Although this approach may not be realistic from a competition policy's perspective, the EC's fiscal State aid investigations undoubtedly adversely affect legal certainty in the Internal Market and that, for many stakeholders, is not a favorable approach to make Europe's tax rules better. Moreover, the importance of fiscal legal certainty was underlined by Mr. Moscovici when he intervened in an informal meeting of the ECOFIN Council.[69] During this intervention, he confirmed on behalf of the EC that it is striving to ensure fiscal

64. Case T-892/16, *Apple Sales International and Apple Operations Europe v. Commission* (December 15, 2017).
65. Case T-892/16, *Apple Sales International and Apple Operations Europe v. Commission* (December 15, 2017), para. 28.
66. *See*, e.g., *Amazon* and *Apple* cases.
67. Samuel Butler (UK satirist), 1612–1680.
68. Gutachten des Wissenschaftlichen Beirats beim Bundesministerium der Finanzen, Steuervergünstigungen und EU-Beihilfenaufsicht: Problematik und Ansätze zur Lösung des Kompetenzkonflikts mit der Steuerautonomie, November 16, 2017.
69. Speech of Moscovici in Malta informal ECOFIN Council intervention on behalf of the European Commission, held on April 8/9, 2017.

legal certainty and recognized that this concept is important in view of the competitiveness of Europe in the world. As Robert Goulder nicely formulated, it seems as if the EC competition policy is used to step in when EC tax policy fails.[70]

4 A C(C)CTB STATUS UPDATE

The CCCTB was relaunched in October 2016 with the aim of eliminating intra-group transactions (and the need for TP in intra-group transactions between Member States). The proposal lays down common rules for computing the tax base of multinational companies within the EU (the Common Corporate Tax Base – CCTB). The Commission also put forward a proposal for a Council Directive on a Common Consolidated Corporate Tax Base. The proposal complements the CCTB proposal with the consolidation element. On December 6, 2016, the ECOFIN Council stated its focus on the elements of a common tax base as a priority which means that the CCTB might be adopted sooner than the CCCTB.

The background and the content were discussed in the previous paper.[71] Critical changes did not take place in the last year, and it seems that the proposal itself has been pushed slightly into the background as the EC agenda is now focusing on the fair taxation of the digital economy. However, a modified CCCTB could serve under the proposal for the fair taxation of the digital economy, as mentioned in the public consultation.[72] The possible solution that is planned is modifying the CCCTB proposal by implementing new PE and profit attribution rules.

Certain flaws of the proposal evidently do not remove the need for the TP such as in the relationship between a group entity within and outside the EU, smaller companies and groups that do not opt-in, and the periods prior to the implementation. Further, the apportionment formula does not take into account the intangibles that can be an important source of value creation. Value creation seems to be ignored on an overall basis as a formulaic allocation obviously fully ignores the productivity of each parameter. As mentioned before, the authors are anxious to see how one can marry this with the arm's length standard that is applied in state aid cases.

5 EU JTPF: RECENT WORK

The EU Joint Transfer Pricing Forum (EU JTPF) is an expert group that assists and advises the EC on TP matters. It provides a platform to develop practical solutions stemming from applying the OECD TP guidelines. An equally important aspect of the JTPF's work is monitoring the EU Arbitration Convention which contributed to the Directive on double taxation dispute resolution mechanisms in the EU. This is explained in the next section.

70. Robert Goulder, Ikea's Royalty Conduit—Some Assembly Required, *Tax Notes International*, January 8, 2018.
71. *See* Verlinden et al., Transfer Pricing Developments in the European Union, pp. 70–74.
72. European Commission, Consultation, Fair taxation of the digital economy, available at: https://ec.europa.eu/eusurvey/runner/Digital_economy (last accessed January 2, 2018).

For further details on the composition and work plan of the JTPF, reference is made to the authors' last year's report.[73] In 2017, the most important achievement of the JTPF is the contribution made to the work on comparables. Following the study on Comparable data used for Transfer Pricing in the EU[74] and detailed discussions at the EU JTPF in March 2017, the EU JTPF agreed on the Report on the Use of Comparables in the EU.[75] The report establishes best practices and pragmatic solutions with various recommendations for both taxpayers and tax administrations in the EU and aims at increasing the objectivity and transparency of comparable searches for TP in practice.

For a detailed review of this study, reference can be made to Chapter 6 of this publication.[76]

6 THERE ARE OFTEN TWO SIDES TO THE SAME COIN: HOW TO AVOID BEING TAXED TWICE (OR MORE)

Policy changes (i.e., ATAD and ATAD2) and new policy initiatives (i.e., proposal for the CCCTB, accepted proposal for Fair Taxation of the Digital Economy) were made to combat tax avoidance. The possibility for these provisions to not be implemented in a coordinated and harmonized way across the entire EU once (if ever) adopted or adopted unilaterally in an uncoordinated way impose a risk of increased double or even multiple taxation disputes. Seemingly, countries are very keen on broadening the tax base and keeping more tax revenue within their own borders. This broadening of the tax base is often combined with an ever reducing corporate tax rate, leaving the corporate tax income for countries stable. This increased desire or obligation to broaden the tax base results in a juridical and economic double taxation that countries have more and more difficulties resolving.

On the international level, the experienced lack of efficiency in tax dispute resolution proceedings is also recognized by the OECD's Committee on Fiscal Affairs which has stressed the difficulties of applying the MAP in cases of double taxation.[77] Under BEPS Action 14, emphasis was put on the fundamental importance of the correct

73. Lang M. et al., Transfer Pricing Developments around the World 2017, pp. 47 et seq.
74. European Commission, *Study on comparable data used for transfer pricing in the EU*, https://publications.europa.eu/en/publication-detail/-/publication/d16d2635-c685-11e6-a6db-01aa75ed71a1 (last accessed January 2, 2018).
75. European Commission. EU Joint Transfer Pricing Forum, Report on the use of Comparables in the EU, JTPF/007/2016/FINAL/EN, available at: https://ec.europa.eu/taxation_customs/sites/taxation/files/jtpf0072017encomps.pdf (last accessed on January 2, 2018).
76. S. De Baets, J. Gao, Recent Developments on Comparability Analysis in Transfer Pricing.
77. To combat these difficulties, some recommendations were offered such as notifying taxpayers of transfer pricing adjustments and providing them with the opportunity to present the relevant facts and arguments. Further, emphasis was given on communication between competent authorities with potential resort to Article 26 of the OECD Model regarding the exchange of information. As for the MAP, in general, the Committee on Fiscal Affairs recommended a minimum level of formal requirements in instituting and operating a MAP. The MAP cases should be settled on their individual merits and not by reference to any balance of the results in other cases, and the competent authorities should, where appropriate, formulate and publish domestic rules, guidelines, and procedures concerning the use of a MAP. More nonbinding documents were released in order to give further guidance, such as the OECD's Manual on

application and interpretation of tax treaties.[78] It seeks to improve the effectiveness and efficiency of the MAP and minimize the risk of uncertainty and unintended double taxation by effective and timely dispute resolution through the MAP. Chapter I of BEPS Action 14 contains a minimum standard on dispute resolution agreed upon by the Contracting States and complementary best practices. It also establishes monitoring mechanisms to ensure fulfillment of the minimum standard. Chapter II of BEPS Action 14 briefly mentions the option of including mandatory and binding arbitration to complement the agreement to the minimum standard.[79] The standard and certain suggestions of BEPS Action 14 were implemented in the Multilateral Convention to Implement Tax Treaty Related Measures to Prevent BEPS (MLI) signed on June 7, 2017.[80] Only a limited number of countries have signed up for mandatory arbitration. While both the Directive and the MLI are important, their application and legal relationship are not straightforward. In the case of a tax treaty being entered into between two EU Member States, the supremacy of EU law over tax treaties follows from the EU Treaties and is confirmed by the CJEU case law. When the Member State has signed the treaty after adoption of the Lisbon Treaty, the supremacy of EU law over the tax treaties can be derived from Article 4(3) of TEU.[81]

As demonstrated below, the Directive manages to address and solve the perpetuating issue of resolving double taxation in a more efficient way compared to the MLI. The Directive provides for detailed rules on mechanisms to resolve disputes between Member States arising from the interpretation and application of agreements and conventions that provide for the elimination of double taxation. The relevant provision ensures a more time-strict and efficient procedure while, at the same time, puts more emphasis on the taxpayer's rights, although these are not always reflected in the procedural rights of the taxpayer under the Directive. Therefore, in the EU context, the double taxation dispute resolution has made an important step forward.

6.1 A Promising Cure: Directive on Tax Dispute Resolution Mechanisms in the EU

Notwithstanding the Arbitration Convention and additional interpretative guidance agreed upon by the EU JTPF through its Report on Improving the Functioning of the Arbitration Convention,[82] double taxation continued to be an issue within the EU. Besides its limited scope (TP and profit allocation issues), the Member States' obligation to resolve TP disputes is not always enforced, and there is often no recourse

Effective Mutual Agreement Procedures (MEMAP) and the Guidelines for Conducing Advance Pricing Arrangements under the Mutual Agreement Procedure (MAP APAs) in the Annex to Chapter IV of the TPG.

78. OECD/G20, *Making Dispute Resolution Mechanisms More* Effective—Action 14 Final Report (OECD 2015), (hereinafter Action 14), Executive Summary, p. 9.
79. Action 14, paras. 62, 63.
80. Multilateral Convention to Implement Tax Treaty Related Measures to Prevent Base Erosion Profit Shifting (November 24, 2016), IBFD Treaties.
81. A. Maitrot de la Motte, Droit fiscal de l'Union européenne, Bruylant, 2012, paras. 132–132.
82. Final Report on Improving the Functioning of the Arbitration Convention (JTPF/002/2015/EN) March 2015.

available to the taxpayer in case the mechanisms are not applied properly and the procedure is prolonged or even blocked. The resolution of the dispute and the accompanying timeline is most often unpredictable, if at all even possible to respect in certain cases.[83]

In order to tackle the double taxation through dispute resolution, the EU is making an important step forward in order to achieve tax dispute resolution procedures that are more effective and efficient. On October 10, 2017, the Council adopted the Directive on Tax Dispute Resolution Mechanisms in the European Union ("the Directive").[84] The Directive builds on the existing Convention on the elimination of double taxation in connection with the adjustment of profits of associated enterprises ("Arbitration Convention")[85] and aims at implementing a harmonized and transparent framework in the EU to cope with an increasing number of double or multiple taxation cases. EU Member States must implement the Directive into their national laws by June 30, 2019 at the latest. The provisions of the Directive will be applicable to any complaint submitted from July 1, 2019 onwards relating to tax disputes concerning income or capital earned in a tax year commencing on or after January 1, 2018. Competent authorities of the Member States that are concerned, however, may agree to apply this Directive with regard to any complaint that was submitted prior to that day or to earlier tax years.

6.1.1 *Enlarged Scope*

The Directive is applicable to disputes arising from the interpretation and application of agreements and conventions that provide for the elimination of double taxation of income and, as the case may be, capital.[86] As opposed to the Arbitration Convention which only applies to the TP adjustments and attribution of profits to PEs, the Directive also applies, for example, to disputes in relation to fiscal residency, the existence/ absence of a PE, or the application of withholding tax in the source State.

The Directive provides for important clarification of the meaning of double taxation by explicitly recognizing that this notion also includes the cancellation or reduction of losses that could be used to offset taxable profits.[87] At the same time, the Directive does not explicitly mention if the taxable subject includes economic double taxation. Given the obvious importance of economic double taxation from a TP perspective, we have to first shed some light on this topic.

83. For evidence on cases where access is denied or procedures are blocked or delayed, *see* Commission staff working document impact assessment accompanying the document Proposal for a Council Directive on Double Taxation Dispute Resolution Mechanisms in the European Union SWD/2016/0343 final—2016/0338 (CNS).
84. Council Directive on Tax Dispute Resolution Mechanisms in the European Union, OJ L 265, (hereinafter "the Directive").
85. Convention 90/436/EEC of 23 July 1990 on the Elimination of Double Taxation in Connection with the adjustment of Profits of Associated Enterprises, OJ L 225 (1990).
86. Article 1 of the Directive.
87. Article 2(1)(c) of the Directive.

The Directive is building on the Arbitration Convention which limits its scope to the TP and PE profit allocation. The Directive is also aimed at extending the possibilities for the elimination of double taxation. The purpose of the Directive is to provide a legally binding instrument for dispute resolution within the EU not only limited to the TP and PE profit allocation issues but to all tax-related issues in the context of the taxable object.

Article 3(1) refers to "*any affected person*" using the singular when referring to the taxable subject. Article 2(1)(d) defines "*affected person*" as "*any person, including an individual, that is resident for tax purposes in a Member State and whose taxation is directly affected by a question of dispute.*" Looking at the definition of both juridical and economic double taxation, the "affected person" in the singular and referring to the same person is only used in the definition of juridical double taxation. This could be interpreted in the sense that the Directive applies to juridical double taxation in the context of the taxable subject.

Further, paragraph 7 of the Preamble to the Directive emphasizes the need to extend the scope of the types of disputes that are covered. This could again be interpreted in a way that the Directive is to extend the scope with regard to the taxable object and not the taxable subject. The object in this case refers to disputes arising from all tax issues (not only TP) suffered by one person as a result of juridical double taxation. Therefore, also taking into account the intention of the legislator leads us to the same conclusion.

However, in our view, the Directive does clearly apply to TP discussions that result in economic double taxation. Indeed, the Directive builds upon the EU Arbitration Convention and, in this manner, covers economic double taxation with regard to TP issues. The authors agree that the Directive does not necessarily include economic double taxation in *all* of the disputes in their dispute resolution system, but the decision to extend the scope to all disputes in case of economic double taxation can be solved by the Member States through mutual agreement procedures (which remains the full competency of the Member States).

The fact that the Directive should also cover the TP adjustments resulting in economic double taxation is further supported by the OECD Model. Most countries consider that economic double taxation arising from the inclusion of profits of associated enterprises under Article 9 paragraph 1 OECD Model is in accordance with the object and purpose of a tax treaty and that these cases should thus be granted access to mutual agreement procedures. For example, both juridical and economic double taxation situations are covered in the Belgian DTTs. The economic double taxation, as a result of profit adjustments made between associated companies, is covered by the Belgian DTTs even in the absence of paragraph 2 of Article 9.[88] In the past, however, some countries took an opposing view and, in the absence of a treaty provision based on Article 9 paragraph 2 OECD Model, believed that they are not under

88. Circ. no. AFZ/2004/0053 (AFZ 5/2004) of 16 January 2004, Bull. no. 846, 2004, 856–894; Circ. no. AFZ/Intern.IB/98-0170 (AFZ 6/2003) of 25 March 2003, Bull. no. 837, 2003, 1369–1375.

a duty to grant access to the mutual agreement procedure in such a case.[89] Under BEPS Action 14, however, as one of the four BEPS Minimum Standards, countries should include "paragraphs 1 through 3 of Article 25 in their tax treaties as interpreted in the Commentary and subject to the variations in these paragraphs provided for under elements 3.1 and 3.3 of the minimum standard; they should provide access to the MAP in TP cases and should implement the resulting mutual agreements (e.g., by making appropriate adjustments to the tax assessed)."[90] This should be applied *inter alia* through Articles 16 and 17 of the BEPS Multilateral Instrument.

In light of the above, following a strict legal approach and taking into account the intention of the legislator, we conclude that the Directive includes economic double taxation in TP cases. As the most complex cases of double taxation are those of economic double taxation, applying such an efficient and significant legal instrument as this Directive to *all* cases of economic double taxation is utmost desirable, if not essentially needed. There is thus an opportunity for the Member States to further confirm the scope of the Directive to cover those situations.

6.1.2 Procedure with Clear Enforceable Timelines

Any person who is a tax resident of an EU Member State and who is affected by a dispute related to double or multiple taxation on his/her income or capital may call on the new procedure. A request (complaint) needs to be lodged within three years from the receipt of the first notification of the action resulting in or that will result in double or multiple taxation. As two or more Member States can be involved in the dispute, the complaint must be filed simultaneously with each of the competent authorities of the Member State concerned.

The complaint is subject to a number of formal requirements with respect to the language and content used. In order to be accepted, the complaint must contain mandatory information such as identification of the persons/companies involved, tax periods concerned, details of the relevant facts and circumstances of the case, and supporting documents should be enclosed. The competent authorities of each of the Member States concerned can request the taxpayer to provide further information within three months from the receipt of the claim. As the taxpayer has no explicit right to provide additional information, it is important to carefully consider which information is useful to provide to the authorities in the initial complaint.

The competent authorities of the Member States concerned will make a decision on the acceptance or rejection of the complaint within six months after receiving it or after receiving the additional information that was requested. In the absence of a decision within this timeframe, the complaint is deemed to be accepted.

Any of the competent authorities concerned may decide to resolve the dispute on a unilateral basis within a period of six months starting upon receipt of all of the necessary documents. If that is not the case, the competent authorities of the Member

89. OECD, Public Discussion Draft, BEPS Action 14: Make Dispute Resolution Mechanisms More Effective, 2014, pp. 6 et seq.
90. OECD BEPS Action 14, Minimum Standard 1.1.

States concerned shall *endeavor* to solve the dispute by means of an MAP within a period of two years. If the competent authorities of the Member States reach an agreement under the MAP within the stipulated timeframe, this will be binding on the competent authorities and enforceable by the taxpayer subject to his acceptance of the agreement.

6.1.3 Mandatory and Binding Arbitration

The Directive contains an explicit obligation of result and introduces certain steps if the competent authorities do not timely resolve the case. For the competent authorities to reach an agreement under the MAP, a strict two-year period is put forward as a deadline starting from the acceptance of the complaint. If the competent authorities of the Member States concerned fail to reach an agreement under the MAP in that timeframe, they need to inform the taxpayer of the reasons thereto.

In the latter case, an Advisory Commission needs to be set up upon a request by the taxpayer to the competent authorities of the Member States concerned. This Commission consists of three to five independent arbitrators and one or two representatives of each Member State. As under the Arbitration Convention, the Directive excludes the arbitration procedure in cases when penalties are imposed for tax fraud, willful default, and gross negligence.

The Directive provides Member States with the flexibility to set up an Alternative Dispute Resolution Commission instead of the Advisory Commission, which may apply to any dispute resolution processes or techniques in order to solve the dispute in a binding manner. The dispute resolution procedure may take the form of a mediation, conciliation, or even "final offer" (i.e., *baseball*) arbitration.[91]

An Advisory Commission or Alternative Dispute Resolution (ADR) Commission shall deliver its opinion to the competent authorities within six months after the date on which it was set up. This period may be extended by three months. Based on this opinion, the competent authorities shall agree on how to resolve the dispute within six months of the notification of that opinion. The competent authorities may make a decision that deviates from the opinion. However, if they fail to reach an agreement, the opinion of the Advisory Commission or ADR Commission becomes binding.

6.1.4 Recourse for the Taxpayer

The involvement of the taxpayers in the dispute resolution mechanism is increased, and an appeal with the national courts is provided to unblock procedures. In the preamble, the Directive also emphasizes the respect of the taxpayers' fundamental rights and the principles recognized by the Charter of Fundamental Rights of the European Union (Charter) and, in particular, the respect of the right to a fair trial and freedom to conduct a business.

91. Article 9(2) of the Directive.

6.1.4.1 *Denied Access*

In case the complaint is rejected by one (but not all) of the competent authorities, the Advisory Commission, which rules on the acceptance of the complaint, is set up. This is in turn followed by the initiation of the MAP in case the Advisory Commission renders a positive decision. If none of the competent authorities initiated the MAP within 60 days, the Advisory Commission shall provide an opinion on the dispute.

If the complaint is rejected by all of the relevant competent authorities, the taxpayer can file an appeal against this rejection to the national courts of the Member States. The national courts are competent to rule on the admissibility of the complaint, can overrule denied access, and have the MAP initiated.

6.1.4.2 *Set-Up of the Advisory Commission*

If Member States fail to agree on the composition or appointment of the Advisory Commission, the taxpayer can request its national court to set it up. In case the competent authorities do not reach an agreement within the prescribed time limit, they must notify the taxpayer stating the reason for such a failure. Following such a failure notification, the taxpayer may request to set up the Advisory Commission within 50 days of receiving the notification and solving the dispute either by means of arbitration or an alternative dispute resolution mechanism. If the Advisory Commission has not been set up in the prescribed time limit of 120 days upon the taxpayer's request due to either one of the competent authorities or all competent authorities failing to appoint at least one independent person, there is a certain guarantee that the Advisory Commission will be set up and that the procedure will actually continue. The taxpayer can apply to a competent court or to any other appointing body or person in accordance with national law to set up the Advisory Commission.[92] The appointment by the competent court should be requested within 30 days after the end of the 120-day time limit for setting up the Advisory Commission.

6.1.4.3 *Obtaining and Implementing the Decision*

Following the opinion of the Advisory Commission or Alternative Dispute Resolution panel, the competent authorities of the Member States concerned have six months after the notification of this opinion to make a final decision on the dispute at hand.[93] After the decision is reached, the competent authority has the obligation to notify the final decision to the taxpayer within 30 days. In case the taxpayer has not received the final decision, he may appeal in the Member State of residence in accordance with the applicable national rules in order to obtain the final decision.

---

92. Article 7 of the Directive.
93. Article 15(1) of the Directive.

Furthermore, the taxpayer even has the possibility to refer to the national court of the Member State if the competent authority of that Member State has failed to implement the final decision reached by the competent authorities.[94]

6.1.5 *Increased Involvement of the Taxpayer*

The Directive requires the competent authorities to inform and involve the taxpayer in several stages throughout the procedure. The taxpayer can participate in the evidence-taking procedure by providing the Advisory Commission or ADR Commission with any information, evidence, or documents that may be relevant for the decision. The taxpayer may also attend or be represented at the hearing upon its request.

Prior to setting up the Advisory Commission (or ADR Commission), the competent authorities need to notify the taxpayer of the date on which the opinion on elimination of double taxation will be adopted, a reference to any applicable legal provision (both domestic and treaty-based), and the rules of functioning for the Advisory Commission.

On the other hand, while the taxpayer's involvement in the proceeding has increased, he still has limited possibilities to intervene and provide additional information as he has not been given full access to the procedure between the competent authorities.

6.1.6 *Transparency Measures*

Enhanced transparency is one of the objectives of the Directive. Therefore, a final decision may be published subject to the taxpayer's agreement. If the taxpayer objects to the publication of the entire final decision, an abstract of the final decision will be published. Before publication, the information to be published is sent to the taxpayer by the competent authorities.

The publication of the decision is used as an incentive and puts more pressure on the competent authorities to propose a diligent decision supported with corresponding arguments already in the MAP phase of the procedure.

6.2 To Prevent Is Better than to Cure

The significant improvement in double taxation dispute resolution in the EU with the Directive provides for a regulated procedure for reaching a guaranteed outcome. The remaining question is whether a bilateral or multilateral APA using the MAP is possible under the Directive. While reading the provisions of the Directive, one may have some doubts since the scope is limited to disputes "when these arise."[95] As bilateral or multilateral APAs are seen as prevention of double taxation and are negotiated in advance, i.e., before any dispute arises, it seems as if the scope of the Directive may not

94. Article 15(4) of the Directive.
95. Article 1 of the Directive.

include bilateral APAs. It is, however, strongly encouraged (also in BEPS Action 14) to enter into bilateral or multilateral APAs as a means to prevent disputes. Also considering the recent changes to the OECD Model Commentary, the question can be raised whether situations that will result in double taxation can fall under the Directive.

When comparing the Arbitration Convention and the Directive, there are differences in wording: Article 6 of the Arbitration Convention refers to cases when an action results or is "likely to result in double taxation." In line with this wording, requests for APAs are possible under the Arbitration Convention. The Final Report of the EU JTPF on Improving the Functioning of the Arbitration Convention specifically addresses disputes that are likely to arise. Conversely, the Directive refers to actions "resulting in or that will result in question of dispute." The difference in wording is in "likely" and "will."

As underlined, there is a distinction between "intends" and "likely to result." It could be argued that "intends" translates into certainty that double taxation will result. Based on this, the wording of the Directive can be read in a sense that one can request MAPs when double taxation has occurred and in cases when one knows it will occur—so if the competent authority makes an adjustment, and the taxpayer has been notified. Under the Arbitration Convention, the APA in the MAP was also available in the case of adjustments. Including bilateral APAs in the scope of the Directive would safeguard the taxpayer's position and his legal certainty. Further clarifications are needed and encouraged. As the Directive does not repeal the Arbitration Convention but builds upon it means that concluding a bilateral APA is still possible in the context of the Arbitration Convention (despite being less "enforceable").

7 (NON-)APPLICABILITY OF TRANSFER PRICING METHODS IN DETERMINING CUSTOM VALUES

In the case *Hamamatsu Photonics Deutschland GmbH v. Hauptzollamt Munchen* decided recently by the Court of Justice of the European Union,[96] it was considered whether TP methodology could be used for custom valuation purposes in certain instances. The case gained quite some attention as it refers to the still unresolved issue of interplay between TP and customs valuation.[97]

Hamamatsu is a company established in Germany that is active in the optoelectronic devices, systems, and accessories industry with a parent entity in Japan. For the purpose of determining intercompany prices for purchasing imported goods from the parent company and establishing the taxable base, Hamamatsu entered into an advance pricing agreement concluded between that group of companies and the tax authorities in Germany. The amounts charged to the German entity by the parent company were established by using the "Residual Profit Split Method" consistent with

96. Case C-529/16, *Hamamatsu Photonics Deutschland GmbH v. Hauptzollamt Munchen*, December 20, 2017.
97. Petruzzi, R., Prasanna, S.; CJEU: *"Restricting the Interplay of Transfer Pricing and Customs Valuation,"* Transfer Pricing International, 1/2018.

the OECD Guidelines. They / the amounts were regularly checked and, if necessary, adjusted to ensure conformity with the arm's length principle.

The specific facts of the dispute concerned a customs declaration made by Hamamatsu in Germany for releasing circulation various goods for free from more than 1,000 consignments received from the parent company in which a customs value corresponded to the price charged. In this period, the operating margin of Hamamatsu fell below the range for the operating margin, and the transfer prices were adjusted. Regarding this adjustment, Hamamatsu applied for the repayment of the custom duties for the imported goods for which there was no allocation of the adjustment amount to the individual imported goods. This application was rejected by the Principal Customs Office in Munich which stated that the method adopted to adjust the amount of the customs duties to be repaid was incompatible with the EU Customs Code, more specifically with Article 29(1) of this Code which refers to the transaction value of individual goods and not of mixed consignment. The case was brought before the German court which decided to stay the main proceeding and refer the following questions to the CJEU: (i) does the Customs Code permit an agreed transfer price which is an amount initially invoiced and declared and a flat-rate adjustment made after the end of the accounting period in order to form a basis for the custom value regardless of whether a subsequent debit charge or credit is made to the declarant at the end of the accounting period? (ii) may the custom value be reviewed and determined using simplified approaches whether the effects of subsequent transfer pricing adjustments can be recognized? The CJEU took a rather rigid approach to interpret the Customs Code and stated that, in circumstances such as in this case, it is not allowed to take into account a subsequent adjustment of the transaction value in customs valuation.

It should be noted that this interpretation applies to this specific situation where it is not permitted that an agreed transaction value that is composed of an amount initially invoiced and declared and a flat-rate adjustment made after the end of the accounting period is taken into account to form the basis for the custom value, especially without the possibility of knowing whether it would be an upward or downward adjustment at the end of the accounting period.

According to the CJEU, this conclusion is derived from the fact that the objective of customs valuation in the EU is to exclude the use of arbitrary or fictitious custom values which instead must reflect the real economic value of an imported good. For that reason, the valuation method that is preferred is the transaction value method under Article 29 of the Customs Code. Other methods subsequently mentioned in the Customs Code can be applied only if the actual price paid or payable cannot be determined by using this method. In this way, the CJEU confirmed that the Customs Code provides for priority methods to establish the transaction value reflecting the real economic value of imported goods. Moreover, under the Customs Code, a subsequent adjustment of the transaction value is limited to certain situations, e.g., to quality defects or faulty workmanship in the goods or damages before their release for which the price can be reduced in proportion to the damage suffered.

Despite the fact that customs authorities across the countries do not follow a consistent approach for evaluating related party pricing for the purpose of customs valuation, this case will certainly have a broader impact for the Member States who would need to follow this interpretation of the CJEU in their custom valuation exercise. To the contrary, it has been recognized by the World Customs Organization[98] that some customs administrations consider both upward and downward price adjustments and make corresponding duty adjustments where appropriate and others do not do so or only consider upward adjustments with additional duty payment. Some consider tax only adjustments whilst others only actual price adjustments. Regarding the TP adjustments that affect only the tax liability in the absence of an actual change to the amount paid for the goods, the World Customs Organization leaves it up to the customs to consider whether it is an indication of price influence. However, it also recognizes that it is a challenge for customs to determine the mechanism and calculation method when they decide that an adjustment to customs value is appropriate because the focus of customs is on individual transactions whereas the TP data are at the aggregate level.

Considering the outcome of this case, one may doubt whether the CJEU is familiar with the TP concepts and methods in the way that TP practitioners are. Despite the fact that the Hamamatsu case concerns the residual profit split method, it makes one wonder if the CJEU would come to the same conclusion if the TNMM method was applied. As a case study of the World Customs Organization[99] illustrates, customs authorities can make use of transfer pricing information based on the TNMM method in interpreting and applying the World Trade Organization Valuation Agreement to verify if the sales prices in question have not been influenced by the relationship between the related parties. These developments demonstrate that alignment of customs valuation with transfer pricing methods is further away than many would have hoped already a decade ago.

8 CONCLUSIVE REMARKS

The year 2017 was again a year which can be called anything but dull for TP practitioners. It was another productive year for the EC. When one would expect that tackling tax avoidance would fall under EC tax policy, it appears as if the EC Competition policy is the easier way as one does not need to put all of the ducks (i.e., the Member States) in one row to "get things done." Fast growing technology giants and well-known B2C companies are in the eye of a storm that intensified around the blurring of tax policy and tax politics. This leads to uncertainty for taxpayers and also for legislators and tax authorities. While coordination of efforts is a noble cause for the EU to work on, there is a need to limit the further proliferation of unilateral domestic (anti-abuse) actions to help all stakeholders navigating through the current complexities. Indeed, not only is the EC acting in a unilateral way toward the global picture, but

98. World Customs Organization, *WCO Guide to Customs Valuation and Transfer Pricing*, June 2015, available at: http://www.wcoomd.org/en/media/newsroom/2015/june/new-wco-guide-to-customs-valuation-and-transfer-pricing.aspx.

99. Case study 14.1 Use of transfer pricing documentation when examining related party transactions under Article 1.2 (a) of the Agreement, available at: http://www.wcoomd.org/-/media/wco/public/global/pdf/topics/valuation/instruments-and-tools/case-study/case-study-14_1-en.pdf?db=web.

individual countries are also introducing significant changes as demonstrated above.[100] Further, while the EC is striving toward a harmonized EU tax policy, the CJEU is on its own path toward negative harmonization in regard to (not) aligning transfer pricing with customs valuation.

These actions resemble a "gotta catch them all" Pokémon game inspired by the concern that profits remain untaxed. However, the increasing risk of these profits being taxed multiple times has been pushed into the background when discussing the proposals impacting the tax base. Uncertainty reigns in the EU TP context and needs to be worked on through a fundamental reflection on the sustainability of a residence based taxation regime instead of being escalated with new proposals that risk becoming sticking plaster solutions serving a political aim. At the heart of the discussion is how to tax remote economic activity by remote sellers. Gross sales thresholds, virtual presences, and the like are hard to understand for a TP practitioner as one cannot jump to conclusions in the absence of a robust functional analysis helping to understand where the sweet spot of the value chain sits. This can and should be analyzed and discussed with an open mind and leading to solutions that ideally combine legal certainty and fairness. This being said, if one has to choose for one over the other, the authors doubt whether anyone would compromise on legal certainty. Also, a more efficient mechanism for dispute resolution of double taxation has been adopted in the form of a Directive. This is a major achievement and deserves praise. Nevertheless, it is not feasible to only solve double taxation after it occurs. Preventing double taxation is essential for the internal market to function at its full capacity.

Finally, amidst the legal uncertainty around TP developments, it may be a good time to express the hopes that stakeholders (will) understand that a respectful dialogue is probably the best foundation for achievement. After all, catching flies with honey is to be preferred over vinegar.

100. *Supra*, section 2.

CHAPTER 3

Transfer Pricing Developments in the United States

Komal Dhall, Prita Subramanian, Cameron Taheri & Marcus Heyland

1 INTRODUCTION

As predicted, U.S. tax reform had the potential to radically impact the entire area of international taxation—and indeed it has. To the surprise of many, after a period of significant uncertainty and speculation, the House and Senate agreed on the text of a tax bill that became the law P.L. 115-97 when signed by the U.S. President on December 22, 2017 (the 2017 Tax Law). It is the first major rewrite of the Internal Revenue Code (IRC) since the Tax Reform Act of 1986. The 2017 Tax Law is complex—eliminating or modifying various sections of the IRC or adding sections to it; and it is broad—including various rules on taxes for business such as changes from a worldwide taxation with deferral towards a territorial system, a reduction in the U.S. business tax rate itself to 21%, mandatory repatriation requirements, and modifications to the treatment of expenses as well as tax changes for individuals and pass-through entities, just to name a few highlights.

Given the complexity and breadth of the 2017 Tax Law, it is important to segue into how and where transfer pricing plays a role. In the main, one would argue the guidance and policies regarding transfer pricing in the U.S. are relatively mature and while, year-over-year, there are a number of important developments, the changes are only of an incremental nature barring, of course, the substantial guidance changes that occur every five to seven years such as the introduction of the broader guidance for intercompany services and the cost sharing rules. Some of the most interesting U.S. developments are on the litigation front where, incidentally, the IRS has lost a number of high profile cases primarily involving intangible property transactions. Any discussion of U.S. transfer pricing developments in 2017, namely, the litigation cases and their impact on the IRS position and future disputes, would be incomplete without considering the lasting impact of the 2017 Tax Law more fully and its potential impact on the tax court cases which many believe frame the new law.

During the year, court decisions were reached in *Eaton Corp. & Subsidiaries v. Commissioner*[1] and *Amazon.com, Inc. v. Commissioner,*[2] while other cases such as *Medtronic, Inc. and Consolidated Subsidiaries v. Commissioner*[3] and *Altera Corp. & Subsidiaries v. Commissioner*[4] are still under appeal awaiting a final court decision. Some of these cases and other landmark cases will be the subject of this chapter as the authors examine the implications on the transfer of intangible property and other relevant aspects of these cases. Likewise, the authors will also examine the 2017 Tax Law where, despite the very few changes to IRC Section 482 or on transfer pricing rules per se, certain new rules will likely have a significant impact on how U.S. domestic corporations and foreign multinationals are motivated to structure and price their intercompany arrangements primarily relating to intangible property.

That is why, for this chapter, the authors take a holistic look at the transfer pricing technical debate around the best method selection and key aspects of deploying those methods as it relates to the evaluation of the arm's length pricing for intangible property. These issues represent longstanding tension between the views of the taxpayer and the IRS. Certain provisions of the 2017 Tax Law are intended to address issues that have come up in tax court disputes between the IRS and taxpayers, and others can be expected to impact the volume of transactions subject to dispute.

Before the authors start their analysis, key provisions of the 2017 Tax Law, in particular as it relates to IRC Section 482, are first described to facilitate the examination of the selection of the best method analysis for licensing arrangements and cost sharing arrangements (CSAs). Later in the chapter and for completeness, the authors make note of certain other changes in the 2017 Tax Law that are also relevant to transfer pricing. Specifically, this chapter will cover the following provisions of the 2017 Tax Law: Global Intangible Low Taxed Income (GILTI), Foreign Derived Intangible Income (FDII), and the Base Erosion and Anti-Abuse Tax (BEAT) in the context of pricing intangible property at arm's length.

For completeness, the authors also touch on two additional topics. One is the question of the binding nature of Advance Pricing Agreements (APAs) in a modernizing tax environment. Here, the authors consider the implications of not only *Eaton Corp. & Subsidiaries v. Commissioner* but also the consequence of greater transparency. Lastly, to round out our discussion of transfer pricing related changes in the 2017 Tax Law, the authors summarize the new limitation of interest deductibility rules as an update per se and not a detailed analysis.

---

1. *Eaton Corp. & Subsidiaries v. Commissioner*, T.C. Memo 2017-147 (2017).
2. *Amazon.com, Inc. v. Commissioner*, 148 T.C. No. 8 (2017).
3. *Medtronic Inc. v. Commissioner*, T.C. Memo. 2016-112 (2016).
4. *Altera Corp. v. Commissioner*, 145 T.C. 91 (2015).

2 SUMMARY OF 2017 TAX LAW PERTAINING TO SECTION 482

The 2017 Tax Law does not alter the fundamental principles of transfer pricing. It carries the language from the prior IRC Section 482 which states the following:

> In any case of two or more organizations, trades, or businesses (whether or not incorporated, whether or not organized in the United States, and whether or not affiliated) owned or controlled directly or indirectly by the same interests, the Secretary may distribute, apportion, or allocate gross income, deductions, credits, or allowances between or among such organizations, trades, or businesses, if he determines that such distribution, apportionment, or allocation is necessary in order to prevent evasion of taxes or clearly to reflect the income of any of such organizations, trades, or businesses. In the case of any transfer (or license) of intangible property (within the meaning of section 936(h)(3)(B)), the income with respect to such transfer or license shall be commensurate with the income attributable to the intangible.

Treasury Regulations Section 1.482 is the legally binding interpretation of IRC Section 482 and puts forth the arm's length principle for transfer prices as the embodiment of the law in IRC Section 482.[5] The Treasury Regulations Section 1.482 also lays out other principles that are consistent with the arm's length principle such as those pertaining to aggregate analyses if those are more reliable or the consideration of realistic alternatives. Since the old language of IRC Section 482 pertaining to transfer pricing is carried over unchanged, as is the Treasury Regulations Section 1.482, the importance of carefully pricing and documenting intercompany cross-border transactions including tangible goods, services, intangibles, and capital is fully preserved in accordance with IRC Section 6662(e). However, while the language in the old law was preserved, the 2017 Tax Law added a sentence to IRC Section 482:[6]

> For purposes of this section, the Secretary shall require the valuation of transfers of intangible property (including intangible property transferred with other property or services) on an aggregate basis or the valuation of such a transfer on the basis of the realistic alternatives to such a transfer, if the Secretary determines that such basis is the most reliable means of valuation of such transfers.

Further, the 2017 Tax Law changes the definition of intangibles in IRC Section 936 which, as noted above, is cross-referenced in IRC Section 482. Thus, while most fundamental aspects of intercompany pricing are unchanged, there are certain provisions in the 2017 Tax Law that directly impact it, particularly the pricing of intangibles. The summary below, therefore, is intended to be narrow as it relates to the changes in the new 2017 Tax Law outside IRC Section 482 that make specific reference to intercompany transactions to define taxes owed.

---

5. With the caveat that taxpayers can and have (e.g., *Altera v. Commissioner*) successfully challenged regulations as being inconsistent with the law.
6. Similar changes were made to IRC Section 367(d) which relates to the outbound transfer of intangible property from a U.S. person.

2.1 Revised Definition Intangibles

The 2017 Tax Law amends the definition of intangible property in IRC Section 936(h)(3)(B) to include workforce in place, goodwill, and going-concern value. *See* below for the updated code where the items in bold were newly added as part of the 2017 Tax Law:

> Intangible property. The term "intangible property" means any—
>
> - patent, invention, formula, process, design, pattern, or know-how;
> - copyright, literary, musical, or artistic composition;
> - trademark, trade name, or brand name;
> - franchise, license, or contract;
> - method, program, system, procedure, campaign, survey, study, forecast, estimate, customer list, or technical data;
> - *any goodwill, going concern value, or workforce in place (including its composition and terms and conditions (contractual or otherwise) of its employment); or*
> - *any other item the value or potential value of which is not attributable to tangible property or the services of any individual.*

The authors address the impact of these changes as it relates to valuing intangible property later in this chapter. In short, however, the authors note the codification of these rules supports the longstanding position of the IRS concerning business synergies and the broader definition of intangibles.

2.2 GILTI

The 2017 Tax Law includes the newly added IRC Section 951A which operates by subjecting certain income, referred to as "global intangible low-tax income" or GILTI, earned by foreign affiliates of U.S. multinationals to current U.S. tax. In general, the GILTI amount is an aggregate foreign profit in excess of a deemed return on tangible assets. The deemed return on tangible assets is measured by reference to a 10% return on foreign tangible property less certain interest expenses. The resulting GILTI amount is then taxed at an effective rate of 10.5% and 13.125% for years beginning before December 31, 2015, and years thereafter, respectively.[7] Importantly, an 80% foreign tax credit is potentially available to offset incremental U.S. taxes.

Intangible property is conspicuously excluded from the base subject to a fixed return. As is apparent from the "GILTI" moniker, the objective of IRC Section 951A is, in fact, to subject the income of foreign related parties associated with valuable intangibles owned by U.S. resident companies to current U.S. taxation. However, it is important to note that the very limited "deemed return on tangible assets" could leave significant income beyond high intangible income subject to U.S. tax.

7. IRC Section 250 allows a 50.0% deduction on GILTI for tax years beginning before December 31, 2025, and a 37.5% deduction thereafter. A 50% deduction implies an effective tax rate of 10.5%, while a 37.5% deduction implies an effective tax rate of 13.125%.

There is the potential of available foreign tax credits to offset the tax burden associated with the provision but certainly high profits earned in very low-tax jurisdictions would be difficult to offset from residual U.S. tax. Therefore, the provision most notably impacts companies that have shifted intangible ownership and profits to zero or very low tax jurisdictions, but there are certainly other circumstances where GILTI can apply given limitations in the offset provisions.

2.3 BEAT

The 2017 Tax Law includes the newly added IRC Section 59A which is designed to prevent the erosion of the U.S. tax base via payments from domestic corporations to foreign related parties. Unlike IRC Section 951A, IRC Section 59A affects non-U.S. multinationals doing business in the U.S. as much or more than U.S.—resident multinationals. Taxpayers that fall within the scope of IRC Section 59A will be subject to a "Base Erosion and Anti-Abuse Tax" or BEAT.

In general, BEAT applies to "base erosion payments" made by a domestic corporation to a foreign related party. Base erosion payments essentially include every payment made by a domestic corporation to a foreign related party with notable exceptions as follows:

- cost of goods sold and other payments that are treated as reductions to gross receipts rather than deductions under US tax accounting rules;
- intercompany service payments eligible for use of the services cost method without regard to the business judgment rule;[8] and
- qualifying derivative payments.

The BEAT is applicable only to the extent that average domestic gross receipts over the last three years exceed USD 500 million and the "base erosion percentage" exceeds 3% (2% for banks). The base erosion percentage is essentially the sum of base erosion payments divided by the sum of all of the deductions that are allowed to the taxpayer.

The BEAT is computed by the difference between 10% (5% in the case of FY2018 and increasing to 12.5% by FY2026) of the domestic corporation's modified taxable income and the corporation's regular tax liability. Modified taxable income, in this case, is essentially the taxable income of the taxpayer with add-backs for base erosion payments. There are multiple complexities to this computation including special rules for related party payments subject to withholding tax and the tax credits taken into account for purposes of computing regular tax liability.

Of all the new provisions, perhaps the BEAT is the most far reaching. To properly address the BEAT would be the subject of a separate chapter altogether as it will impact multinational corporate business structures for years to come. The BEAT is the subject of short-term action as well as more long-term planning as the end of deferral in the

8. Treasury Regulation Section 1.482-9.

U.S. tax system, the lower headline U.S. tax rate, and new tax provisions will motivate all companies to revisit their operating models.

This said, in brief, certain observations can be made. The transfer prices paid by domestic corporations to foreign related parties in the form of royalties or service payments will be of great consequence since the intercompany price is determinate of taxes owed. Thus companies may look to mitigate exposure to the incremental tax on such outbound payments or in any restructuring of transactions or supply chains.

The BEAT only applies to payments made to related parties. Thus, the provisions will have differential impact on taxpayers who do business as integrated multinationals versus those who, for example, sell to unrelated distributors.

The provisions may have significant impact on U.S. companies (headquartered or sub of a foreign multinational) that make large services payments to offshore related parties, such as technology or life sciences companies that have large R&D workforces in India and other jurisdictions. If these payments are not eligible for the services cost method, the entire service charge will be subject to the BEAT.[9]

This is, of course, only a summary and does not adequately cover the various scenarios to which the BEAT is potentially applicable and the extent to which the BEAT would, in fact, be ultimately applied.

2.4 FDII

The 2017 Tax Law includes the newly added IRC Section 250 which allows a deduction of 37.5% and 21.875% for years beginning before December 31, 2015, and years thereafter, respectively, for "foreign derived intangible income" (or FDII) booked by a U.S. domestic corporation. Thus, in effect, IRC Section 250 creates a preferential tax rate of 13.125% and 16.406% for years beginning before December 31, 2015, and years thereafter, respectively, for foreign derived intangible income.[10]

Under IRC Section 250, foreign derived intangible income is computed in accordance with a complicated formula. The first step is to compute the "deemed intangible income" of the domestic corporation which, generally speaking, is the profit of the domestic corporation in excess of a 10% return on domestic tangible property. Next, the resulting amount is multiplied by the ratio of "foreign derived deduction eligible income" and "deduction eligible income." Foreign derived deduction eligible income is the amount of income recorded by the domestic corporation in connection with property sold to a foreign party (related party or third party) for foreign use or services provided by the domestic corporation to a foreign party (related party or third party). Deduction eligible income is essentially the total income recorded by the domestic corporation excluding Subpart F income, dividends, and a few other items.

9. See Treasury Regulation Section 1.482-9 for more information on the SCM and services eligible for this method.
10. IRC Section 250 allows a 37.5% deduction on FDII for tax years beginning before December 31, 2025, and a 21.875% deduction thereafter. A 37.5% deduction implies an effective tax rate of 13.125%, while a 21.875% deduction implies an effective tax rate of 16.406%.

It is important to note that IRC Section 250 creates a preferential rate for foreign derived intangible income thus incentivizing U.S. multinationals to keep intangible property in the U.S. or potentially migrate intangible property back to the U.S. However, IRC Section 250 has been criticized by U.S. trading partners as an export subsidy; thus companies need to consider the potential for other countries to implement counter measures, e.g., disallow a deduction for royalty payments made to the U.S.

Similar to IRC Section 951A, IRC Section 250 uses blunt mechanics to compute intangible income, i.e., intangible income is computed as the residual income in excess of a small return on tangible property.

In theory, the combined effect of IRC Section 951A (after taking into account foreign tax credits) and IRC Section 250 is to equalize the tax treatment of intangible income earned domestically and offshore. However, in practice, such equalization will not always be the case, for example, since U.S. companies with a high foreign effective tax rate will not trigger a GILTI related tax so they will continue to have an incentive to offshore intangible property to pursue a lower tax rate than the rate available in the U.S. (with the added incentive of tax free repatriation).

3 INTANGIBLE PROPERTY AND THE SELECTION OF THE BEST METHOD

As noted above, intangible property in IRC Section 482 is defined by cross reference to IRC Section 936. Prior to the 2017 Tax Law, intangible property was defined in terms of certain specified identifiable intangible property and similar items. The 2017 Tax Law significantly expands the definition to include workforce in place, goodwill, and going-concern value.

In addition to providing regulations around the transfer pricing of intangibles, Treasury Regulations Section 1.482-7 as updated in 2011 includes the concept of "platform contribution transactions" ("PCTs") in the context of a CSAs. The platform contribution concept also broadened the definition of intangible property compared to what existed in the old IRC Section 936 and is more aligned with the new intangible definition. Hence, the new 2017 Tax Law gives the 482-7 position significantly greater legal authority. Further, the new law potentially provides an even more expansive definition of intangibles than 482-7 did in that it applies more widely than just to CSAs.

From experience, given that many court cases have dealt with such transfers, the authors know transfers of intangibles and the issue of platform contributions are challenging and contentious. The periods covered in court cases to date are pre-2011, hence, transfers of intangible property are defined under the old IRC Section 936 definition and were completed before the updated cost sharing regulations were finalized. Below, the authors discuss the issues that are central to the court cases involving intangibles in the following two sections: (i) licensing of intangibles; and (ii) transfers of intangibles under a CSA. The authors discuss a seminal court case for each—*Medtronic, Inc. & Consolidated Subsidiaries v. Commissioner* for licensing of intangibles and *Veritas Software Corp. & Subsidiaries v. Commissioner*[11] for the transfer of intangibles under a CSA[12]—to illustrate the key issues. Common issues are the selection of best method, aggregation and, in the case of the transfer of intangibles under a CSA, certain key inputs in the valuation model.

3.1 Licensing Arrangements and U.S. Case Law

A licensing arrangement involves a controlled transfer of intangible property.[13] Treasury Regulation Section 1.482-4(a) provides the following methods to compute the arm's length consideration for the transfer of intangibles:

- Comparable uncontrolled transaction (CUT) method[14]
- Comparable profits method (CPM)
- Profit split method (PSM)
- Unspecified method.

The best method rule requires that the method employed provides the most reliable measure of an arm's length result under the facts and circumstances. No priority of methods is provided nor is one method considered to be more reliable than others. Treasury Regulation Section 1.482-7 provides the applicable methods available in the case of a CSA, and the authors discuss these later in this chapter.

Licensing arrangements are nearly ubiquitous today as a result of the expansion of U.S.-parented multinationals overseas. As these firms expanded geographically, intangible property such as trade names originally developed in the U.S., and manufacturing processes were licensed throughout the global operation. One of the most common licensing structures involves a U.S.-parent that licenses intangibles to a controlled foreign manufacturer (often located in jurisdictions with low labor costs) in exchange for consideration (typically a royalty expressed as a percentage of sales). The fact pattern of a U.S.-parent licensing its intangibles to a controlled foreign manufacturer is littered with historical disputes and litigation. In these disputes, the principal underlying technical issue is the selection of best transfer pricing method and related issues such as aggregation of intercompany transactions and applicability of realistic alternatives.

11. *Veritas Software Corp. v. Commissioner*, 133 T.C. 297 (2009).
12. Note that, in principle, *Veritas Software Corp. & Subsidiaries v. Commissioner* involved intangibles under the old IRC Section 936 definition under a cost sharing arrangement. However, the IRS essentially treated the transfer as a PCT, highlighting some key points of contention in valuation models.
13. Treasury Regulation Section 1.482-4.
14. Similar to the comparable uncontrolled price (CUP) method in the OECD Guidelines.

3.1.1 Background U.S. Litigations

The IRS litigation position in several historical cases has been to apply the CPM.[15] Taxpayers, on the other hand, commonly apply the CUT method. The CPM evaluates whether the amount charged in a controlled transaction is arm's-length based on objective measures of profitability (profit level indicators) derived from uncontrolled taxpayers that engage in similar business activities under similar circumstances. Under the comparable profits method, the determination of an arm's length result is based on the amount of operating profit that the tested party would have earned on related party transactions if its profit level indicator were equal to that of an uncontrolled comparable (comparable operating profit).[16] The CUT method evaluates whether the amount charged for a controlled transfer of intangible property is arm's length by reference to the amount charged in a CUT.[17]

In the cases discussed below, the IRS selected the CPM with the controlled foreign manufacturer as the tested party on the basis that the controlled foreign manufacturer is merely a routine manufacturer (akin to a contract manufacturer) and all non-routine contributions are performed in the U.S. In computing an adjustment, the IRS has aggregated all intercompany transactions involving the controlled foreign manufacturer. For example, the controlled foreign manufacturer may sell tangible goods to the U.S.-parent in addition to paying a royalty to it. In this sense, the IRS adjustment is premised upon the IRS' determination of the total profit to which the controlled foreign manufacturer is entitled (under a CPM approach) without determining the appropriate price for each intercompany transaction. In performing such an aggregation, the IRS cites the U.S. transfer pricing regulation that states multiple transactions can be combined if when taken together, i.e., looked at as whole, such transactions are so interrelated that combining them yields the most reliable means of determining the arm's length consideration. This regulation has been amended over time but is relevant for the cases discussed in this chapter:[18]

> The combined effect of two or more separate transactions may be considered if such transactions taken as a whole, are so interrelated that consideration of multiple transactions is the most reliable means of determining the arm's length consideration for the controlled transaction.

The IRS also commonly uses a realistic alternatives argument to support its aggregated CPM approach. In particular, the IRS argues that the realistic alternative available to the U.S.-parent is to make the products themselves (as opposed to the controlled foreign manufacturer) or, perhaps more practically, to engage a third-party contract manufacturer. The IRS contends that its aggregated CPM approach takes into account the realistic alternative principal because the CPM uses third-party contract manufacturing companies as comparables which theoretically serve as a proxy for

15. *Bausch & Lomb, Inc. & Consolidated Subsidiaries v. Commissioner; Sundstrand Corp. v. Commissioner; Medtronic, Inc. & Consolidated Subsidiaries v. Commissioner.*
16. Treasury Regulation Section 1.482-5(a), Treasury Regulation Section 1.482-5(b).
17. Treasury Regulation Section 1.482-4(c)(1).
18. Treasury Regulation Section 1.482-1(f)(i)(a); this regulation is no longer in effect.

what the U.S.-parent would pay a third-party contract manufacturer acting as a substitute of the controlled foreign manufacturer. In making this argument, the IRS cites the following U.S. transfer pricing regulation regarding realistic alternatives:[19]

> the Commissioner may consider the alternatives available to the taxpayer in determining whether the terms of the controlled transaction would be acceptable to an uncontrolled taxpayer faced with the same alternatives and operating under comparable circumstances. In such cases the Commissioner may adjust the consideration charged in the controlled transaction based on the cost or profit of an alternative as adjusted to account for material differences between the alternative and the controlled transaction, but will not restructure the transaction as if the alternative had been adopted by the taxpayer.

Taxpayers have rebutted both the aggregation and realistic alternative argument on the basis that the foreign manufacturer is not a contract manufacturer at all but a manufacturer bearing material risk by citing the following regulation which requires the IRS to respect the taxpayer's transactions as structured unless the structure has no economic substance:[20]

> The Commissioner will evaluate the results of a transaction as actually structured by the taxpayer unless its structure lacks economic substance.

In the next section, the authors summarize the *Coca-Cola Co. & Subsidiaries v Commissioner*[21] case first involving a similar dispute involving the IRS position of aggregation and application of the CPM that is still under litigation and dive into more detail using *Medtronic, Inc. and Consolidated Subsidiaries v. Commissioner* (which is under appeal) to further illustrate how the court has interpreted the technical tension described above.

3.1.2 Summary of Coca-Cola Co. & Subsidiaries v. Commissioner

In *Coca-Cola Co. & Subsidiaries v. Commissioner*, Coca-Cola is challenging the IRS determination that royalties paid by related party licensees to Coca-Cola for use of trademarks and formula rights were less than arm's length for 2007–2009. The licensees manufactured a concentrate product that was for sale to bottlers outside the United States. The IRS made a USD 9.4 billion income adjustment based on the CPM testing the licensees' return on operating assets against that of the selected unrelated companies. The taxpayer had followed the methodology set forth in a 1996 closing agreement for the payment of royalties as well as intercompany charges for headquarters' expenses.

In its Tax Court petition, Coca-Cola contends that the IRS improperly applied the CPM to the licensees. The Taxpayer claims that the licensees substantially bore all entrepreneurial risk and responsibility for their businesses with important decision-making authority for their operations, the licensees invested more than USD 45 billion

19. Treasury Regulation Section 1.482-1(f)(2)(ii).
20. Treasury Regulation Section 1.482-1(f)(2)(ii).
21. *Coca-Cola Co. & Subsidiaries v. Commissioner*, T.C. No. 031183-15 (2017).

in preroyalty operating and marketing expenses, and that the IRS' CPM analysis used inappropriate comparables, i.e., beverage bottlers rather than manufacturers like the licensees. The case is pending in Tax Court, and the trial is scheduled for March 2018.

3.1.3 *Summary of Medtronic, Inc. and Consolidated Subsidiaries v. Commissioner*

In *Medtronic, Inc. and Consolidated Subsidiaries v. Commissioner*, Medtronic challenged the IRS determination that royalties paid by the indirectly owned Puerto Rican manufacturing entity of Medtronic U.S. (MPROC) were deficient in tax for 2005 and 2006, respectively. The IRS calculated these deficiencies using the CPM with MPROC as the tested party and third-party contract manufactures as comparables. The subject key issue was whether income related to intercompany licenses for the intangible property required to manufacture devices and leads should be reallocated under Section 482 to Medtronic U.S. from MPROC, for tax years 2005 and 2006.[22]

3.1.3.1 Facts

Intercompany Agreement: **Devices and leads license.** Medtronic U.S. and MPROC entered into license agreements for the intangible property used in manufacturing devices and leads. Under the devices and leads licenses, MPROC obtained the exclusive right to use, develop, and enjoy the intangible property used for manufacturing devices for sale to customers in the United States and its territories and leads for sale to customers worldwide. In accordance with the devices and leads licenses, MPROC agreed to pay a royalty of 29% to Medtronic U.S. on its U.S. net intercompany sales of devices and 15% to Medtronic U.S. on its net intercompany sales of leads. Medtronic U.S. and MPROC later entered into amended license agreements to reflect agreements reached in a memorandum of understanding (MOU) between Medtronic U.S. and the IRS. The amended agreements included a profit split methodology that changed the royalty rates. Ultimately, MPROC would pay a 44% royalty rate to Medtronic U.S. on its net intercompany sales of devices and a 26% royalty to Medtronic U.S. on its net intercompany sales of leads.

3.1.3.2 Medtronic Position

Medtronic U.S. argued that MPROC paid Medtronic U.S. arm's length royalties for the intangible property licensed pursuant to the devices and leads licenses on the basis that MPROC was comparable to that of a full-fledged entrepreneurial licensee responsible for its own success. Using the CUT method, Medtronic U.S. argued that royalties of

22. *Supra* n. 3, 70–71.

29% of net device intercompany sales and 15% of net leads intercompany sales was arm's length (these royalty rates were the original royalty rates used by Medtronic prior to the MOU-based amendment).[23]

In its application of the CUT method, Medtronic U.S. used an agreement between Medtronic U.S. and Pacesetter (a third party) as its primary means of supporting a starting royalty rate and then made various adjustments to account for differences in contractual terms. In its analysis, which extensively relied upon the Pacesetter agreement, Medtronic U.S. determined that the arm's length royalties were 29% for devices and 15% for leads.[24]

3.1.3.3 *IRS Position*

The IRS was dismissive of the functions carried out by MPROC and determined that the CPM was the best method (with MPROC as the tested party) to determine the arm's length royalty rates. Importantly, as part of its position, the IRS contended that aggregating the various intercompany transactions entered into by MPROC with Medtronic U.S. into one CPM was the most reliable method. This approach was plainly shaped by the IRS' view that MPROC was merely a routine manufacturer akin to a contract manufacturer.[25] Regarding realistic alternatives, the IRS argued that the aggregated CPM approach considered Medtronic' realistic alternatives. Specifically, the IRS asserted that MPROC was replaceable and that Medtronic U.S.' realistic alternative was to outsource manufacturing to another Medtronic entity, to a third party, or to one of its U.S. plants, or to build a new plant.[26]

3.1.3.4 *Decision*

The court concluded that the IRS' aggregated CPM approach was not the best method because it overly diminished the importance of MPROC's quality function,[27] i.e., doctors would stop using Medtronic's products if any material portion of the products were defective. The court also concluded the IRS unnecessarily aggregated transactions.[28] The court determined that each of the four transactions should be analyzed separately because the structure did not lack economic substance. The court did not directly address the point of realistic alternatives but tacitly rejected the IRS position on the basis that, again, the IRS was too dismissive of the function of MPROC. As for the devices and leads license transaction, the court concluded that appropriate adjustments should be made to Medtronic U.S.' CUT approach.

23. *Supra* n. 3, 120–121.
24. *Supra* n. 3, 72.
25. *Supra* n. 3, 88–89.
26. *Supra* n. 3, 91.
27. *Supra* n. 3, 117.
28. *Supra* n. 3, 116.

The court accepted the Pacesetter agreement and Medtronic U.S.' adjustments to this rate for a starting royalty rate of 17%.[29] The court then made several additional adjustments for: (i) know-how to account for exclusivity; (ii) profit potential to account for the difference between the pacesetter product and devices and leads; and (iii) product range to align the breadth of the devices and leads license versus the limited product range compared to the pacesetter agreement:[30] The IRS has now appealed the decision. In its appeal brief, the IRS contended that the court erred as a matter of law in its adoption of the CUT method and failed to apply regulatory standards. In particular, the IRS cited numerous issues with the Pacesetter agreement for which the court relied including different payment terms (the Pacesetter agreement featured a partial up-front payment which the IRS asserted the court ignored), differing functions, and differing intangibles.[31] The IRS may have been partially motivated to appeal the decision since the technical issues in *Coca-Cola Co. & Subsidiaries v. Commissioner*, i.e., the characterization of the foreign entity and the extent to which it bears risk, the aggregation of multiple transactions, and selecting the CPM as the best method over the CUT, are similar to *Medtronic, Inc. and Consolidated Subsidiaries v. Commissioner*.

3.1.4 *Key Themes from the Medtronic, Inc. and Consolidated Subsidiaries v. Commissioner Case*

Medtronic, Inc. and Consolidated Subsidiaries v. Commissioner demonstrates certain failings on the part of the IRS in selecting and applying the best method as determined by the courts in their interpretation of the relevant legal authorities.

3.1.4.1 *Characterization*

An appropriate understanding of the risks managed by a tested party informs the best method selection process. A tested party managing risks that are key to the business has the potential to substantially reduce the reliability of the CPM. A fuller understanding of the risk profile might alternatively have yielded another best method altogether. The court, in this case, rejected the CPM as applied by the IRS because of a number of comparability shortcomings. Instead, the court found the CUT to yield a more reliable result. Every transfer pricing method splits profit between parties. When the court reviewed the implied allocation of profits to MPROC under the IRS proposed CPM analysis, it was clear to the court that the relative allocation of profit to MPROC given its risk profile as a licensee and important contributor to the value chain was too low when benchmarked using a set of contract manufacturers.

29. *Supra* n. 3, 134.
30. *Supra* n. 3, 135–137.
31. *Supra* n. 3, appellate brief.

3.1.4.2 Aggregation

Aggregation as a tool that can be useful to explore when transactions are interrelated and to analyze if, when taken together as a whole, the allocation of profit using individual transactions yields relatively reasonable results. Said differently, when there are multiple transactions between related parties, the CPM is commonly used as a reasonableness check to consider if the allocation of profit between the two parties yields sensible results. Aggregation can also be applied as a primary method if the multiple transactions, when taken together, yield results that are more reliable than those that are possible by evaluating the transactions separately. However, to emerge as a primary method, an accurate understanding of the functions, assets, and risks must be fully understood. An unclear understanding of the facts and circumstances may compromise the relevance of any benchmarking carried out at the aggregate level.

3.1.4.3 Comparability

The courts demonstrated yet again that an adjusted imperfect internal CUT (with potentially imperfect adjustments) is capable of delivering the most reliable measure of arm's length pricing. In analyzing comparability between internal CUTs and the tested transaction, differences are often identified. The courts provide for a: (i) know-how adjustment to quantify the exclusivity of know-how being shared with MPROC; (ii) profit potential adjustment recognizing the difference between devices and leads from the Pacesetter products; and (iii) product range adjustment to compensate for the broader range of products in the internal CUT. In carrying out the comparability analyses clear differences like those identified in the *Medtronic* case emerge. Commonly, however, internal agreements are not adjusted to appropriately account for differences in facts and circumstances between the tested transaction and those entered into with third parties but rather rejected altogether. While the court's decision lacked a clear analysis supporting the quantification of its adjustments, the authors are reminded of the rich pricing data available in arrangements directly with third parties and that such data and its potential comparability to the tested transaction should be fully evaluated.

3.1.5 Implications Looking Forward

U.S. Tax Reform is likely to change the dynamic which underlies historical licensing disputes including the best method selection.

One question is how the interpretation of the new definition of intangibles will impact the applicability of the CUT method. Where the earlier definition of intangibles allowed for the discrete identification of the transfer of intangibles, the new inclusion of workforce, goodwill, and going-concern value make it potentially harder to take a more narrow definition of the subject transaction. Said differently, will it continue to be possible to determine the value of the transfer of an intangible by reference to a third-party transaction transferring a similar intangible under similar circumstances, and will this be interpreted as sufficiently adequate under the new IRC Section 482? Or, is there additional value under the broader definition of intangibles, substantially impairing the comparability of potential CUTs, and requiring a greater allocation of income?

As the U.S. Treasury begins to interpret the new IRC Section 482, it may deliver more clarity through revisions to the Treasury Regulations Section 1.482 or other guidance. Until then, interpretation of the new law will to come to light by IRS examiners, the IRS appeals process, and potentially by the courts.

3.2 CSAs and U.S. Case Law

Transfers of intangibles under CSAs have been a significant source of controversy. A CSA is an arrangement by which controlled participants share the costs and risks of developing cost shared intangibles in proportion to their reasonably anticipated benefit (RAB) shares.[32] CSAs are widely used by taxpayers particularly in the technology, software, and pharmaceutical industries.

The transfer of intangibles in the Veritas case took place prior to the introduction of the updated CSAs; however, arguments raised by the IRS were often based on the updated cost sharing regulations that were proposed in 2009. The U.S. Treasury released temporary cost sharing regulations in Treasury Regulation Section 1.482-7 which introduced the concept of platform contribution as a broader alternative to the term intangible property that was already in place. These regulations were finalized without substantive changes in 2011. A platform contribution is any resource, capability, or right that is reasonably anticipated to contribute to developing intangibles under a CSA. One of the substantive requirements of a CSA is that all controlled participants must engage in platform contributions transactions (PCTs)[33] to the extent that there are platform contributions, i.e., if a participant to a CSA contributes any resource, capability, or right that is reasonably anticipated to contribute to developing intangibles under the CSA, then all of the controlled participants must enter into a PCT to make use of the platform contribution and must make an arm's length payment to the participant making the platform contribution.[34] Prior to 2009, instead of the requirement of a PCT when a controlled participant made a platform contribution to the development of the cost shared intangible, the earlier cost sharing regulations required a "buy-in payment" for any preexisting intangibles contributed by a controlled participant to the development of the cost shared intangible.

Similar to transfers of intangibles under licensing arrangements, buy-in payments or PCTs have been the subject of extensive controversy and litigation. Cases that were

32. Treasury Regulation Section 1.482-7(b).
33. A platform contribution is defined by Treasury Regulations Section 1.482-7 as any resource, capability, or right that a controlled participant has developed, maintained, or acquired externally to the intangible development activity (whether prior to or during the course of the CSA) that is reasonably anticipated to contribute to developing cost shared intangibles. Further, "PCT" is a term that was developed as a result of the final Treasury Regulations Section 1.482-7 regulations issued in 2011. Prior to that, the equivalent term was "buy-in payment."
34. Treasury Regulation Section 1.482-7(b)(1)(ii).

previously argued in Tax Court include *Veritas* and *Amazon* both of which included transfers of intangible property prior to the introduction of the revised cost sharing regulations.

There are numerous underlying technical differences between taxpayers and the IRS that drive these disputes, some of which can be attributed to new concepts like PCTs emerging in the new cost sharing regulations. The most significant of the disputes have centered around three main themes:

(1) Method selection. Did the taxpayer apply the most appropriate transfer pricing method based upon the facts and circumstances?
(2) Useful life. Do the platform contributions have a longer useful life than the average useful life of the taxpayer's current products?
(3) Discount rates. Did the taxpayer apply the proper discount rates to determine the PCT payment?

The issue of method selection is similar to the issue arising in the licensing of intangibles wherein the IRS has favored an approach that assigns all projected residual profits to the platform contribution made by the U.S. cost sharing participant. The IRS has done this using the income method as specified in the cost sharing regulations or a variant of it.

Under the income method, as specified by the cost sharing regulations, the arm's length PCT payment is determined by reference to a controlled participant's best realistic alternative to entering into a CSA. The arm's length charge for a PCT will be an amount such that a controlled participant's present value, as of the date of the PCT, of its cost sharing alternative of entering into a CSA equals the present value of its best realistic alternative.[35] While the cost sharing regulations include the income method as a specified method for evaluating the arm's length pricing of a PCT, this income method is one application of what has more broadly been referred to as the income approach in the valuation literature. At the heart of any income approach for valuing an asset is a two-step process: (i) estimate the stream of income from the asset over the life of the asset; and (ii) discount the stream of income back to the present at an appropriate discount rate.

Central to the disputes between taxpayers and the IRS on determining arm's length PCT payments using an income approach have been two of the key parameters required for applying these steps.

The first step involves projecting the income expected to be generated by the platform contribution over its economically useful life. A key sticking point between taxpayers and the IRS has been the determination of the economically useful life of the platform contribution, i.e., the period over which it would continue generating residual income. The longer the economically useful life of the platform contribution, the higher would be the value of the platform contribution and the higher the PCT payment.

35. Treasury Regulations Section 1.482-7(g)(4)(i).

Taxpayers and the IRS have tended to take differing views of the useful life of the platform contributions with the IRS favoring long or infinite lives and the taxpayers arguing for finite lives.

In the second step, once the income stream attributable to the asset is determined, it needs to be discounted to the present at an appropriate discount rate. The higher the discount rate on an income stream, the lower its present value. The discount rate has been another point of contention between the IRS and taxpayers. Taxpayers have favored higher discount rates on projected income from platform contributions than the IRS.

The authors discuss the three central points of contention between the taxpayers and the IRS—selection of method, useful life, and discount rate—in greater detail below. This is followed up with a description of the *Veritas Tax Court* case that illustrates these issues.

3.2.1 Selection of Method

The application of the income method (or slight variations thereof) has been the historic IRS litigation position for payments related to preexisting intangibles or platform contributions in a CSA. The IRS has argued, as in the *Veritas* case discussed below, that the income method is the best method because the transfer of preexisting intangible rights (or the platform contribution of the U.S. cost sharing participant) to the foreign CSA participant is akin to the sale of a business and hence needs to be valued in accordance with the net present value of the profits of the business being "sold." This reasoning for selecting the income method by the IRS has also been intimately tied to its application of a perpetual useful life for the platform contribution. Further, the IRS has preferred the income method because it implicitly picks up the value of all forms of intangibles (whether transferred or not) including synergy, goodwill, and going-concern value. This is important because these concepts argued by the IRS can be found in the updated 2011 cost sharing regulations but not before then.

Taxpayers, on the other hand, have typically applied the CUT method in litigation. The CUT method evaluates whether the amount charged for a controlled transfer of intangible property was arm's length by reference to the amount charged in a CUT.[36]

The IRS has historically rejected the CUT method on the basis that the transaction at issue (the transfer of intangible rights as part of a CSA) is rarely if ever observed in an uncontrolled context; thus there are not sufficiently comparable transactions in order to apply the CUT method. Further, the IRS contends that the CUT method, as employed by taxpayers, values each intangible separately and, as a result, does not consider the synergy value of the various forms of intangibles being used in conjunction.

36. Treasury Regulations Section 1.482-4(c)(1).

3.2.2 Useful Life

Under the income method, the useful life assumption of the subject intangible is highly determinate of the resulting intangible value. As a result, the useful life assumption has been central to disputes. In the CSA cases that have been litigated, the IRS has argued that the subject intangible is long lived or even perpetual lived. Taxpayers, on the other hand, have argued that useful life is finite reflecting obsolesce and decay of preexisting intangibles over time. This fundamental difference in assumptions has led to multi-billion dollar valuation differences.[37] The CSA regulations include minimal guidance on the concept of useful life. The updated 2011 CSA regulations do provide the following brief guidance which supports the IRS' position of long-lived intangibles:[38]

> If the cost shared intangibles themselves are reasonably anticipated to contribute to developing other intangibles, then the (CSA activity) includes the period, reasonably anticipated as of the date of the PCT, of developing and exploiting such indirectly benefited intangibles.

In addition, the IRS provides the following summary of its position on useful life in the Practice Unit which further elaborates on the concept of long-lived intangibles:[39]

> The conventional concept of useful life in intangibles looks to the period of time economic benefits are derived from the current technology. The useful life is therefore helpful in determining the period of analysis for valuing an existing resource, capability, or right without further development (i.e., make-sell rights). However, the value of the make-sell rights of the current technology or product does not take into account all of the resources, capabilities, and rights made available to a CSA. The make-sell rights do not take into account the benefits associated with the future products or technology that build upon the current version. Successful efforts and experience need to be considered. At arm's length, parties will analyse their investments given all the future income to be generated from those investments. Determining resources, capabilities, or rights reasonably anticipated to contribute to developed intangibles requires that future income beyond the current generation of product or technology be considered. Therefore the value of the make-sell rights does not satisfy the required PCT payment. The value of all platform rights must also be considered.

Taxpayers have historically employed a variety of techniques to counter the IRS position and evidence the finite life of intangibles. In some cases, taxpayers have relied upon external license agreements which incorporate a declining royalty. Taxpayers contend that such declining royalties show that third parties acknowledge that intangibles lose their value over time. In other cases, taxpayers have relied upon internal data such as the declining proportion of sales derived from a certain product release over time or the number of unique lines of code developed each year in a software application.

---

37. See *Veritas Software Corp. & Subsidiaries v. Commissioner* and *Amazon.com, Inc. v. Commissioner.*
38. Treasury Regulations Section 1.482-7(g)(2)(ii)(A).
39. IRS. LB&I International Practice Service Transaction Unit: "Pricing of Platform Contribution Transaction (PCT) in Cost Sharing Arrangements (CSA)—Initial Transaction". p. 16.

3.2.3 *Discount Rate*

Similar to useful life, the discount rate materially influences the intangible value. In general, the IRS and taxpayers both compute discount rates using a weighted average cost of capital (WACC) derived under the capital asset pricing model (CAPM). Thus discount rate disputes tend to be limited to inputs to the WACC computation such as risk free rate, equity risk premium, beta, etc.

Separate from the general WACC computation as computed under CAPM, the application of the income method has unique discount rate considerations that can potentially generate disputes. In the application of the income method, taxpayers typically use two separate discount rates: one for the cost sharing alternative and one for the licensing alternative. The CSA regulations accept the concept of different discount rates for each alternative:[40] The point of controversy is determining the appropriate difference (often referred to as "differential") between the two discount rates. All else equal, the higher the differential, the lower the intangible value. On the topic of discount rate differentials, the IRS provides field examiners the following caution in the Practice Unit dealing with PCTs:[41]

> some taxpayers may exaggerate the differences in risk between the two alternatives to justify a lower discount rate for the licensing alternative and a higher discount rate for the cost sharing alternative. By doing this a taxpayer can drive the PCT value down significantly.

3.2.4 *Summary of Veritas Software Corp. v. Commissioner*

Though old, *Veritas Software Corp. & Subsidiaries v. Commissioner* remains a landmark case decided in 2009 dealing with intangible valuation for cost sharing purposes. The case dealt directly with all of the technical schisms described above including: best method, useful life, and discount rates. There have been other cost sharing intangible valuation cases in litigation since *Veritas Software Corp. & Subsidiaries v. Commissioner*,[42] and these cases have relied, in part, upon the decision reached in *Veritas Software Corp. & Subsidiaries v. Commissioner*. In the sections below, the authors begin with a brief background of the case and then examine the major technical issues.

Importantly, *Veritas Software Corp. & Subsidiaries v. Commissioner* was subject to the cost sharing regulations that were in place prior to 2009. Prior to the 2009 cost sharing regulations, there was no concept of platform contribution in the regulations, only the narrower intangible property term. Therefore, instead of the requirement of a PCT when a controlled participant made a platform contribution to the development of the cost shared intangible, the earlier cost sharing regulations required a "buy-in payment" for any preexisting *intangibles* contributed by a controlled participant to the development of the cost shared intangible. This distinction was an important one for

40. Treasury Regulations Section 1.482-7(g)(2)(v)(B)(1).
41. IRS. LB&I International Practice Service Transaction Unit: "Pricing of Platform Contribution Transaction (PCT) in Cost Sharing Arrangements (CSA)—Initial Transaction". p. 27.
42. *Amazon.com, Inc. v. Commissioner.*

the outcome of the case. As discussed below, the IRS selected the best method and determined the buy-in payment as if it were a PCT payment under the 2009 cost sharing regulations. The taxpayer and the Tax Court disagreed with this approach. The authors use the term "buy-in payment" in the narrative below since that was the language used in the case.

3.2.4.1 Background

In 1999, Veritas Software Corp (Veritas U.S.) entered into a CSA with Veritas Ireland, its foreign subsidiary, to develop and manufacture storage management software products. Veritas U.S. retained the rights to the cost shared intangibles in the Americas, and Veritas Ireland obtained the rights to the cost shared intangibles in the rest of the world. Veritas U.S. granted Veritas Ireland the right to use its preexisting intangibles including trademarks, trade names, inventions, patents, and other technology intangibles in its territory. As consideration for the transfer of preexisting intangibles, Veritas Ireland made a USD 166 million buy-in payment to Veritas U.S. Veritas U.S. employed the CUT method to calculate the payment.[43]

In a notice of deficiency issued to Veritas U.S., the IRS employed an income method and determined a requisite buy-in payment of USD 2.5 billion which it later reduced to USD 1.675 billion. The IRS further determined that the requisite buy-in payment must take into account access to Veritas U.S.' research and development team; access to Veritas U.S.' marketing team; and Veritas U.S.' distribution channels, customer lists, trademarks, trade names, brand names, and sales agreements. Veritas U.S. contended that the IRS' determinations were arbitrary, capricious, and unreasonable, and the CUT method was the best method to calculate the requisite buy-in payment.[44]

3.2.4.2 Method to Derive Arm's Length Intangible Value

The IRS contended that, because "the assets collectively possess synergies that imbue the whole with greater value than each asset standing alone," it is appropriate to apply the akin to a sale theory and aggregate the controlled transactions rather than value each asset. The IRS asserted that such an approach "produces the most reliable means of determining the arm's-length consideration for the controlled transactions."[45]

The court rejected the notion that the akin to a sale approach produced the most reliable result on the basis that it assumes perpetual lived intangibles (the court concluded the intangibles were, in fact, short lived; *see* next section) and takes into account intangibles that were subsequently developed rather than preexisting.[46] Further, the court determined that the transaction at issue did, in fact, have economic

43. *Supra* n. 11, 18-19.
44. *Supra* n. 11, 1.
45. *Supra* n. 11, 39.
46. *Supra* n. 11, 40-41.

substance and was structured as a license of preexisting intangibles, not a sale of a business. Thus, the court determined that the IRS was not authorized to aggregate the transactions and treat them as a sale.[47]

Veritas U.S. used the CUT method to calculate the buy-in payment. The IRS contended that the CUT method was not the best method and that Veritas U.S. did not present CUTs to prove that its buy-in payment was arm's length. The IRS asserted that agreements between Veritas U.S. and unrelated parties were not CUTs because they either involved rights that were not comparable to those licensed under the CSA or licensees who were not comparable to Veritas Ireland. The court agreed with the CUT method. It determined that some of the agreements selected by Veritas U.S. were not comparable but used others as CUPs for the buy-in payment valuation.

3.2.4.3 Perpetual Versus Finite Useful Life

In valuing the buy-in payment, the IRS assumed a perpetual useful life for the transferred intangibles. Veritas U.S., on the other hand, assumed the useful life was two to four years and, further, the value decayed over those two to four years such that the starting royalty rate should decrease over the period.

Veritas U.S. evidenced that, at the time of the CSA, Veritas U.S. products had a limited useful life in part by showing that the source code used in its products completely turned over every three to four years. In the end, the court held that the appropriate useful life of the preexisting product intangibles was four years.[48]

Veritas U.S. also argued that the starting royalty rate should decline or decay over the four-year period to account for obsolesce and decay of the technology over the period. This assertion was based upon agreements that Veritas U.S. had with third-party OEMs that paid for a custom built product that Veritas would not further develop. In these instances, the OEM agreements contained a royalty degradation or technology aging discount provision to account for obsolescence and decay.[49]

The court held that the starting royalty should be ramped down starting in year 2 at a rate of 33% per year from the then-current percentage (32% in year 1; 21% in year 2; 14% in year 3; and 10% in year 4). This decline was based upon an analysis of the turnover of the underlying product source code over the four-year period.[50]

3.2.4.4 Applicable Discount Rate

The IRS applied the CAPM and concluded that 13.7% was a reasonable estimate for Veritas U.S.' WACC. Veritas U.S. also applied the CAPM but concluded that 20.47% was a reasonable estimate of Veritas U.S.' WACC.

47. *Supra* n. 11, footnote 29.
48. *Supra* n. 11, 54.
49. *Supra* n. 11, 54.
50. *Supra* n. 11, 67.

There were two differences between the IRS' and Veritas U.S.' applications of CAPM: the estimate of the beta and the equity risk premium. The court ultimately held that 20.47% was the correct WACC since Veritas U.S., unlike the IRS, used reliable data to calculate both variables.[51]

3.2.5 Looking Ahead

The dramatic cut to the U.S. corporate tax rate, the introduction of a preferential tax rate for foreign source intangible income, and a global minimum tax regime (coupled with BEPS related changes) will generally reduce incentives for U.S. companies to transfer or keep intangibles offshore. Thus, it is likely that companies will enter into fewer CSAs or, more generally, intangible transfers out of the U.S. in the coming years. This said, there are a number of CSAs already in existence and disputes underway regarding PCTs and more.

As illustrated by the *Veritas* case, a fundamental disagreement between the IRS and the Tax Court/taxpayer has been their views on which preexisting rights or assets are transferred in a CSA that need compensation.

The IRS has consistently taken an expansive view of what needs to be compensated in a PCT or buy-in payment. In Veritas, the IRS argued for the inclusion of workforce in place, goodwill, and going-concern value in the buy-in payment, but the Tax Court overruled the IRS noting that the regulations during the years at issue included no explicit authorization for their inclusion.

The Tax Court also dismissed the IRS' argument in *Veritas Software Corp. & Subsidiaries v. Commissioner* that the intercompany arrangement was akin to a sale of the Veritas non-Americas business since the assets collectively possess synergies that imbue the whole with greater value than each asset standing alone. Further, the Tax Court noted that the regulations allow for aggregating transactions if that produces the most reliable means for determining the arm's length consideration. However, the IRS' aggregate "akin to sale" valuation did not provide the most reliable arm's length consideration since it simply served as a means of aggregating the value of preexisting intangibles and intangibles that still needed to be developed.

As mentioned earlier, the codification of the expanded definition of intangible property bolsters the longstanding arguments raised by the IRS in past disputes but historically rejected by the courts. In the Explanatory Statement to the 2017 Tax Law, Congress notes that the revised definition along with the changes to IRC Sections 367 and 482 address definitional and methodological issues that have arisen in controversies, citing the *Veritas* and *Amazon* cases, in both of which the Tax Court ruled that goodwill and going-concern value fell outside the legal definition of intangible property. The 2017 Tax Law explicitly includes goodwill, going-concern value, and workforce in place within the definition of intangibles. It also codifies the principles of aggregation and realistic alternatives in the valuation of intangibles under IRC Sections 367(d) and 482. Under the added provisions, the Secretary shall require the valuation

51. *Supra* n. 11, 71.

of transfers of intangible property (including intangible property transferred with other property or services) on an aggregate basis or the valuation of such a transfer on the basis of the realistic alternatives to such a transfer if the Secretary determines that such a basis is the most reliable means of valuation of such transfers. These changes explicitly address some of the greatest points of contention between the IRS and taxpayers and may have the result of increasing PCT values which may even further reduce taxpayer incentives to engage in CSAs.

3.3 Binding Nature of APAs or Prior Agreements with the IRS

Prior to the introduction of the 2017 Tax Law, a fundamental challenge regarding the binding nature of an IRS agreement was already called into question. With the various new tax provisions under the 2017 Tax Law, it is further unclear how taxpayers in existing APAs or those currently in APA negotiations nearing conclusion will address these new provisions and whether any treaty provisions can be availed. The authors deal with each of these challenges in turn.

In three separate cases, the IRS decided to depart from an agreement with a taxpayer and take a different approach in examining their transfer pricing. Unsparingly, these departures have led to litigation. In *Coca-Cola Co. & Subsidiaries v. Commissioner*, the IRS and taxpayer executed a closing agreement in 1996 to settle an intercompany licensing dispute for the years 1987 through 1989. The closing agreement provided that, for the years after 1995, no penalties would be assessed in connection with the taxpayer's transfer pricing if the taxpayer followed the methodology set forth in the closing agreement. For its post-1995 tax years, Coca-Cola applied the closing agreement methodology, and the IRS audited and accepted the taxpayer's use of the methodology in every tax year from 1996 to 2006. However, the IRS proposed a different methodology, discussed in more detail above, for the tax years 2007 through 2009, resulting in a USD 9.4 billion income adjustment.

As noted in the intercompany licensing disputes section, in *Medtronic, Inc. and Consolidated Subsidiaries v. Commissioner*, the taxpayer was compliant with a prior MOU with the IRS covering the royalty rates on devices and leads, yet the IRS decided to change its position. While an MOU is an informal agreement between the IRS and taxpayers and a closing agreement is only binding for the years under examination, in *Eaton Corp. & Subsidiaries v. Commissioner*, the IRS decided to cancel and revoke two unilateral advance pricing agreements and propose subsequent transfer pricing adjustments for the years covered under the agreements. In the section below, the authors use *Eaton Corp. & Subsidiaries v. Commissioner* as a guide to illustrate how the court held on this issue. More broadly, these IRS actions, coupled with the European Commission's state aid investigations has put the spotlight on unilateral agreements with tax authorities around the world.

3.3.1 *Summary of Eaton Corp. & Subsidiaries v. Commissioner*

In 2003, Eaton and the IRS reached an agreement on the terms of Eaton's first APA (APA I) which covered the 2001–2005 tax years. Eaton renewed APA I (APA II), which covered the 2006–2010 tax years. APA II was executed on December 20, 2006.[52] In attempting to renew APA I (APA II) in 2009, Eaton informed the IRS that it would withdraw its request for a renewal.[53]

3.3.1.1 *Background*

In 2010, Eaton discovered data and computational errors after two of its transfer pricing managers took over responsibility following the departure of the prior tax manager. When Eaton's new transfer pricing managers and their team began working on the APA transfer pricing method, they noticed a difference between the manufacturing costs that were computed using the plant variance and freight factor and the actual manufacturing costs reflected in the ledgers. In April 2010, Eaton notified the IRS that it had identified certain errors in its APA transfer pricing method computations and was in the process of correcting them.

On December 16, 2011, the IRS notified Eaton that APA I and APA II would be cancelled effective January 1, 2005, and 2006, respectively. The IRS' letter stated specifically:[54]

> These cancellations are based on numerous grounds, including the failure of a critical assumption, misrepresentation, mistake as to a material fact, failure to state a material fact, failure to file a timely annual report, or lack of good faith compliance with the terms and conditions of the APA.

As a result of cancelling APA I and APA II, the IRS determined that, under Section 482, an adjustment was necessary to reflect an arm's length result for intercompany transactions that Eaton and its U.S. subsidiaries entered into regarding breaker products and related electrical components and products produced in the Island plants' manufacturing and assembly operations. On December 19, 2011, The IRS issued a notice of deficiency to Eaton determining deficiencies in tax totalling USD 19,714,770 and USD 55,323,229 for 2005 and 2006, respectively, and penalties of USD 14,281,960 and USD 37,329,600 for 2005 and 2006, respectively.[55] In its notice of deficiency, the transfer pricing methodology used by the IRS was the CPM with Puerto Rico and the Dominican Republic manufacturing operations selected as the tested parties. Any additional profit above a routine manufacturing return was allocated to Eaton's U.S. operations.

52. *Supra* n. 1, 40.
53. *Supra* n. 1, 111.
54. *Supra* n. 1, 112.
55. *Supra* n. 1, 113.

3.3.1.2 Decision

The court concluded that it was an abuse of discretion for the IRS to cancel APA I for tax year 2005 and APA II for tax year 2006. The court noted the IRS had many opportunities not to agree to APA I and APA II and, further, during the APA I and APA II negotiations, the IRS never suggested a different transfer pricing method as an alternative. The court went on:[56]

> [the IRS] had an opportunity not to renew APA I and enter into APA II if [the IRS] wanted to change the [transfer pricing methods]. APA II provided an opportunity to look at the agreement de novo. After completing the APA II negotiations, [the IRS] should have had a clear understanding of [Eaton's] transactions and should not have entered into APA II if the APA II team was concerned that [Eaton] was omitting or misrepresenting information.

As for the computation errors, the court noted:[57]

> [Eaton] made immaterial and inadvertent errors that do not fit the APA governing revenue procedures' definition of "material." [The IRS] should not be able to use these errors as grounds for switching to a [transfer pricing method] that was contemplated during the APA I and APA II negotiations.

In the end, the court concluded that the IRS' cancellation of APA I and APA II was arbitrary and unreasonable, holding:[58]

> An APA is a binding agreement and it should be cancelled only according to the terms of the revenue procedures. It should not be cancelled because of a desire to change the underlying methodology of a method that would result in a significantly different profit split. For these reasons the cancellation of the APAs was arbitrary and unreasonable. We do not sustain [the IRS'] determination to cancel APA I and APA II.

3.3.2 Implications of Court Findings and Context Given Tax Modernization

Eaton Corp. & Subsidiaries v. Commissioner provides taxpayers some level of assurance of the binding nature of the agreement reached with the IRS. This said, facts and circumstances matter, and the Court's decision is heavily predicated on the specific facts of the taxpayer. As a result, reliance on this opinion may not provide a great deal of benefit. One important distinction to note in *Eaton Corp. & Subsidiaries v. Commissioner* as well *Coca-Cola Co. & Subsidiaries v. Commissioner*, and *Medtronic, Inc. and Consolidated Subsidiaries v. Commissioner* is that all of the agreements were unilateral with the IRS.[59] Similarly, the European Commission's state aid investigations have

56. *Supra* n. 1, 192-193.
57. *Supra* n. 1, 193.
58. *Supra* n. 1, 193.
59. The counterparty to the transactions covered by the various agreements were primarily located in jurisdictions in which the U.S. does not have a treaty. As a result, a bilateral agreement was generally not available to the taxpayers.

focused on rulings or unilateral APAs granted by various countries. In light of the impetus to revisit such agreements, is a unilateral APA of any real value?

The Organisation for Co-operation and Development's ("OECD") Base Erosion and Profit Shifting ("BEPS") has increased transparency on multinational enterprises' transfer pricing. This spotlight extends to unilateral rulings and APAs. BEPS Action 5 is one of the four BEPS minimum standards which all-inclusive framework members have committed to implement. One part of the Action 5 minimum standard is the transparency framework for compulsory spontaneous exchange on certain rulings which, in the absence of transparency, could give rise to BEPS concerns. In 2017, the OECD released a peer review of 44 countries to assess countries' compliance with Action 5. The peer review included the following five factors: information gathering process; previous exchange of information; confidentiality of the information received; statistics on the exchanges of rulings; and transparency on certain aspects of intellectual property regimes.[60] The jurisdictions reviewed in the report had issued a combined total of 10,000 tax rulings, which included issues related to past rulings between January 2010 and March 2016 as well as future rulings between April 1, 2016, and December 2016.[61]

In 2016, the IRS agreed to exchange information on unilateral advance pricing agreements with foreign tax authorities but decided not to send the full APA documents abroad.[62] Instead, the material exchanged was a summary containing basic information on the unilateral APA.[63] As part of the OECD peer review, the report provided that the U.S. received no recommendations as it met all aspects of the terms of reference for the 2016 year in review.

At the same time, while the OECD has been pushing for the spontaneous exchange of unilateral APAs, BEPS Action 14 has been focused on making dispute resolution more effective. Action 14 develops solutions to address obstacles that prevent countries from solving treaty-related disputes under mutual agreement procedures via a minimum standard in this area as well as a number of best practices including arbitration. As part of that effort, Action 14 provides that a best practice is that countries should implement bilateral APA programs.[64] Likewise, the IRS' Revenue Procedure for APAs states that "to minimize taxpayer and governmental uncertainty and administrative cost, bilateral and multilateral APAs are generally preferable to unilateral APAs."[65] Moreover, the IRS APA office "may reject a taxpayer's unilateral APA request for various reasons, particularly when accepting it would contravene procedures and practices established with particular treaty partners."[66]

---

60. OECD. Harmful Tax Practices—Peer Review Reports on Exchange of Information on Tax Rulings. December 4, 2017.
61. *Id.*
62. "IRS to Exchange Summaries of Unilateral APAs Abroad," BNA Transfer Pricing Report, 25 Transfer Pricing Report 783 (October 28, 2016).
63. *Id.*
64. OECD. Action 14 Final Report, Making Dispute Resolution Mechanisms More Effective, p. 30. October 5, 2015.
65. Rev. Proc. 2015-41, Section 2.02(4)(2).
66. *Id.*

The world is moving towards scrutinizing unilateral agreements. Consequently, taxpayers should consider pursuing bilateral agreements such as APAs rather than unilateral agreements to obtain additional certainty. Under a bilateral APA, if one tax authority believes that the agreement is too one-sided for the taxpayer, the tax authority would need to renegotiate with their treaty partner before moving to set aside such an agreement. The overall treaty relationship would suffer should a tax authority seek to reopen bilateral APAs. Consequently, they are recommended in both the U.S. and abroad as a tool to solve transfer pricing disputes.

3.3.3 Looking Ahead

For those APAs already signed, there are some open questions. For example, questions regarding existing APAs range from: (i) has a critical assumption somehow been triggered such that it cancels the existing agreement; to (ii) does an additional payment, either GILTI, BEAT, or FDII incentive, require further negotiation with treaty partners and, if so, what impact, if any, does it have on the terms of the APA? Questions such as these and more mean that taxpayers will need to work closely with tax authorities to ensure their APAs are appropriately preserved, modified, or cancelled. All APAs are unique, therefore, there is no single answer. Each will need to be considered under its own facts and circumstances. For some taxpayers, the cancellation of an APA might be a good thing as it will allow the freedom necessary to restructure transactions. Yet, for others, the dissolution of an existing APA may trigger unforeseen tax liabilities.

Every taxpayer is urged to review the terms of their APAs to ensure that any short-term steps taken in response to the 2017 Tax Law do not violate the terms of the APA or the critical assumptions they are predicated on. In the near term, the APA and Mutual Agreement ("APMA") office itself may not have clear answers right away.

3.4 Limitation on Interest Deductibility

Prior to the 2017 Tax Law, thin capitalization rules and the potential threat of recharacterization of debt as equity put constraints on the ability of a U.S. taxpayer to take on debt. The new Treasury Regulations Section 385 issued in 2016 represented a further attempt to limit what was perceived by the U.S. Government as excessive leverage of the U.S. taxpayer. There is speculation that Treasury Regulations Section 385 may be rescinded, however, no action has yet been taken, and the documentation provisions are expected to come into effect in 2019.

3.4.1 Overview

The 2017 Tax Law would further limit deductibility of business interest under IRC Section 163(j). For U.S. corporations, the existing IRC Section 163(j) disallows deduction of net interest expense above 50% of EBITDA. This current limitation applies to corporations with debt/equity ratios exceeding 1.5 to 1.0.

The revised IRC Section 163(j) would disallow tax deductions for net business interest expense of any taxpayer (regardless of business form) in excess of 30% of a base that approximates earnings before interest, taxes, depreciation, and amortization (EBITDA) (plus floor plan financing interest) starting in 2018, switching to the stricter standard of 30% of a base that approximates earnings before interest and taxes (EBIT) in 2022. Importantly, the limitation applies to debt held by both related and unrelated parties and that debt existing prior to 2018 will not be grandfathered. The test is performed at the level of the tax filing entity (i.e., the consolidated tax return for corporations). Any disallowed business interest would be carried forward indefinitely, though there will be no carry forward of excess limitation.

Taxpayers with average annual revenues for the three-year period ending with the prior tax year that do not exceed USD 25 million or are regulated public utilities and electric cooperatives are exempted from the limitation. Also, certain real estate businesses could elect for the interest expense limitation not to apply and would consequently be required to use the alternative depreciation system (ADS) to depreciate certain property.

3.4.2 Comparison with BEPS Interest Limitation

BEPS Action 4 recommendations include a Fixed Ratio Rule as well as a Group Ratio Rule. The Fixed Ratio Rule aims to limit a taxpayer's net interest expense that is paid to both related and unrelated parties to a fixed percentage of EBITDA or EBIT. The recommended percentage range is 10%–30%. As such, the 2017 Tax Law interest limitation provision is broadly consistent with the BEPS guidance.

The Group Ratio Rule allows for an additional interest deduction based on group-wide financial metrics such as the ratio of net third-party interest expense to EBITDA. The 2017 Tax Law includes no such accommodation; consequently, each tax filing entity is held to the same standard with no regard to the financial requisites or common practice of its industry.

Many countries already have thin-cap rules in place that are applicable to either total or related-party debt and, therefore, the introduction of this provision in the 2017 Tax Law brings the U.S. onto similar ground.

4 CONCLUSIONS

This chapter is focused on transfer pricing and, therefore, the analysis of the 2017 Tax Law is narrow and centered on the new definition of intangible property and the impact that the 2017 Tax Law potentially has on future transfers of intangible property, APAs, and new guidance pertaining to the limitation of interest deductibility. This said, the 2017 Tax Law is new, complex, and includes a number of significant changes to the current US tax law. Further clarifications from U.S. Treasury on the 2017 Tax Law are expected in the coming year, with more guidance expected to drip through over the next several years. While the biggest changes seem to have been announced already, any new developments later this year will be watched very closely.

CHAPTER 4

Transfer Pricing Developments in Developing Countries and Emerging Economies

Giammarco Cottani

> Global trade must be simple and modernized; it must be inclusive so everyone has the same opportunity. The next generation of globalization must be inclusive.
>
> Jack Ma, AliBaba Founder, at World Economic Forum in Davos, 2018

> […] The forces of protectionism are raising their heads against globalization. Their intention is not just to avoid globalization, but to reverse its natural flow. The solution to this worrisome situation against globalization is not isolation. The solution is in understanding and accepting change.
>
> Narendra Modi, PM of India, at World Economic Forum in Davos, 2018

1 INTRODUCTION

This chapter addresses the initiatives that emerging economies and developing countries have taken in the course of 2017 in the field of transfer pricing. In this respect, according to the author, the first step is to make clear that an accurate definition of what is meant by the term "developing" vis-à-vis "developed" country cannot be found in tax-relevant publications of international organizations.[1] Therefore, the chapter will assume the terms "emerging economy" and developing "country" having the same meaning from a transfer pricing standpoint.

It is also true, though, that the obstacles in accurately delineating the difference (if any) between a "developing" and an "emerging economy" makes the work of transfer pricing specialists easier in asserting that the arm's length principle is neutral in its application, i.e., it is immaterial whether it is the tax administration of a developed or developing economy that carries out a comparability analysis based on the arm's length principle. What can be significantly diverging between the tax administrations of an OECD, *rectius*, developed country/economy, and a developing/emerging one is the level of administrative resources to be deployed in guaranteeing a proper enforcement of any legislation.

Arguably, "emerging" and "developing "tend to be construed as synonyms when it comes to assessing that, since the late 1990s, the economies of these countries presented higher growth rates than developed ones.[2] In this respect, countries like Brazil, China, and India but also countries like Russia and South Africa (the latter countries collectively labelled as "BRICS") whose tax administrations have played a significant role in shaping the international tax policy landscape in recent years seem to express the view that—within their domestic boundaries—the arm's length principle may be construed in a way that best fits their sovereign national interests.

Therefore, this paper will discuss the key areas of transfer pricing developments intervened within each of the above-mentioned countries and/or regions but with a focus on Brazil, China, and India as the latter countries present rather peculiar features when it comes to the transfer pricing legislative setting and actual enforcement.

To this end, the above-mentioned analysis is performed in order to assess whether consistency or, rather, subtle contradiction exists with the internationally endorsed principles and administrative practices that the OECD and the United Nations tried to lay down.

As a general remark, what seems rather odd—yet very significant in terms of geopolitics—is the fact that, on the one hand, the OECD is in full swing in deploying all of its resources to guarantee a swift and sound implementation of the BEPS Action Plan irrespective of whether or not a country is part of such an international organization. In this regard, the initiative falling under the OECD "Inclusive Framework"[3] tries to

1. To understand the difficulties linked with drawing a clear distinction between "developed" and "developing," it is worth noting that, in the 2016 edition of its World Development Indicators, the World Bank made a decision to no longer distinguish between "developed" and "developing" countries in the presentation of its data.
2. *See* the anecdotal evidence shown by Korotayev A., Zinkina J. [http://cliodynamics.ru/index.php?option = com_content&task = view&id = 361&Itemid = developing country. The term implies inferiority of a developing country or undeveloped country compared with a developed country, which many countries dislike.
3. The OECD, as a response to the call of the G-20 Leaders, OECD members, and G-20 countries, has developed an Inclusive Framework ("IFW") on BEPS which allows interested countries and jurisdictions to work with the OECD and G-20 members on developing standards on BEPS related

respond to such a challenge; as of January 2018,[4] more than 100 countries have agreed to develop consistent BEPS standards in their own domestic legislation. Yet Brazil, China, and India have given their own—at times contradictory—interpretations of such international commitment in managing their domestic transfer pricing systems.

Moreover, the work of the United Nations in funneling a consistent approach to transfer pricing legislation should also be taken into account. In this regard, the significant achievement of the 2017 update of the United Nations Transfer Pricing Manual reflects the consistent approach taken by the UN Committee of Experts on Taxation matters of which the Transfer Pricing specialist constitutes its Subcommittee. Next to that, the recently created Capacity Development Unit, formed in 2012, has a close relationship with the Committee of Taxation Experts, and much of its work is targeted at disseminating the results of the Committee's work to developing countries through publications, training programs, and technical assistance. For example, the Capacity Development Unit has designed and delivered several courses on transfer pricing for developing countries in Africa and South America based on the Committee's *United Nations Practical Manual on Transfer Pricing for Developing Countries*. In addition, a successful pilot technical assistance project on transfer pricing has been carried out with Ecuador and will be extended to other countries.

Along the line of these initiatives, it came as no surprise then that, in April 2016, the United Nations, the OECD, the International Monetary Fund (IMF), and the World Bank Group (WBG) formed "The Platform for Collaboration on Tax" (the "Platform") as the institutional framework for enhanced cooperation by the four international organizations in delivering assistance to developing countries to strengthen their tax systems, including their transfer pricing systems.

Notwithstanding the above, the relationship between the Platform and the OECD "Inclusive Framework" is somewhat unclear. The Inclusive Framework is meant to be responsible for monitoring and supporting the implementation phase of the BEPS Project; it is open to all countries that are prepared to commit to the BEPS minimum standards. Developing countries can participate in the Inclusive Framework with equal rights and are entitled to receive capacity-building assistance from international organizations that will allow them to implement BEPS countermeasures effectively. The Platform and the Inclusive Framework are intended to cooperate closely. The activities of the Inclusive Framework will inform the work of the Platform, and the Platform will bring issues arising from its work to the attention of the Inclusive

---

issues and reviewing and monitoring the implementation of the whole BEPS Package as monitoring implementation and the impact of the different BEPS measures is a key element of the work ahead. The Inclusive Framework is a new global tax governance network created by the OECD to facilitate implementation of its signature tax coordination project, i.e., the OECD/G-20 Base Erosion and Profit Shifting (BEPS) initiative. The OECD intends the Inclusive Framework to engage participating states in "an inclusive dialogue on an equal footing to directly shape standard setting and monitoring processes." This entails, without expressly defining, a vision of international tax policy negotiation in which all participating states have a meaningful say in the decision-making that affects them. Should this be the actual goal, achieving an equal footing will require a significant institutional commitment to overcome the vast differences in resources, capacity, and relative bargaining strengths of the participating states.

4. For further references, *see* http://www.oecd.org/tax/beps/beps-about.htm.

Framework. However, at this stage, it is unclear how the relationship between the Platform and the Inclusive Framework will operate in practice.

As a result, despite this rather odd tension between the international organizations in dealing in a concerted manner with transfer pricing policy legislation and enforcement, a number of the major countries and regions representing the emerging economies of this world followed their own path in managing their domestic transfer pricing practices.

The next paragraphs will then address how Brazil, China, India, and some relevant economies from the Africa region took a position vis-à-vis the above-mentioned initiatives of such prominent international organizations in the area of transfer pricing.

2 SIGNIFICANT TRANSFER PRICING DEVELOPMENTS IN THE COURSE OF 2017: THE IMPACT OF PART D OF THE 2017 UNITED NATIONS MANUAL

Brazil, China, and India present certain similarities as well as certain differences when it comes to transfer pricing enforcement. Recent years of tax policy in these countries witnessed the circumstance that the approach to the interpretation and implementation of the arm's length principle is very much related with the economic policy considerations of each country's foreign policy.

In order to understand the magnitude of the discussion, it is necessary to focus on the economics at stake to realize why they achieved such prominence from a tax and transfer pricing standpoint.

First, China and India are cumulatively home to 40% of the world's population.[5] In 2014, China had the world's largest number of middle-class households, standing at 112 million, and the number is expected to reach 137 million by 2030.[6] Craving lucrative opportunities, investors are entering into the emerging markets. As a result, the global economy has observed a huge influx of FDI into these markets.

In this regard, looking at the BRICS countries, China and Brazil are amongst the most popular countries in which foreign investors are more willing to have their businesses in place. At a global level, the FDI inflow of BRICS countries in total accounts for almost 10% of the global FDI from 1970-2016.

In this regard, while all three jurisdictions were featuring themselves as capital importing countries, in the last five to ten years, such a trend reversed, particularly for China and India.[7] China somehow replaced India as the major funder of foreign direct

5. *See* US Central Intelligence Agency (CIA), World Factbook, 2015 statistics.
6. *See* Middle-class consumers are defined as those with 75.0%-125% of the median income. The source of data is Euromonitor International, *Top 5 Emerging Markets with the Best Middle Class Potential*, which can be assessed at: http://blog.euromonitor.com/2015/09/top-5-emerging-markets-with-the-best-middle-class-potential.html.
7. In this regard, the circumstance that China somehow surprised investors by issuing three new transfer pricing regulations during 2016 and 2017 that can be considered as some of the OECD BEPS Action Plan's international front-runners is significant. The newly introduced regulations, namely, Bulletins 42, 64 and 6, were issued related to the reporting of related-party transactions,

investment in the region of South-East Asia because of its significant donation of surplus capital to invest and started a very aggressive economic foreign policy campaign known as the "Belt and Road Initiative" (or BRI). India as well started to characterize itself as a capital exporter and a number of significant acquisitions by Indian conglomerates of foreign targets, which simply were unthinkable years ago, became a reality in recent years.[8]

From a purely transfer pricing standpoint, however, there is an underlying aspect that the above-mentioned countries share and is given by the slightly diverging interpretation of the arm's length principle as endorsed both at the OECD and at the United Nations levels.

It is not a case, indeed, that in the 2017 update of the UN Transfer Pricing Manual, part D on "Country Practices" entailed the existence of doubts as to whether Brazil, India and China wanted to clearly distance themselves from the arm's length principle.

In this regard, the 2017 version of the UN TP Manual expressly stated such diverging positions[9] when, by referencing to the foreword to the first edition of the UN TP Manual, it held the view that "[..]*While consensus has been sought as far as possible, it was considered most in accord with a practical manual to include some elements where consensus could not be reached, and it follows that specific views expressed in this Manual should not be ascribed to any particular persons involved in its drafting. [Part D]1 is different from other chapters in its conception, however. It represents an outline of particular country administrative practices as described in some detail by representatives from those countries, and it was not considered feasible or appropriate to seek a consensus on how such country practices were described. [Part D] should be read with that difference in mind.*" (NdR: emphasis added).

Based on the above premise, the following features represent, in the author's view, some of key elements where the countries listed below take their own views when it comes to transfer pricing policy design and implementation, namely:

(i) **Brazil**: being one of the first countries in South America that introduced transfer pricing legislation, despite its full involvement in the BEPS project, reiterated that the comparability analysis under the arm's length principle

the administration of APAs and rules for improving the administration of special tax investigations, and adjustments and MAPs, respectively. Dr Liao Tizhong, Director of the International Tax Division in the State Administration of Taxation (SAT), notes that China is increasingly eager to become an active participant in the international tax reform process. Such a position is in line with China's flourishing development of its transfer pricing regulations, in particular from the issuance of its first APA rule in 1998 to the latest Bulletin of 2017. Along the way, China has actively engaged in APAs and MAPs and produced significant results, as it had signed 51 bilateral APAs and made 43 transfer pricing corresponding adjustments by the end of 2015. Furthermore, during its Five-Year Plan (2011–2015) period only, the SAT eliminated international double taxation exposures of RMB 18.7 billion for MNEs. *See also* https://economictimes.indiatimes.com/news/international/business/china-expected-to-become-worlds-largest-importer-in-5-years-investment-firm/articleshow/61919413.cms.

8. For an example of such a trend, *see* the 2008 completion of the acquisition by Tata Motors of the Jaguar Land Rover businesses from Ford Motor Company for a net consideration of US $2.3 billion. For further information, *see* http://www.tatamotors.com/press/tata-motors-completes-acquisition-of-jaguar-land-rover/.
9. *See* Foreword, page V, of the 2017 Manual.

falls short of achieving market results. Therefore, it adopts methods with predetermined profit margins as well as rejecting the possibility of performing corresponding adjustments under its tax treaties in the same way that this is recommended by Article 9(2) of the OECD Model Tax Convention.[10]

(ii) **China**: the most active of the emerging economies in the field of transfer pricing, its State Tax Administration ("SAT") always stressed the relevance of the market of distribution (and associated proximity to customers) to be treated in a manner akin to an intangible rather than a comparability factor. This views found its expression in the notion of "location-specific advantages" or "location rents where China made it clear that they will construe the recommendations of Actions 8-9-10 of the BEPS Action Plan in a manner consistent to what is reflected in their own domestic administrative practice.

(iii) **India:** the country has always been characterized, more than any other jurisdiction, by a "hypertrophic" production of its courts in the field of transfer pricing. The attention of Indian judges was on every single facet of transfer pricing legislation but, more than any other country, the importance given by its administration toward the notion of intangibles (and an alleged economic ownership notion underlying every distribution activity taking place within its domestic boundaries) as well as the approach to intercompany services stood out when compared to any other transfer pricing issue.

(iv) **Mexico:** like the above-mentioned countries presented earlier, Mexico shares a common goal with these jurisdictions which is securing tax revenues from base erosion and profit shifting phenomena. This situation particularly concerns developing countries and emerging economies which collect the most significant portion of their revenue as corporate income tax from multinational groups. Significant tax noncompliance concerns as well as the political challenge of imposing general indirect taxes in developing countries such as Mexico have forced the latter jurisdiction to revisit its tax collection strategy.

Notwithstanding the above, the BEPS approach to transfer pricing may not necessarily benefit Mexico which—among OECD countries—has the lowest tax to gross domestic product (GDP) ratio (19.5% in 2014, compared to the OECD average of 34.4%).[11]

Because of tax collection pressure, Mexican tax authorities may seek to adhere strictly to the recommendations coming out of the BEPS Final Report to transfer pricing audits that do not necessarily always reflect the principles agreed at the OECD level. In fact, recent experience in transfer pricing audits in Mexico has revealed the potential for differing interpretations of the arm's length principle, although the Mexican SAT generally guarantees a consistent application of transfer pricing provisions. For instance, should the BEPS approach for properly understanding value creation be

10. *See* Oliveira, A. Gomes de; Moreira, F. Lisboa, *The Brazilian Transfer Pricing Regime*, in Bulletin for International Taxation, IBFD, 2017 (Volume 71), No. 6.
11. *See* OECD, Revenue Statistics, available at http://www.oecd.org/tax/tax-policy/revenue-statistics-ratio-change-latest-years.htm.

applied in a way aiming at highlighting, e.g., solely headcount or payroll expenses, such an approach would likely lead to double taxation as developed economies may rely on other value contribution assets (e.g., R&D activities, marketing functions, depending on the circumstances and the industry sector at stake) to justify the attribution of residual margins.

Although Mexico is very well represented in transfer pricing issues by skilled officials at both the OECD and United Nations fora, the reality of transfer pricing audits in the country do not seem to always be reconciled with sound tax policy approaches. For instance, certain foreign-owned MNEs with subsidiaries in Mexico have reported that, during past audit activities, Mexican tax authorities, at times, have requested information in the course of an audit on payroll expenses of the top executives of the Mexican subsidiary and its counterparts.

Such information, on top of the data collected on head counts provided in the country-by-country reporting, might lead to a distortion in profit attribution or to a complete recharacterization of the actual substance of the transactions by Mexican tax authorities. However, such an approach would not be consistent with the arm's length principle and, therefore, could lead to double taxation.

The following paragraphs will review each of these relevant developments in detail. However, the author believes that a significant aspect to focus on in identifying a sound conceptual framework for understanding the transfer pricing approach applied in the above-mentioned countries is how Brazil, China, and India look at the notion of "risk." In particular, the tax administrations of the latter countries generally aim at construing it in a more economical manner vis-à-vis the OECD and UN position as expressed in the notion of risk management and financial capacity to assume risk.[12]

More in detail, markets (and proximity to them) play an indispensable role in the business life of MNEs. MNEs make decisions with regard to which market and in what form they would like to establish their businesses after assessing the relative strengths and weaknesses of them. The consideration of which market to choose in the business setting of MNEs has given rise on how to consider the notion of location-specific advantages (LSAs) in the field of transfer pricing. "Location savings", lacking an official definition, is in transfer pricing parlance often understood both as: (i) (net) cost savings realized by an MNE exploiting price differences in the factors of production between alternative jurisdictions; and (ii) as any extra profits arising thereof.

The discussion of the identification and allocation of location savings in the past was mostly related to the relocation of manufacturing activities from a "high-cost" to a

12. The concepts of "risk management" (embedding within it that of control over risk) and "financial capacity to assume risk" are contained in Chapter I of the 2017 update of the OECD Transfer Pricing Guidelines, in the new Section D2, at para. 1.60 onwards. The above-mentioned concepts lie at the heart of the revamp of the "BEPS" transfer pricing analysis in requiring an accurate delineation of the transaction by going through of a six-step approach to risk allocation. This is where, in the author's view, Brazil, China, and India approach the issue in a substantially different manners in trying to attribute a greater economic premium to the market where profit economically arises.

"low-cost" location and raised interest both from MNEs that were involved in business restructurings and relocation of activities and from tax administrations in both types of countries that were concerned.

Despite the rather significant amounts at stake, the subject appears to have attracted relatively little attention from the transfer pricing community with some exceptions in the nineties but again with little public awareness since then. However, its importance gained prominence again given the explosive growth of Foreign Direct Investments (FDIs) in emerging economies with the BRICS countries (led by China and India) emphasizing the importance of fair treatment (i.e., taxation in the "market country") of location savings in transfer pricing matters.

In this context, the term location savings appears to have a broader meaning and go beyond the situation of relocating a plant from a "high-cost" to a "low-cost" jurisdiction. On the contrary, it relates to any net cost advantage that a company involved in any activity in a certain country may benefit from and the impact it should have on the transfer pricing dealings it has entered into with other related companies.

This entails that, along with the rapid economic growth, emerging countries are big advocates of the concept of LSAs. China and India in particular are known for holding strong views regarding LSAs, but also African countries (e.g., South Africa), Asian (e.g., Vietnam), and some other developing countries are currently considering implementing specific transfer pricing rules regarding LSAs. The emerging markets, in general, contend that the additional profits attributable to LSAs should accrue to the jurisdiction in which the business operations actually take place as they are physically closer to the source of income and, therefore, the associated premium profit margins arising therefrom should be taxable by that very jurisdiction, i.e., the market country.

Notwithstanding the above, it is worth mentioning that LSAs do not involve solely emerging markets but, rather, are a more generic item relevant to all types of economies with regard to transfer pricing, and countries that are more capital importers than capital exporters tend to maintain similar views.

Stated otherwise, it seems that LSA is a notion to be construed as a by-product of the economic argument whereby risks are economically shared irrespective of their "legal segregation" by means of contractual arrangements and, therefore, the economic impact of certain risks is translated at a separate entity level irrespective of their transfer pricing labeling.[13]

For instance, assume that a US MNE active in the automotive business and characterized as a "principal" for transfer pricing purposes experiences a significant crisis in the industry, triggering a dramatic reduction in sales. Such an external factor (i.e., the market demand reduction leads to a contraction of the production capacity at the group level, leading to a business restructuring requiring the closure of

13. Interestingly enough, it seems that such a view is held by the OECD itself in the 2010 Report "Attribution of Profits to Permanent Establishments" that is currently a subject of review by WP6 in the wake of the follow-up work to BEPS Final Report on Actions 8-9-10. In Part I of the Report, it is clearly argued that, in Step I of the Authorized OECD Approach, ("AOA") risks—absent binding legal arrangements between the head office and the rest of the enterprise of which it is a part—always follow functions, i.e., can never be separated from the source-generating activities of income.

manufacturing plants due to production overcapacity (and associated increase of inventory costs)). Such an externality would arguably affect the remuneration that is left at the level of both related party or third-party contract or toll manufactures, although such entities are being—in the transfer policy of the group—generally treated as low-risk entities entitled to routine margins. In light of the surge of the LSA argument, the position of the tax administration of BRICS countries is questioning the legitimacy of such a widely accepted notion.

3 BRAZIL

As a capital importing country, Brazil has always imposed measures of protection of its corporate tax base. These measures include limitations on remittances abroad and the deductibility of royalty payments on top of the introduction of the transfer pricing legislation in 1996. In this regard, Brazil was one of the first Latin American countries to enact such legislation, together with its unique worldwide income taxation regime for companies which goes far beyond the usual controlled foreign company (CFC) regimes to include taxing income earned offshore, the concepts of black and grey lists, the application of the concept of beneficial ownership, and thin capitalization rules that incorporate a flat debt-to-equity ratio. From a policy perspective, these rules are Brazil's defense against tax evasion even if they can result in double taxation.

As far as transfer pricing is concerned, Brazil stands out in a category of its own. Almost 20 years after the introduction of Law 9,430/1996, the term "arm's length" was incorporated into the doctrine to denote a principle to comply with in respect of a transaction between related parties under which the parties have to act as if they were independent. According to some literature,[14] the fixed margins introduced by the Brazilian legislator in applying the transfer pricing methods have the following three main objectives, namely: (i) countering tax avoidance; (ii) guaranteeing predictability regarding the attraction of foreign investment; and (iii) assessing the respect of the principle of strict legality. Therefore, there are already two elements which make Brazil's position with respect to transfer pricing different than the internationally accepted standards, namely:

(i) The fact that transfer pricing provisions have been introduced targeting tax avoidance and not a proper allocation of taxable income, in mind; and
(ii) The use of fixed margins and industry weighted averages rather than a proper comparability analysis.

Defining the concept of cost to determine the comparable arm's length price is difficult. Specifically, in transactions between independent parties, it is not the cost incurred on which comparability is based but rather a planned cost that has benefit, sometimes nonmonetary or nondisbursed, which is the basis for third parties to add to their profit margin. Consequently, the predetermined margins adopted by Brazil are an

14. *See* M. Ilarraz, *Drawing upon an Alternative Model for the Brazilian Transfer Pricing Experience: The OECD's Arm's Length Standard, Pre-fixed Profit Margins or a Third Way?*, Brit. Tax Rev. 2, pp. 227–228 (2014).

attempt to capture what the intercompany prices would have been had the transactions in question occurred between independent parties.[15]

In the following, a more detailed description of the recognized transfer pricing methods according to domestic Brazilian legislation is provided:

The *preços independentes comparados* (independent comparable prices, PIC) method is defined as the arithmetic mean of the prices of identical or similar goods, services or rights, ascertained in the Brazilian market with regard to purchase and sale transactions under similar payment conditions. The details of the PIC are contained in Article 18, first paragraph of Law 9,430/1996.

As can be appreciated from its legal definition, the PIC method is a comparison between the transaction conducted by the related party domiciled abroad and a Brazilian, unrelated company or between a Brazilian company and a foreign, unrelated company on the basis that such transactions must be identical or similar in relation to transactions between a related foreign company and an unrelated third party. The related company located outside Brazil must provide the relevant information.

In order for the PIC method to apply, the products compared in the transactions used as standards and the transactions in question must be similar. The definition of similarity for comparability purposes is set out in Article 42 of IN 1,312/2012 and must "have the same nature and function; may be mutually replaced in the function for which they were produced; and have equivalent specifications."

Certain adjustments are possible with regard to transactions arising out of business. These may be physical or content-related in nature. The purpose of this is to make the transactions compatible. If the PIC with the OECD comparable uncontrolled price method ("CUP") are compared, minor differences seem to exist with the internationally accepted guidance reiterated also within the UN Practical Manual on Transfer Pricing for developing countries, although the strict requirement of retrieving information from the entity located abroad may present some difficulties from a strict compliance standpoint.

The *preço de revenda menos lucro* (resale price less profit method, PRL) is defined in Article 18, item II of Law 9,430/1996, as being the weighted arithmetic mean of the resale prices of the goods, services, or rights in Brazil calculated in accordance with a specific method, i.e., a formula, that is intended to compare the participation in the cost of the goods, services, or rights sold of the imported input and apply such a percentage to the sale price of the finished goods, services, or rights.[16]

In general, the PRL is the method applied in most of the situations in which a Brazilian importer has difficulties in obtaining the supporting documentation required

15. Such a position has been argued by L. Schoueri, in *O arm's length como Princípio ou Standard Jurídico*, in *Estudos de Direito Tributário em Homenagem ao Professor Gerd W. Rothmann*, pp. 203–230 (L.E. Schoueri et al. eds., Quartier Latin 2016).
16. The difference is the profit, which must fall within the appropriate fixed profit margin, which depends on the sector involved. The fixed profit margins are as follows: (1) 40% in respect of pharmaceuticals, tobacco, optical, photographic, and cinema equipment and tools; medical-hospital machinery including dental machinery, equipment and tools; natural gas and oil extraction, and petroleum derivatives; (2) 30% in respect of chemical products, glass and glass products, cellulose, paper and paper products, and metallurgy; and (3) 20% in respect of all the other sectors.

by the tax administration in respect of the other methods, such as the PIC. The PRL has also attracted the most criticism in terms of noncompliance with OECD or UN standards as no value chain analysis is undertaken in determining the minimum profitability required for the Brazilian party in question. In most situations, especially when the Brazilian entity is a limited-risk distributor or a contract manufacturer, it is very complicated to meet even the lower fixed margin of 20%.

In addition, the PRL is the method that has been most scrutinized by the administrative and judicial courts. The relevant discussions date back to the initial years of application of the transfer pricing rules in Brazil. In this context, the original wording of the method was then simpler and stated that the sales price, as adjusted for the unconditional discounts, taxes, and contributions, applied to sales and commissions and brokerage fees paid, less a 20% fixed profit margin, was compared with the import price. However, IN 38/1997 limited the application of the method to straightforward import-resale transactions and did not apply when the imported item was used as stock in the production of other goods, services, or rights sold. This was a limitation only contained in the administrative practices and not in the law.

The *custo de produção mais tributos e lucro* (production cost plus profit, CPL) method is defined as the average production cost of identical or similar goods, services, or rights in the country in which they were originally produced plus the taxes and fees charged on the export operation in the country in question. The CPL contains a profit margin of 20% calculated on the price so determined.

At first sight, the CPL method would appear to be easy to use provided that companies have the necessary information to support it. However, companies can encounter substantial challenges in gathering evidence in respect of the costs incurred abroad by the related party.

In this regard, it should be noted that the local tax administration (*Receita Federal do Brasil—RFB*) is strict in demanding reliable accounting information from abroad, including contacting the companies that wish to keep their price formation data confidential. The CARF has also often held in favor of the tax authorities thereby further hindering the application of the CPL method. As a result, when applying the method, a great deal of documentation and information from the foreign related party is necessary to sustain the application.

The fourth method is the *preço sob cotação na importação* (price under quotation on import, PCI) method and mandatorily applies to goods or rights that are subject to public prices in internationally recognized mercantile and future exchanges as defined in Article 18, sixteenth paragraph of Law 9,430/1996. Although there is no clear definition in law, all of the regulatory rules on the issue refer to its application to commodities traded on internationally recognized exchanges. IN 1,312/2012, which regulates the application of the transfer pricing rules, includes a list of goods in Appendix I, as well as their relevant *Nomenclatura Comum do MERCOSUL* (tariff classification numbers, NCMs) which, if traded on international exchanges, must be subject to the PCI method.

The *preço de venda nas exportações* (export price method, PVEx) is contained in Article 19, third paragraph, numeral I of Law 9,430/1996. The PVEx is defined as the arithmetic mean of the sale prices charged by the company to other customers or by another national exporter of identical or similar goods, services or rights, in the same income tax calculation period and under similar payment conditions.

For the purposes of the consistent use of the PVEx, the free on board (FOB) price must be used in the comparison. If the transaction is conducted according to the cost, insurance, and freight (CIF) standard, the freight and insurance costs must be excluded. With regard to taxes, the comparability must follow the provisions of Article 19, second paragraph, numeral I of IN 1,312/2012, the price of which, in the Brazilian market, shall be deemed net of any unconditional discounts granted, of ICMS [state VAT], of the Municipal Service Tax (ISS), COFINS and PIS/PASEP.[17]

As far as transfer pricing of intercompany financing is concerned, the domestic provisions regarding intercompany financing transactions have changed over the years. When the first rules were issued in the initial version of Law 9,430/1996, all of the interest paid on intercompany loans was deductible provided that the contract was properly registered with the Brazilian Central Bank.

In its original text, Law 9,430/1996 established the following:

(a) an objective limit in respect of the deductibility of interest where the debtor was a tax resident in Brazil;
(b) a taxable amount where the creditor was resident in Brazil; and
(c) that, with regard to contracts registered with the Brazilian Central Bank, interest should be considered to have been agreed, i.e., a "safe harbor." In practice, as almost the entire loan transactions between Brazilian companies and foreign-related parties were registered with the Brazilian Central Bank, the safe harbor provision applied in almost all situations.[18]

In 2012, with the amendments made to Article 22 of Law 9,430/1996, the express reference to contracts not registered with the Brazilian Central Bank was withdrawn which established the use of the rate provided for in the registered agreement. In doing so, these changes excluded the use of the "safe harbor" in respect of interest deductibility in Brazil.

Consequently, with regard to *Lei* (Law) 12,766/2012, the limit for deductibility of interest expenses became: (1) a preestablished interest rate; and (2) a spread margin that would be defined by the Ministry of Finance. In particular, the *Portaria* (Edict)

17. There is, nevertheless, a limitation relating to the PVEx. This is that the comparison can only be made with regard to the national company, i.e., the party in question, or any other Brazilian exporter. Such an unrelated Brazilian exporter can sell to other unrelated parties, and this price can be used for comparison despite the fact that it may not be possible to collect data from a foreign company selling to an unrelated third party with regard to the application of the PVEx.
18. The original wording of Art. 22 of Law 9,430/1996 was an effective measure aimed at guaranteeing consistency with the arm's length standard as the registration of intercompany loans was carried out manually and the Central Bank undertook a double-check and/or review of the relevant rate. This persisted until 2007, when the *registro declaratório eletrônico* (electronic registration module, RDE-IED) was set up and the previous verification of the rates was removed from the system. In addition, as the hyperinflation and weak currency that existed prior to 1995 had long past, the rules regarding transfer pricing verification on intercompany loans were in need of revision.

427/2013 establishes a spread margin of 3.5% when the Brazilian party is the borrower and 2.5% when the Brazilian party is the lender. The preestablished interest rate is the interest rate paid by Brazilian sovereign bonds with prefixed rates in US dollars or Brazilian reals or the six-month London Interbank Offered Rate (Libor) rate in respect of other transactions in foreign currency.

Comparing the changes in Brazilian transfer pricing rules introduced by Law 12,766/2012 with the international practice as adopted by the OECD Transfer Pricing Guidelines reveals that the Brazilian legislation is still far from the arm's length principle due to certain fundamental differences such as the lack of commitment to market variables that directly affect the interest rates charged on financial transactions. Stated otherwise, rather than enforcing the arm's length principle adopted by the OECD Model and followed in international practice, the Brazilian transfer pricing legislation attempts to establish a maximum deductibility standard or minimum revenue to be recognized.

With regard to the deductibility limit as set out in Article 22, paragraph 6 of Law 9,430/1996, interest paid or credited to a related party abroad can only be deducted up to the following limits:

- the market rate in respect of Brazilian sovereign bonds issued in the foreign market in US dollars for transactions in US dollars at a prefixed rate;
- the market rate in respect of Brazilian sovereign bonds issued in the foreign market in Brazilian reals for transactions in reals at a prefixed rate; and
- the six-month Libor in all other cases.

The predetermination of the interest rates may also give rise to controversy. Fixed income investments yield an interest rate which may be pre- or post-fixed. The prefixed interest rate is agreed at the time of signing the loan agreement, but the post-fixed interest rate only becomes known on the return of the investment. While the rules established a prefixed interest rate for Brazilian sovereign bonds in US dollars or Brazilian reals or the Libor for transactions in other currencies, they failed to establish a post-fixed interest rate for use in floating rate transactions.

More importantly, Brazil has expressly stated its position of not taking into account corresponding adjustments affecting the other contracting party resulting from the application of transfer pricing rules in the context of a tax treaty. None of the tax treaties that Brazil has concluded contain an equivalent of Article 9(2) of the OECD Model. In this respect, Brazil has stated its reservations on the contents of *OECD Model Tax Convention on Income and on Capital* Article 9(2) but is now attempting to align its laws with Action 14 of the OECD/G-20 BEPS initiative, although it is not possible to say when such measures will be fully implemented by Brazil.

Other interesting transfer pricing areas where Brazil took its own views are those related to services and royalty payments.

According to Article 18, paragraph 9 of Law 9,430/1996, Brazil's transfer pricing rules do not apply to royalties and technical, scientific, administrative, or similar assistance that remain subject to the deductibility conditions stipulated by the current legislation.

With regard to such issues, it is interesting to note that Brazilian tax law contains objective limitations on the deductions of royalties and related technical and/or administrative assistance. In particular, a limit of 5% deductibility for royalty and assistance, i.e., technical, scientific, administrative, and related payments based on the revenues arising from the intangible or technology that is used has been always in place.[19]

Generally, the costs relating to royalties including the technical, scientific, or administrative assistance and rents relating to such royalties should only be deductible when a contract is registered with the *Instituto Nacional de Propriedade Intelectual* (National Industrial Property Institute, INPI), i.e., the Brazilian patent and trademark office, and the Brazilian Central Bank. The deductible amount is established at 1% of the net sales for trademarks or up to 5% of the net sales depending on the economic sector, for patents, industrial processes, and manufacturing formulas and the corresponding technical, scientific, administrative, or similar assistance payments.

In this context, it should be noted that, as an importer of technology, Brazil limits the deductibility of the amounts paid as royalties in order to protect its taxable base. it could be argued that these provisions could fully meet the underlying rationale of the BEPS project, but the objective is achieved at the expense of applying the arm's length principle. As a result, the transfer pricing rules do not apply on such costs/payments for this reason.

Regarding safe harbors, Brazilian legislation covers safe harbors in a simple way with regard to related-party transactions. The first safe harbor applies whenever the average cost of goods sold to related parties in export transactions is equal to or exceeds 90% of the average cost of goods sold in the Brazilian market to unrelated parties. In such circumstances, taxpayers are not covered by the transfer pricing export methods.

The second safe harbor relates to the materiality of the export revenues. This applies when the net export revenues are equal to or less than 5% of the total net revenue of the entity in the period and the relevant documentation is sufficient to prevent any adjustment.

The third safe harbor relates to a stimulus for the exports of Brazilian companies. When the party in question can demonstrate that it has realized a net profit before corporate income tax and social contributions that is equivalent to or greater than 10% of the export revenue, taking the average of the previous two years, and provided that the total export revenues do not exceed 20% of the total net sales of the company, the transfer pricing methods do not apply.

Finally, when the parameter price differs by up to 5% of the actual price or 3% in the case of the PCI or PECEX methods, no adjustment is made.

For the transfer pricing analysis of intercompany services, Brazil approaches as follows: The tax administration has always imposed a high tax burden on the import of services. With regard to intra-group services or the low value-added services between Brazilian companies, it should be noted that, when the centralizing entity consolidates the costs of administrative functions such as accounting, legal, financing, etc., and the

19. *See* BR: Lei (Law) 3,470/1958 of November 28, 1958, Art. 74).

cost is recovered without a markup being applied, the majority position of the doctrine of legal scholars and the prevailing jurisprudence of the courts hold that it should be accepted as the reimbursement of costs or cost recovery.

The recent review of the transfer pricing guidelines promoted by Action 8 to 10 of the OECD/G-20 BEPS initiative prompted a domestic review of how the tax administration should approach the issue of low value-added services. In this respect, such services have a close proximity to the Brazilian concept of *atividade-meio* (ancillary activity) and, as such, could be subject to the reimbursement of expenses.[20] It is not possible to reimburse the costs of operations that represent the main activity of the entity and, in such cases, transfer pricing provisions apply. The treatment of the "importation of services" which is broadly subject to taxation in Brazil at total combined rates ranging from 39.25% to 49.25% should also apply when the Brazilian entity is subject to a cost contribution agreement (CCA) and benefits from services provided abroad.

Based on the above-mentioned analysis, it is possible to conclude that, although inspired by the OECD and the arm's length standard, Brazil's transfer pricing legislation positions itself far from the practices adopted in international taxation. It remains to be seen how the implementation of the BEPS recommendations will be taking place within the country as Brazil is a full member of the OECD "Inclusive Framework."

4 CHINA

In 1991, China introduced its first transfer pricing provisions under the Income Tax Law for Enterprises with Foreign Investment and Foreign Enterprises which—in a way similar to Brazil- were thought of initially more as an anti-tax avoidance measure.[21]

The emergence of the Chinese transfer pricing provisions was heavily influenced by the phenomenon that more than half of the foreign-invested enterprises reported an operating loss in the 1980s. Indeed, the tax policy in China during that time was strongly pro-FDI with the aim of attracting foreign investments and strengthening the Chinese economy. In the 1990s, the tax incentives provided to foreign-invested enterprises in China were enormous. One of the incentives for foreign-invested industrial enterprises scheduled to operate for a period of ten years or more included exemption from income tax for the first two profit-making years and a 50% tax reduction for the following three years with the possibility to carry forward operating

20. *See*, for further details, E.P. Bifano, *Apuração de Preços de Transferência em Intangíveis, Contratos de Prestação de Serviços, Intragrupo e Cost Sharing Agreements* (L.E. Schoueri ed.) 3 Tributos e Preços de Transferência p. 45 (2009).
21. *See* K.H. Chan & L. Chow, International Transfer Pricing in China (Sweet & Maxwell Asia 1998); K.H. Chan & L. Chow, An Empirical Study of Tax Audits in China on International Transfer Pricing at 83–112, 23 Journal of Accounting and Economics (1997); M. Huang & H. Yu, China: Transfer Pricing at 21–26, International Tax Review (1997); H. Sun, DFI, foreign trade and transfer pricing at 362–382, 29 Journal of Contemporary Asia 3 (1999); J. Li, Transfer Pricing in China at 565–576, 54 Bulletin International Taxation. 11 (2000), Journals IBFD; J. Li, Transfer Pricing Audits in Australia, China and New Zealand: A Developed VS. Developing Countries Perspective at 21–28, 32 Intl. Tax J. 21 (2006); and D.H.K. Ho & P.T.Y. Lau, A Tax Study of Transfer Pricing in China at 62–78, 28 International Tax Journal 62 (2002).

losses at the starting stage for five years. Empowered by the domestic transfer pricing provisions, the Chinese tax authorities can conduct a transfer pricing adjustment when the payment or receipt of charges in transactions between a foreign-invested enterprise and its foreign associated enterprises is not at arm's length, which ultimately results in a tax revenue loss in China.

However, it was not until 2008 that the workload of transfer pricing cases of the Chinese tax authorities had substantially increased. To some extent, the tightened rule toward foreign-invested companies resulted in these companies generating more and more tax revenues in China. The year of 2008 was also a milestone because the State Administration of Taxation (SAT) began introducing transfer pricing concepts, such as LSAs, that were new to the OECD standards and encouraged the local taxation bureaus to explore and apply the concepts in their tax audits.[22]

One year later, the Chinese tax authorities successfully collected the overdue taxes of CNY 544 million (around EUR 74 million) during the fiscal year of 2009 by applying concepts such as location savings, market premiums, etc. in the negotiations of bilateral advance pricing agreements (BAPAs).

Following this line of reasoning, the SAT believed that the notion of LSAs emphasized the advantages of emerging markets, i.e., the purchasing powers and the cheap labor force, the contributions of which should be acknowledged and respected in value creation.

In 2009, China introduced a comprehensive anti-avoidance regime into the legislation—including the transfer pricing articles—for the first time through the "Special Tax Adjustment" provision in Chapter 6 of the Enterprise Income Tax Law and its Implementation Regulation. In 2009 (but retroactively effective from 2008), the SAT released the Implementation Measures of Special Tax Adjustments (Trial Version), better known as Circular 2.[23]

In September 2015, the SAT released the Consultation Draft Circular entitled "Implementation Measures for Special Tax Adjustments" or Draft Circular 2.[24] The latter administrative documents aim at amending and updating Circular 2 by implementing the latest OECD BEPS developments. Throughout Draft Circular 2, the role of location savings, market premiums, and other LSAs in value creation is frequently emphasized. Draft Circular 2 was finalized through three publications, namely: (i) Bulletin 42, "About Improving Reporting and Filing of Related Party Transactions and Contemporaneous Documentation" in July 2016; (ii) Bulletin 64, "Improving the Administration of Advanced Pricing Arrangements" in October 2016; and (iii) Bulletin 6, "Implementation Measures for Special Tax Adjustments and Mutual Agreement Procedure" in April 2017.

The interesting common feature of the above-mentioned documents is that these bulletins show that the Chinese tax authorities are gradually toning down the emphasis

22. *See* Notice of the SAT's Work on the Anti-Tax Avoidance in 2008, Guo Shui Han [2009] 106, March 6, 2009.
23. *See* Implementation Measures for Special Tax Adjustments (Trial), Guo Shui Fa [2009] 2, January 8, 2009.
24. *See* Implementation Measures for Special Tax Adjustments (Draft), September 17, 2015.

on LSAs. Such a reduction in emphasis on the notion of LSAs may be possibly justified by the endorsement by China of the BEPS Inclusive Framework.

However, there are no specific transfer pricing rules concerning LSAs in the domestic legislation even after the finalization of Draft Circular 2. Instead, the Chinese tax officials have made a self-statement in Chapter D.2. of the UN Manual, "China Country Practice," providing input on how the Chinese tax authorities address the issue of LSAs in their tax audits.

Within the country chapter, the Chinese tax authorities adopted a four-step approach on the issue of LSAs, namely: (i) identifying whether an LSA exists; (ii) determining whether the LSA generates additional profit; (iii) quantifying and measuring the additional profits arising from the LSA; and (iv) determining the transfer pricing method for allocating the profits arising from the LSA.

If the Chinese approach on location savings and the OECD position on "local market features" as a comparability factor are compared, certain similarities exist. However, it seems that the OECD's approach is more prescriptive as the determination of the additional profits arising from LSAs should take into account whether the LSAs are passed on to independent customers or suppliers and, if so, to what extent. The thought behind of the OECD's approach is that LSAs may not necessarily generate location rents and, therefore, market premiums to be remunerated.

When determining LSAs and their impact on transfer pricing, the Chinese tax authorities raise two factors in particular for consideration, namely, the industry analysis and the quantitative analysis.[25] However, further information on how to conduct the analyses is missing. In the absence of detailed guidance, taxpayers may face difficulties in practice when dealing with LSAs, especially for the quantitative analysis.

With regard to whether LSAs exist and what they are, the Chinese tax authorities refer to the automotive industry as an example.[26] It is believed that there are six types of LSAs existing in the automotive industry in China, as follows, and that the benefits derived from those LSAs should accrue to the Chinese enterprises:

- the foreign enterprise offering lower prices for the provision of technologies in return for the limited market access opportunities;
- the foreign enterprise charging premium prices in China due to the Chinese consumers having general preferences for foreign brands and imported products;
- a large number of potential customers;
- capacity constraints on the supply of domestically assembled automotive vehicles;
- lower duty savings if imported car parts are assembled domestically; and
- a large supply of high-quality and low-cost parts manufactured by Chinese suppliers.

25. In this respect, *see* 2017 UN Manual, at para. D.2.4.4.
26. *See* 2017 UN Manual, at para. D.2.4.4.7.

It is clear that the listed items are the general industry conditions that a foreign automotive company may encounter in China and hence are the LSAs. The first four items are market-related LSAs, i.e., market premiums, while the last two are cost-related LSAs, i.e., location savings.

The contributions of a Chinese enterprise in an independent joint venture in the automotive industry include the local distribution network, intimate knowledge of the local market, and the right market access.

In the example by China in the UN TP Manual, the Chinese enterprise usually claims 50% of the total profits of the joint venture. The SAT then concludes that this 50%, as an arm's length result, reflects the contributions of the LSAs. Therefore, when a comparable transaction takes place between a Chinese enterprise and its foreign affiliate in the automotive industry, the remuneration to the Chinese enterprise should reflect the contribution of LSAs.

With specific reference location savings, the SAT uses the contract R&D as an example to demonstrate how to calculate the amount of location savings and the transfer pricing impacts (*see* the six-step calculation in Table 4.1 below). Oddly enough, the approach as presented by China in the UN TP Manual country examples seems detrimental to the protection of local taxable bases. In fact, rather than allocating all the cost savings (e.g., 50) to the Chinese enterprise, the Chinese six-step calculation in effect allocates only part of the cost savings (e.g., 4 = 8% × 50) to the Chinese enterprise. The application of the Chinese six-step calculation gives rise to the outcome that location savings are shared between the Chinese enterprise and its foreign affiliate. However, justification is missing as to why that portion of location savings should accrue to the Chinese enterprise.

Possibly, the major weak point of the Chinese approach is the adoption of foreign comparables to determine the full markup on costs. An implicit assumption in this example is that the domestic comparables are absent. In such a scenario, a legitimate question to pose would be whether cost-related market features are the most relevant circumstance to consider when determining the arm's length transfer price based on foreign comparables. It seems that the Chinese six-step calculation recognizes only cost as the circumstance under which material differences between the controlled transaction and the foreign comparables arise.

Table 4.1 Six-Step Calculation of the Location Savings

Steps		*Calculations*
i	Calculate the arm's length range of full cost markups (FCMUs) based on foreign comparables, mostly in developed countries	Assume the median FCMU is 8%
ii	Calculate the difference between the cost base of the Chinese taxpayer (e.g., 100) and the average cost base of the foreign companies (e.g., 150)	150 – 100 = 50
iii	Multiply the arm's length FCMU (e.g., 8%) by the difference in the cost bases (50)	8% × 50 = 4

Steps		*Calculations*
iv	The resulting profit is the additional profit (i.e., 4) attributable to China for location savings	4
v	Determine the total arm's length profit for the Chinese taxpayer	4 + 8% × 100 = 12
vi	Determine the adjusted arm's length FCMU for the Chinese taxpayer	12 ÷ 100 = 12%

More broadly, it has to be determined whether the notion of LSA includes, in the Chinese tax authorities position, also that of market premium. The answer seems to be affirmative in the event a broad definition of the economic term "LSA" is adopted. To this end, market premiums seem to be broadly related to "the additional profit derived by an MNE by operating in a jurisdiction with unique qualities impacting on the sale and demand for a service or product."[27] In light of the example concerning the automotive industry introduced by the SAT in the UN Manual, the market premiums include the consumers' general preferences for foreign brands and imported products (which is different from loyalty to a specific brand) and the large population with growing wealth.

From the Chinese SAT transfer pricing standpoint, the market premium should be linked to the local marketing endeavors, which may even create local marketing intangibles. The SAT adopts the view that additional profits derived from the unique characteristics of the Chinese market should be taxed in China. In this regards, such unique characteristics include consumers' preferences for a specific brand or product that is attributable to the local marketing and promotion activities performed by the local entities. The argument of the SAT is that the significant promotion activities effectively increase the brand recognition of a particular product or service in the local market which is the main reason why the local entities experience a great increase in sale revenues. The effects of the market premiums should take into account the domestic sales in China and the overseas sales to the Chinese consumers as well. Given this argument, it is concluded that the Chinese understanding of "market premium" includes not only the market-related LSAs, i.e., the market itself that allows the generation of a premium, but also the premium caused by the local endeavors.[28]

Such a position should lead to the conclusion that Chinese-related parties must be appropriately remunerated for their location-specific advantages and should be entitled to additional profit when they improve their foreign-related party's original intangibles including global brand names, technical expertise, and business processes. This view seems to be in line with the aim of the BEPS Project to align the transfer pricing result with value creation.

27. *See* 2017 UN Manual, at para. D.2.4.4.4.
28. J. Li & S. Ji, Location-Specific Advantages: A Rising Disruptive Factor in Transfer Pricing, 71 Bull. International Taxation. 5 (2017). *See also* Peng, C. (X.), *China (People's Rep.)/International—A Rethink of Location-Specific Advantages with an Analysis of the Chinese Approach,* in International Transfer Pricing Journal, IBFD, 2017, (Volume 24), No. 6.

One interesting question in this regard is whether the value-adding factor is indeed the marketing activities carried out by: (i) the Chinese affiliates; (ii) the LSAs generated by the exploitation of the Chinese market; or (iii) both. According to the Chinese view as expressed in the UN TP Manual,[29] it seems that the existence of marketing intangibles and the LSAs are often so closely integrated that they should be considered together.

Interestingly enough, with the release of its latest Bulletin 6,[30] the SAT retains the proposal in Draft Circular 2 that LSAs are one of the comparability factors falling under the category of "economic circumstances." Furthermore, Bulletin 6 confirms that the application of the transactional profit split method should particularly look into the LSAs in the determination of the relative contributions of the transacting entity to the residual profits.

From the above, it can be argued that, with respect to the Chinese view on LSAs, the view after the reshaping of Bulletin 6 is closely linked to the internationally agreed position as expressed by the OECD and the United Nations. Nevertheless, such alignment with the international standard does not seem to be consistent with the new wording under Bulletin 42 which contains revised transfer pricing documentation requirements in China.

As stated in Bulletin 42, taxpayers, on the one hand, should properly document factors with an effect of influencing the transfer prices, including LSAs, in the Local File. On the other hand, taxpayers are required to present a value chain analysis in the Local File in which they need to quantify and allocate the contributions to value creation attributable to LSAs. Such documentation obligations seem to go beyond the requirement of the BEPS initiatives.

In conclusion, it seems that conflicting views on the treatment LSAs in the three bulletins still exist. Nevertheless, as can be seen from the most recent release of Bulletin 6, one may draw the conclusion that the Chinese approach is becoming more and more consistent with the internationally agreed approach, i.e., treating LSAs not as "something of value" akin to an intangible but rather as a comparability factor.

In the context of market premiums, the special market features along with the striking economic performance of Chinese-related businesses have increased the attention of the Chinese tax administration. This administration tends to increase the assessment of Chinese affiliates that act as an interface of the Chinese market in the MNE group. This assessment is focused on the marketing and promotional activities made by Chinese enterprises in China.

With specific reference to the treatment of intangibles, it is interesting to note that, in Bulletin 6, an additional letter "P" (referring to "promotion" on top of "protection") has been added so as to enlarge further the OECD's DEMPE concept. In particular, the function referred to the "P" letter—as one of the important value-creating factors when determining profit allocation of intangible-related income, has been highlighted. According to Bulletin 6, contributors to the *DEMPEP* of the

29. *See* 2017 UN Manual, at para. D.2.4.5.1.
30. *See* Implementation Measures for Special Tax Adjustments and Mutual Agreement Procedure, SAT Bulletin [2017] 6, April 1, 2016.

intangibles will be granted proper intangible-related returns; otherwise, the Chinese tax administration will be entitled to perform a transfer pricing adjustment. It is expected that the Chinese enterprises undertake certain promotions of the foreign intangibles in the Chinese market, and it is thus claimed that the Chinese enterprises will add value and increase the margins associated with the commercial exploitation of the intangible as initially developed. Accordingly, the Chinese enterprises should be allocated the part of the intangible-related returns corresponding to their contributions. In a nutshell, promotion is officially recognized as a separate function that is instrumental for the value creation of intangibles. It indicates that China is putting more and more emphasis on the marketing activities conducted locally and the marketing intangibles created locally in the tax audit.

A comparison of Draft Circular 2 and the three finalized bulletins concludes that the approach that the Chinese tax authorities take regarding LSAs seems nowadays more aligned with the mainstream view of the OECD and the United Nations, notwithstanding that some contradictions still exist. In particular, location savings are going to be assessed more and more from the perspective of comparability factors. With regard to market premiums, the Chinese approach, to a large extent, focuses on assessing the local marketing activities carried out by Chinese enterprises and partly distancing themselves from the OECD view by introducing the "DEMPEP" concept unlike the OECD's DEMPE.

5 INDIA

India has always been particularly active in the field of transfer pricing and voiced its position several times both within the fora of the OECD as well as that of the United Nations.

In India's country-specific chapter in the updated UN Manual, the Indian tax authorities have also revised and updated their comments on a number of transfer pricing issues being relevant from their own perspective. The Indian chapter of the updated UN Manual also contains an acknowledgment of India's endorsement of the recommendations contained in the final reports for all of the Actions under the OECD Base Erosion and Profit Shifting (BEPS) Project including actions concerning transfer pricing.

In particular, while India tried to distance itself in 2012 from the OECD position as far as policymaking is concerned,[31] today India is an active member as well of the BEPS inclusive framework, and it is supposed to endorse the recommendation arising from the Final Reports of the 15 Action items.

31. Reference is made in particular to the letter sent by India in August 2012 to the United Nations Committee of Taxation Experts where it is stated that "*We reiterate our views stated under General Comments and Recommendations that UN should take the lead in developing standards and guidance on Transfer Pricing issues. The advice of the former Group of Experts to follow OECD principles set out in OECD Transfer Pricing Guidelines should be ignored and the current Commentary on Article 9 be substituted by guidance worked out afresh through UN work.*"

The strongest position held by India was related to the treatment of marketing intangibles. In the past, and as will be seen by analyzing significant domestic case law, the local tax authorities argued that Indian subsidiaries (which claimed to be no-risk and limited-risk-bearing distributors by the parent MNE in order to justify a low cost-plus return) have incurred and borne very large expenditures for the development of marketing intangibles. These entities, therefore, generally incur very significant losses or disclose very nominal profit.

As a result, the tax authorities compute the arm's length price in cases involving marketing intangibles by applying a so-called bright-line test to establish whether the advertisement, marketing, and promotional (AMP) expenditure incurred by the taxpayer is higher than that incurred by comparable companies operating in a similar industry. The bright-line test involves a ratio-based analysis wherein the ratio of AMP expenditure to sales of the taxpayer is compared with the ratio of average AMP expenditure to sales of comparable companies operating in a similar industry. Should the taxpayer's ratio be higher than the average ratio of the industry, the conclusion is that the taxpayer has incurred excess AMP expenditure that effectively amounts to brand building on behalf of its associated enterprise.

Such Indian entities (which incur excessive AMP expense, bear risks, and perform functions beyond what an independent distributor with a similar profile would incur or perform for the benefits of its own distribution activities) should be compensated for the return on their intangibles. Such compensation would be in the form of reimbursement of excess AMP expenditure plus a markup. Alternatively, the Indian entity should be entitled to share profits related to the marketing intangibles.

If no reimbursement plus markup is made in such cases or the related party does not receive an arm's length return for the development of marketing intangibles in the form of its entitlement to share profits, the tax authorities will make an adjustment because of reimbursement of excess AMP expenditure plus a markup.

The above-mentioned position was reflected in two significant cases decided in India, namely: (i) the "Sony Ericsson Mobile Communications India"[32] case; and the (ii) "Maruti Suzuki India" case.[33]

The former case dealt with the following situation. The taxpayer acted as a distributor in India. The tax authorities applied the bright-line test and alleged that the taxpayer incurred AMP expenditure in excess of that of comparable companies. The tax authorities passed an order upholding that the foreign company must reimburse the excess AMP expense (computed by applying the bright-line test) plus a markup for the alleged provision of services in developing the brand of the foreign company in India.

When the matter reached the High Court, the Court rejected the application of the bright-line test as advanced by the tax authorities for determining whether the taxpayer

32. For further references, *see* IN: HC Delhi, March 16, 2015, Sony Ericsson Mobile Communication India Pvt. Ltd. v. CIT, ITA 16/2014.
33. For further references *see*, IN: HC Delhi, December 11, 2015, Maruti Suzuki India Ltd. v. CIT, ITA 110/2014 & ITA 710/2015, Tax Treaty Case Law IBFD.

needs to be compensated for its promotional efforts. The Court recognized the concept of economic ownership of a trade name or trade mark as intrinsic to the determination of transfer prices

The facts in the *Maruti Suzuki India* case, instead, were as follows. The taxpayer is engaged in the manufacture of passenger cars in India. The tax authorities undertook a benchmarking analysis by applying the bright-line test and compared the AMP expenses incurred by the taxpayer with those incurred by comparable companies. As the ratio of AMP expenses as a percentage of sales of the taxpayer was higher than that incurred by the comparable companies, the tax authorities concluded that the excess was incurred for promotion of the Suzuki brand (owned by a related party). Accordingly, an adjustment on account of AMP expenses was computed. The taxpayer was not successful before the Income Tax Appellate Tribunal (the Tribunal).

When the taxpayer appealed before the High Court, the Court pointed out that the bright-line test was applied by the tax authorities to the AMP expense to: (i) determine the existence of an international transaction; and then (ii) to make a quantitative "adjustment" to the arm's length price to the extent of excessive AMP of the taxpayer vis-à-vis the comparable entities. The High Court held that, once the bright-line test was ruled out by the *Sony Ericsson* judgment, the existence of an international transaction on account of the incurring of the AMP expenses cannot be established based on the bright-line test. Furthermore, the AMP expenses incurred by the taxpayer substantially benefitted only the taxpayer and thus no separate compensation is required to be paid by the associated enterprise to the taxpayer.

The tax authorities filed a special leave petition before the Supreme Court against various High Court rulings (in which the High Court ruled in line with the *Maruti* and *Sony* cases). The Supreme Court admitted the petition, and a hearing is awaited. What stood out is the fact that the bright-line test is rejected at the OECD level as well as the concept of "economic ownership" of intangibles which the OECD maintained only for purposes of Step 1 of the Authorized OECD approach.

The approach of the tax authorities, as stated in the Indian chapter of the Manual, is to carry out a detailed functional analysis to identify all of the functions of the taxpayer and an associated enterprise pertaining to all international transactions and examine whether the marketing activities, marketing research, market development, distribution channel, dealers channel, customer list, etc. (i.e., DEMPE functions) reflected by the expenditure incurred by the taxpayer and an associated enterprise in India are in conformity with the functional and risk profiles and the benefits derived by the taxpayer and an associated enterprise.

From anecdotal evidence collected with Indian colleagues, the author's view is that the tax authorities generally believe that Indian taxpayers are incurring AMP expenses for and on behalf of brand owners outside India. They also assert that these expenditures provide both direct (e.g., increase in royalties during the launch of new products) and indirect (e.g., enhancement to the value of the brand) benefits to the brand owner and, therefore, the Indian entity must be compensated for this. The most appropriate method to remunerate the Indian entity would depend on the facts of the case.

The adjustments made by the tax authorities have been subject to judicial reviews in India and, although the matter is still to be finally adjudicated by the Supreme Court, the above principles are aligned with the decisions of the High Courts as well as with the recommendations contained in the Action 8-10 Final Reports.

The author believes that the issue of marketing intangibles becomes significant in the case of a distributor (as also stated in the OECD Guidelines and the UN Manual) that buys products from the manufacturer and sells the same in its jurisdiction under a license to exploit the trademark or brand belonging to the legal owner. In such cases, it is essential to select appropriate comparables with the same intensity of functions (including AMP) so that the distribution margins of the taxpayer can be correctly compared with the comparables that have the same intensity of functions and so that no separate adjustment with respect to AMP would be required.

However, the tax authorities have taken the position that they will use a bright-line test for all types of taxpayers, namely, licensed manufacturers and distributors without considering their characterizations that are based on functional, asset, and risk analyses and the methods adopted for benchmarking the transactions for transfer pricing purposes.

The tax authorities are welcome whereby they have acknowledged that a detailed functional, asset, and risk analysis must be conducted to ascertain whether marketing efforts are in line with the functional and risk analyses. However, it seems that, in recently concluded audit activities, while efforts have been made by the tax authorities to engage in a detailed evaluation of functions, assets, and risks, adjustments have been made nevertheless using the same approach as the bright-line test because the tax authorities are still on appeal before the Supreme Court with regard to this issue.

India, like China, also believes in the relevance of the notion of LSAs but, at times, they take a more aggressive stance particularly for purposes of selecting the profit split method as the most appropriate to the circumstances of the case.

According to the tax authorities, the expression "location savings" has a much broader meaning than that accorded by the United Nations transfer pricing manual as it goes beyond the issue of relocating a business from a "high-cost" to a "low-cost" location and relates to any cost advantage that a jurisdiction can provide.

The tax authorities believe that it is possible to use the profit split method to determine an arm's length allocation of location savings and income in cases when comparable uncontrolled transactions are not available. In these circumstances, it is considered that the functional analysis of the parties to the transaction and the bargaining power of the parties (which—at arm's length—would be determined, for example, by the competitiveness of the market, the availability of substitutes, and the cost structure) should both be considered as appropriate factors.

According to the tax authorities, a comparability analysis and benchmarking by taking local comparables will determine the price of a transaction with a related party in a low-cost jurisdiction. However, the tax authorities believe that this comparability analysis will not take into account the benefit of location savings that can be computed by taking into account the cost difference between costs in the low-cost country and in the high-cost country from which the business activity was relocated.

The "*Watson Pharma*"[34] case was the first ruling on location savings. The taxpayer was engaged in contract manufacturing for its associated enterprises and provided contract research and development (R&D) services to its associated enterprises. For these transactions, the taxpayer was compensated by its associated enterprises on a total operating cost-plus arm's length markup basis. During an audit, the transfer pricing officer made an adjustment on account of alleged locations savings accrued to associated enterprises owing to the transfer of these activities from the United States (location of the associated enterprise) to India. The transfer pricing officer made an adjustment on the basis of articles available in the public domain which contained an analysis of costs undertaken in different jurisdictions. The transfer pricing officer concluded that there was a significant reduction in costs in India vis-à-vis those in the United States. Based on this, location savings were computed and then allocated equally between the taxpayer and the associated enterprise, because—in the view of the transfer pricing officer—the taxpayer and the associated enterprise had similar bargaining power owing to their individual strengths.

The Income Tax Appellate Tribunal rejected the adjustment, citing several reasons including the following:

- both the taxpayer and the associated enterprise operated in a perfectly competitive market, and the taxpayer did not have exclusive access to factors leading to location-specific advantages. Therefore, the taxpayer did not have any unique advantage, and there was no excessive profit arising in the entire supply chain; and
- where local market comparables were available and used, a specific adjustment for location savings was not required. Any benefit or advantage to the associated enterprise was irrelevant if the profit level indicator of the taxpayer was within the range of comparables.

According to the author, the judgment in *Watson Pharma* goes against the principle asserted by India in the Indian chapter of the 2013 version of the UN Manual.

India continues to believe that the profit split method should be considered for the allocation of location savings and income where comparables are not available. However, India has revised its position on using local comparables. Earlier, the local tax administration had believed that using local comparables would not take into account the location savings; however, now India states that, where comparable uncontrolled transactions are available, the comparability analysis and benchmarking that uses the results/profit margins of such local comparable companies will determine the arm's length price of a transaction with a related party in a low-cost jurisdiction. If good local comparables are available, the benefits of location savings can be said to have been captured in the arm's length price so determined. However, if good local comparables are not available that could capture the benefits of location savings or

34. For further references, *see* IN: ITA Mumbai, January 9, 2015, Watson Pharma Pvt. Ltd. v. DCIT, ITA 1423/Mum/2014, Tax Treaty Case Law IBFD.

when the overseas associated enterprise is chosen as the tested party, the issue of capturing the benefits of location savings would remain an issue in determining the arm's length price.

According to the 2017 position of India in the UN TP Manual, there is acknowledgement that location savings—if any—would be factored in the results of proper local comparables and thus no separate adjustment would be required. This revision by India seems to bring the country in line with the above-mentioned Tribunal decisions as well as with the OECD Guidelines.

More than any other emerging economy, though, India has considered the area of intra-group services as a particularly relevant one for appropriately managing its own transfer pricing regime. To this end, Indian tax authorities deem intra-group services as one of the most high-risk areas in Indian taxation. Thus, the tax authorities evaluate the receipt of services in detail including the following:

- the nature and details of the services including the quantum of services received;
- whether the services are duplicative (i.e., whether the Indian subsidiary receives services that are similar to services that it performs itself);
- whether the Indian subsidiary has the capacity to absorb the services provided by the associated enterprise;
- the economic and commercial benefits derived by the recipient of intra-group services;
- whether an independent third party would be willing and able to provide such services; and
- identification of costs (including pass-through costs) incurred by an associated enterprise in providing the intra-group services as well as the basis for allocation of such costs and markup, if any.

India also acknowledges that shareholder services, duplicative services, and incidental benefits from group services do not constitute intra-group services requiring arm's length remuneration.

The observation of the tax authorities in the updated Indian chapter of the 2017 UN TP Manual remains broadly the same as in the earlier version of the chapter. However, one major change in the revised chapter is the statement that, even if an arm's length result is achieved in respect of intra-group payments from India, an additional protection in the form of an overall ceiling on the amount of such payments may be required. This may be justified because even an arm's length payment might result in either an erosion of all of the profits of the Indian entity or an increase in the losses of the Indian entity thereby rendering the arm's length nature of such payments as being questionable. Thus, an overall ceiling on such payments in the form of a certain percentage of the sales or revenue of the Indian entity is being used in the appropriate cases. The latter conclusion may lead to wondering whether, with intra-group services, one can talk of safe harbors or measures going beyond the arm's length principle. In the author's view, pragmatism in managing the remuneration of inter-company services should be appreciated, but it cannot justify a rigid application disregarding the industry sector at stake.

The Final Report on OECD BEPS Actions 8-10 on low-value-adding services provides a simplified approach for determining arm's length charges for low-value-adding services. However, the Indian chapter of the updated UN Manual states that India has not endorsed the guidance under Action 10 for low-value-adding services and, therefore, has not opted for the simplified approach.

In addition, applying a cap on payments for intra-group services does not appear to be a reasonable approach on the part of tax authorities. Furthermore, it seems that applying a cap on intra-group services will have the following implications for taxpayers: (i) the disallowance of payments beyond a certain percentage; and (ii) such additional payment (i.e., beyond a certain percentage) is subject to corresponding and secondary adjustment issues.

Thus, this could cause administrative difficulties for genuine taxpayers, for example, if a taxpayer in the initial phase of business would need intra-group services but its payment for such services would not be allowed as it would not have enough revenue to support the arm's length nature of such payments.

Nonetheless, MNEs in India seem to always be required to maintain robust documentation substantiating the arm's length price of intra-group services as such transactions are often placed under the spotlight by the tax authorities.

6 CONCLUSIONS

The outcome of this comparative exercise led the author to conclude that Brazil, China, and India tend to have a slightly different approach when it comes to proper transfer pricing implementation. More in particular, although two out of the three tax administrations, i.e., China and India, tend to adhere to consistent tax policy principles revolving around the arm's length principle, Brazil seems to sit on a league of its own as a fixed margin methodology seems to be the key feature of its domestic legislation, although a possible alignment regarding the latter country may be achieved insofar as the OECD project recently launched with the country will prove fruitful.[35] From an implementation standpoint, though, each of the above countries present specific peculiarities which may be particularly related to:

---

35. It should be noted, though, that Brazil quite surprisingly launched a joint project on February 28, 2018 to examine the similarities and differences existing between the Brazilian and OECD approaches to valuing cross-border transactions between associated firms for tax purposes. The project will also assess the potential for Brazil to move closer to the OECD's transfer pricing rules, which are a critical benchmark for OECD member countries and followed by countries around the world. For further information, *see* http://www.oecd.org/tax/transfer-pricing/oecd-and-brazil-launch-project-to-examine-differences-in-cross-border-tax-rules.htm.

The 15-month work program will analyze the legal and administrative framework behind the Brazilian transfer pricing system as well as its implementation. It will examine strengths and weaknesses in the Brazilian approach while exploring options for greater alignment with the OECD's internationally accepted standard, the OECD Transfer Pricing Guidelines, which would be an important element of any future process of accession to the Organisation.

(1) Regarding Brazil, the current legislation made clear that the scope of its provisions is to counter tax avoidance and not act as an income allocation rule. To this end, the adoption of fixed margins introduced by the Brazilian legislator in applying the transfer pricing methods have pursued the following objectives of:
   (i) countering tax avoidance;
   (ii) guaranteeing predictability regarding the attraction of foreign investment; and
   (iii) assessing the respect of the principle of strict legality. Therefore, there are already two elements that make Brazil's position with respect to transfer pricing different than the internationally accepted standards, namely:
      (a) the fact that transfer pricing provisions have been introduced targeting tax avoidance and not a proper allocation of taxable income, in mind; and
      (b) the fixed margins and industry weighted averages rather than a proper comparability analysis.

(2) Concerning China, the SAT acted swiftly in implementing the BEPS recommendations, but- as has been the case for India—the local tax administrations tried to somehow "customize" some significant OECD transfer pricing principles to the local interest. In the latter regard, reference is made to the notion of "local market features" as an intangible warranting a premium return as well as to the (re)interpretation of the notion of DEMPE. More in detail, in the context of market premiums, the special local market features along with the striking economic performance of Chinese-related businesses have increased the attention of the Chinese tax administration. The Chinese tax administration tends to increase the assessment of Chinese affiliates that act as an interface of the Chinese market in the MNE group. This assessment is focused on the marketing and promotional activities made by Chinese enterprises in China. With specific reference to the treatment of intangibles, it is interesting to note that the letter "P" (referring to "promotion" on top of "protection") has been added so as to further enlarge the OECD's DEMPE concept. In particular, the function referred to the "P" letter—as one of the important value-creating factors when determining profit allocation of intangible-related income, has been highlighted. Such a variation in the notion of "DEMPE" might entail that, e.g., local distributors operating on Chinese soil may be positioning themselves on the upper quartile of an interquartile range to remunerate what—according to the local tax administration—is a distribution function warranting a premium return.

(3) Along the same line of reasoning, India is also of the view that LSAs are relevant but, at times, they take a more aggressive stance particularly for purposes of selecting the profit split method as the most appropriate to the circumstances of the case. In particular, according to the tax authorities, the expression "location savings" has a much broader meaning than that accorded by the United Nations transfer pricing manual as it goes beyond the

issue of relocating a business from a "high-cost" to a "low-cost" location and relates to any cost advantage that a jurisdiction can provide.

Moreover, it seems to the author that India tends to depart from a consistent OECD interpretation of fundamental principles such as the application of the profit split. According to such a (biased) view, the tax authorities believe that it is possible to use the profit split method to determine an arm's length allocation of location savings and income in cases where comparable uncontrolled transactions are not available. In these circumstances, it is considered that the functional analysis of the parties to the transaction and the bargaining power of the parties (which—at arm's length—would be determined, for example, by the competitiveness of the market, the availability of substitutes, and the cost structure) should both be considered as appropriate factors. According to the author, such a position defies the recent view expressed by the OECD in its latest Discussion Draft on the application of the profit split[36] whereby the absence of comparables should not be the automatic trigger to resort to such a method.[37]

Therefore, according to the author, it seems quite obvious to conclude that, although the tax policy world on transfer pricing has the same starting point, i.e., the arm's length principle, its practical implementation seems slightly different in the economies that are growing faster than the rest of the G-20 countries. From a taxpayer's standpoint, such developments are not welcome, at best, as the risk of double or multiple taxation is greater than twenty years ago when transfer pricing expertise was just at its beginnings.

36. *See* Discussion Draft on BEPS ACTION 10 Revised Guidance on Profit Splits, available at http://www.oecd.org/ctp/transfer-pricing/Revised-guidance-on-profit-splits-2017.pdf.
37. *See* para. 6 of the Discussion Draft, where it is stated that, "*6. The main strength of the transactional profit split method is that it can offer a solution for cases where both parties to a transaction make unique and valuable contributions (e.g. contribute unique and valuable intangibles) to the transaction.*"

CHAPTER 5

Recent Developments on Transfer Pricing Documentation and Country-by-Country Reporting

Oliver Wehnert

1 INTRODUCTION

1.1 History of Developments in Transfer Pricing Documentation Requirements

Since the first implementation of transfer pricing documentation regulations in the United States (US) back in 1994, the scope, depth, and level of detail of the information to be provided by taxpayers about their transfer pricing was a permanent area of dispute between taxpayers and tax authorities. This is due to the purpose of transfer pricing documentation. As transfer pricing is about the exchange of goods, services, and assets between related parties, there is the rebuttable assumption that, because of the lack of a conflict of interest between the parties, transfer prices are set so that taxpayers optimize their tax position. Thus, the purpose of transfer pricing documentation is that taxpayers give reasons for why they believe their transfer prices are in line with the arm's length principle as stipulated in Article 9 of the OECD Model Tax Convention (MTC). However, as transfer pricing is accepted as not being an exact science, the OECD[1] and numerous national States have established regulatory frameworks about which information taxpayers have to provide in their documentation from a qualitative and quantitative perspective. Once such transfer pricing documentation was presented to the tax authorities, taxpayers had the burden of proof to determine whether or not transfer prices comply with the arm's length principle.

1.2 Need for Documentation Reforms

The challenges for tax authorities in this context were predominantly related to the difficulty and factual impossibility of examining the correctness and accuracy of information provided by the taxpayer about, e.g., functions performed, risks assumed, and assets employed in foreign countries, i.e., beyond the borders of responsibility of a particular tax authority. This continuously led to the assumption of tax authorities that taxpayers are hiding certain relevant information or at least holding it away from a tax authority in a particular country. Further, local country tax authorities tended to overstate Multinational Enterprises' (MNE) operations in their country. In short, tax authorities continuously complained and tried to overcome the perceived lack of transparency of taxpayers' operations and were always striving to get as much information about the taxpayer as possible.

For taxpayers, on the other side, the major challenges with the pre-BEPS fragmented regulatory environment were related to the enormous administrative burden to comply with the various widely similar, but often different in detail, transfer pricing documentation requirements around the world. These differences existed both

1. The OECD has laid down transfer pricing documentation obligations in Chapter V of the OECD Guidelines (GL) 1995.

regarding the level of detail of qualitative information as well as to the way quantitative analyses were to be provided to justify the arm's length nature of the transfer pricing. Thereby, taxpayers usually tried to disclose as little information as possible to comply with local regulations so that penalties,[2] if any, were avoided.

The attitude of taxpayers toward transfer pricing documentation was also driven by the perception that there was not a lot to win with preparing comprehensive and extensive documentation other than to obtain penalty protection. This is because there was and still is no regulatory framework in place that stipulated that, in the case that such comprehensive documentation existed, the arm's length nature of transfer pricing is evidenced and thus accepted by tax authorities without any further examination. Rather, the transfer pricing documentation prepared by the taxpayer was and still is, in fact, the starting point of the examination by the tax authorities in scope of tax audits where typically a significant amount of additional information was to be provided to substantiate the conclusions drawn in the transfer pricing documentation. As experience showed that, usually, almost every tax audit finally resulted in an income adjustment and thus double taxation, many taxpayers applied transfer pricing documentation strategies where only the very minimum of information was provided, typically just enough to get over the penalty protection hurdle as more information was to be provided in later tax audits anyway. Further, in light of the ever increasing number of countries with transfer pricing documentation regulations, taxpayers were striving for a consistent way to document intercompany relationships which became more and more of a challenge because of local country deviations in transfer pricing documentation requirements.

As a result, between the mid-1990s and the beginning of the BEPS project in 2013. It could be said that there was a high level of frustration about transfer pricing documentation on both sides with taxing authorities looking for more transparency and taxpayers looking for more consistency to reduce the administrative burden related to transfer pricing documentation.

2 KEY OBSERVATIONS ON BEPS ACTION 13

2.1 Overview of the New Documentation Requirements

In scope of the OECD/G20 BEPS project, Action 13 dealt with transfer pricing documentation. The goal of Action 13 was to develop "rules regarding transfer pricing documentation to enhance transparency for tax administration, taking into consideration the compliance costs for business. The rules to be developed will include a

2. Many countries have enacted penalty regimes together with transfer pricing documentation requirements. Such regimes can basically be distinguished in: (i) regimes where (monetary) penalties apply if taxpayers provide no or incomplete documentation; and (ii) those where penalties are assessed as a surcharge on the tax that occurs on a transfer pricing adjustment.

requirement that MNEs provide all relevant governments with needed information on their global allocation of the income, economic activity and taxes paid among countries according to a common template."[3]

As a result of Action 13, a three-tiered standardized approach to transfer pricing documentation was developed that is deemed to require taxpayers to articulate consistent transfer pricing positions and will provide tax administrations with useful information to assess transfer pricing risks, i.e., to determine whether taxpayers have used transfer pricing to shift portions of income into so-called tax advantaged environments.

Action 13 resulted in a full revision of Chapter V of the OECD TPG which was published by the OECD in July 2017.

According to the new Chapter V, transfer pricing documentation consists of three elements, i.e., the so-called master file, the local file, and Country-by-Country Report ("CbC Reports"). Once implemented, the new transfer pricing documentation approach will provide a level of transparency about a taxpayers' global operations for tax authorities that was never in place before. This clearly accomplished overcoming the above-mentioned deficit perceived by taxing authorities of former transfer pricing documentation regulations regarding the lack of transparency. If properly and consistently implemented on a global scale, the new set of rules has some potential to address a taxpayer's demand for regulations that are more consistent on a worldwide level although the overall scope of the documentation has clearly increased which will require additional efforts on the taxpayers' end.

2.2 Master File and Local File

The first component of the documentation is the master file which is supposed to provide high-level information regarding an MNE's global business operations and transfer pricing policies. Notably, the master file shall be made available to all relevant tax authorities. As the term "master file" was in use in transfer pricing long before the BEPS project started, many taxpayers only realized rather late that the information to be provided within the master file according to the new Chapter V significantly exceeds what they might had included in their master files prior to the BEPS project. Inter alia, the (new) master file is supposed to include a description of the (global) supply chain for the group's five largest products and/or service offerings, information on R&D and intangibles transfer pricing policies, information on the MNE's intra-group financing policies and, last but not least, a list and brief description of existing unilateral advance pricing agreements and other tax rulings relating to the allocation of income among countries.[4] In particular, the aforementioned information was typically not included in transfer pricing documentation prior to the BEPS project and may provide the basis for intense local country examination activities going forward.

3. OECD (2017), BEPS Action 13 on Country-by-Country Reporting—Guidance on the appropriate use of information contained in Country-by-Country reports, OECD/G20 Base Erosion and Profit Shifting Project, OECD, Paris, Action 13: 2015 Final Report; p. 9.
4. Annex I to Chapter V OECD TP GL 2017.

The second component of the documentation is the so-called local file requiring a detailed transactional transfer pricing documentation specific to each country that identifies material related party transactions and the taxpayer's analysis of the transfer pricing determinations they have made with regard to those transactions. It could be stated that the scope of information to be included in the local file according to Chapter V OECD TP GL 2017 does not significantly exceed the usual level of information required in local country regulations prior to the BEPS project. However, it needs to be considered that the new Chapter V only sets minimum standards. That is, local countries can regulate that additional information needs to be included in the local file.

2.3 Country-by-Country Reporting

The third and most controversial component of the new transfer pricing documentation approach is the so-called country-by-country report (CbC Reports) which provides for a standardized format that obliges taxpayers with consolidated revenues of more than EUR 750 million[5] to disclose financial information about their global group by country and qualitative information about the activities of legal entities within the global group by entity. The financial information to be provided in the CbC Reports by country includes revenues with related and unrelated parties, profits and losses before taxes, cash and accrued taxes paid, stated capital, number of employees, and tangible assets. Obviously and intentionally, this information provides full transparency about the MNE's global allocation of income by country. It also allows tax authorities around the globe to determine all kinds of more or less meaningful ratios for risk assessment purposes, like profit per employee, return on equity, return on assets, etc. Therefore, it can be expected that CbC Reports will be a powerful basis for tax authorities to challenge a taxpayer's global income allocation and the transfer pricing system. Together with the second form about qualitative information regarding the activities of group entities in various countries, tax authorities will have an unseen level of transparency about a multinational group.

To ensure that CbC Reports are implemented by countries in a consistent manner, Action 13 also resulted in draft Model legislation related to Country-by-Country Reporting (CbCR).

In terms of submitting the three components of transfer pricing documentation to tax authorities, the master file and local file are to be submitted to local country tax authorities based on the local country regulatory framework whereas CbC Reports are only to be submitted by the ultimate parent entity to its tax administration which will then exchange the CbC Reports with other tax administrations. In this respect, Action 13 also produced a so-called Multilateral Competent Authority Agreement which stipulates how the exchange of information is to be conducted automatically between countries that are parties of or territories covered by the Convention on Mutual

5. The appropriateness of this threshold is highly questionable because it does not say anything about the magnitude of cross border intercompany activities. If, e.g., a company makes EUR 800 million of global sales EUR 799 million EUR of which would be in one country and EUR 1 million in a subsidiary abroad, it would still have to submit a CbC Reports.

Administrative Assistance in Tax Matters. Further, Action 13 also drafted a (bilateral) Competent Authority Agreement on the Exchange of Country-by-Country Reports on the basis of a Double Taxation Convention.

As with many other areas of the BEPS project, the in depth advice on implementation produced in the scope of the 2015 Final Report documented very clearly that it was the strong intent of the countries participating in the BEPS project to enact the new concept.

Although the business community was continuously involved during the BEPS project, at least in form of public hearings, they were not able to prevent the introduction of CbC Reports. For most multinationals, the strong opposition against CbC Reports was not driven by an intention to hide certain tax structuring but rather the expectation that CbC Reports will result in even more transfer pricing controversy. This expectation is grounded on the fact that it does not really matter for any local country whether profits not shown in their jurisdiction are low or high taxed somewhere abroad. Rather, transfer pricing controversy experience over the last twenty years clearly demonstrates that each local country tries to maximize its piece of the global profit pie of an MNE and thus its own tax revenues. CbC Reports will, for the first time ever, provide information on which parts of the global profit of an MNE are realized in which country and what group entities located in each country do. And as a matter of fact, this will trigger discussions about why a profit (margin) in country A is higher than in country B despite a similar functional and economic profile of entities located in both countries.

Further, it can be stated that mature developed industrial countries like, e.g., Germany, France, or Japan, underestimated the potential impact of CbC Reports for too long. As factual data will evidence, MNEs headquartered in such countries typically realize a significant portion—often above 50%—of their global consolidated profit in their rather high tax home countries although the home market often only represents less than 10% of the global revenues with unrelated parties. It is, therefore, fair to expect that such MNEs will face much more transfer pricing controversy than in the past.

Lastly, it has to be taken into consideration that the BEPS project clearly put international tax matters and, in particular, transfer pricing into the spotlight on a global scale. Consequently, the global coverage of countries with transfer pricing (documentation) regulations increased significantly since the BEPS project started. This also means that, for MNEs, transfer pricing documentation has to be produced in even more countries than before the BEPS project. As documentation will remain the starting point for any tax authority to examine an MNE's transfer pricing system, it is to be expected that more controversy will take place in significantly more countries, many of which will not be very experienced in handling such cases.

As a result of BEPS Action 13 and other parallel developments on regional levels (e.g., in the EU), taxpayers will have to cope with the challenge of an unseen transparency about their global operations, financial structure, and tax position.

3 GLOBAL IMPLEMENTATION OF BEPS ACTION 13

3.1 Emerging Implementation Challenges

Since the OECD published the final report on Action 13 including the revised language of Chapter V of the OECD TP GL, countries around the world started to implement the new three-tiered approach to transfer pricing documentation consisting of a master file, a local file, and CbC Reports. As of December 31, 2017, more than 60 countries enacted transfer pricing documentation regulations accordingly.

Although it can be observed that most of the countries adhered to the OECD language in their implementation efforts, it needs to be noted that many countries considered Chapter V of the OECD TP GL as the minimum standard and added additional documentation requirements in their local regulations. Such additional requirements relate typically to the local file. In particular in countries which had transfer pricing documentation regulations before the BEPS project, it can be noted that governments complemented the OECD language by additional requirements which they deem to be important in their countries.

Deviations in regulations on local files, however, result in a lack of consistency on a global scale which clearly undermines the goal of BEPS Action 13 to strive for consistent transfer pricing documentation approaches to keep the administrative burden and the resulting compliance costs for taxpayers at a reasonable level.

Regarding the master file, fortunately, the worldwide implementation seems to be pretty consistent with the OECD approach. This is important for taxpayers as the intention of the new regulatory framework is that taxpayers prepare such a master file only once for the entire group and submit it in each country together with the individual local file for the group entity located in this country. This generally good idea, however, results in some practical difficulties in particular for global groups comprising various different business units or subgroups. In such MNEs, group entities belonging to one business unit or subgroup have typically very little interaction with other business units or subgroups. To prepare one master file for the entire MNE containing information about all of the different business units or subgroups does not make a lot of sense because it provides a lot of irrelevant information to taxing authorities. In such cases, it can be observed that MNEs with such structures prepare master files by business unit or subgroup which should be acceptable to taxing authorities as they do get all of the necessary information to examine and evaluate the relevant MNE's transfer pricing.

As to be expected, the implementation of CbC Reports was and still is the biggest challenge for both taxpayers and tax authorities.

3.2 Challenges for Taxpayers

For taxpayers, the biggest challenges are related to obtaining the right data. According to the OECD regulations,[6] CbC Reports were intended to be used by tax authorities mainly for risk assessment purposes. Therefore, the requirements for CbC Reports as to data are not really detailed in terms of an accounting standard. Basically, CbC Reports assume that financial data by country that need to be reported represent the sum of the relevant data of the group entities within a country. This sounds simple, in the first place, but turned out to be a larger problem in particular for MNEs in which reporting systems or consolidation groups no longer follow geographies.

The second challenge for taxpayers relates to the fact that, according to the regulations, the reporting entity is the ultimate parent entity of an MNE group. Again, many larger MNEs consist of business units or subgroups who have little to no interaction with each other. Still though, if such different business units and subgroups are finally owned by the same parent entity, they would have to be combined in the CbC Reports, e.g., their financial data would have to be added up by country. An example in this regard may be the companies in the automotive industry where the ultimate parent company typically owns the traditional automotive businesses (i.e., manufacturing and sales entities) and also owns a financial services arm comprising banks or leasing companies where customers can obtain loans to finance car purchases or conclude leasing contracts. For CbC Report purposes, the financial data of both subgroups would have to be added up. Obviously, it is highly questionable to what extent such information is suited to serve the purpose of a risk assessment. Clearly, it would have been preferred if MNEs with such a structure would have had the possibility to follow their business structure in the CbC Reports. However, this is not the case and might lead to a lot of confusion at the level of tax authorities once they review the first CbC Reports.

3.3 Challenges for Legislators and Policy Makers

On the tax authority side, the biggest challenges in terms of implementation were, on the one hand, related to establishing the technical platform, i.e., the IT infrastructure to be able to receive the CbC Reports from the taxpayers in their countries. In that respect, it was also important to ensure a globally consistent IT infrastructure so that the reports could indeed be exchanged automatically. Over the last two years, the OECD has provided a lot of support in this regard and has created a globally consistent html format for this purpose. Still, it can be observed that the submission of CbC Reports in that format does not work (yet) in one or another country. However, experience shows that such technical difficulties will be overcome over time.

6. *See* OECD (2017), Chapter V, *OECD Transfer Pricing Guidelines for Multinational Enterprises and Tax Administrations 2017*, OECD Publishing, Paris, para. 5.5.

Obviously, the necessary technical efforts by country differed significantly from country to country. Due to the applicable threshold of consolidated revenues of EUR 750 million regarding the obligation to submit CbC Reports, smaller countries had to deal with a handful of relevant MNEs in their countries whereas only mature industrial countries needed to build the infrastructure for hundreds of taxpayers. Regarding the exchange of information, the situation is different as the number of MNEs being active in a country often does not differ in relation to the size of the country.

However, the technical challenges for certain countries resulted in differences as to the effective date for submitting the first CbC Reports. Whereas the OECD recommended that the first CbC Reports should be filed for MNE fiscal years starting on or after January 1, 2016, [7] many mature industrial countries in particular moved the effective date to MNE fiscal years starting on or after January 1, 2017 or even later. As the CbC Reports are basically only to be filed once by the ultimate parent entity (UPE) in its country of residence, the situation can occur where a subsidiary of a UPE is resident in a country where Action 13 was fully implemented with effect for fiscal year 2016 whereas its UPE is resident in a country where the effective date for the first CbC Reports submission is for fiscal year 2017 or even later. In these cases, it is important that such subsidiaries do not run a noncompliance or penalty risk in their countries of residence. In cases where the country of residence of the UPE does not enact any CbC Reports obligation, the regulatory framework foresees that another group entity has to be appointed that falls under the CbC Reports obligations.

The second major challenge for tax authorities related to CbC Reports implementation was to establish the legal framework to be able to exchange the CbC Reports information. This was considered to be a very critical issue in particular in countries with strict tax secrecy laws. More than two years after the final report on Action 13 was issued by the OECD, however, it can be stated that the legal implementation was very successful on a global level. On December 21, 2017, the OECD released additional exchange relationships that have been activated under the Multilateral Competent Authority Agreement (MCAA) on the Exchange of Country-by-Country (CbC) Reports. Currently, together with the exchange relationships under the European Union (EU) Council,[8] there are over 1,400 automatic exchange relationships established among jurisdictions committed to exchanging CbC Reports as of mid-2018. The full list of automatic exchange relationships that are in place and an update on the implementation of the domestic legal framework for CbCR in jurisdictions are available on the OECD website. With this update, Argentina, Bulgaria, Cayman Islands, Colombia, Croatia, Czech Republic, Hungary, India, Lithuania, Malta, Russia, and Sweden have been included on the list of countries that have activated exchange relationships for CbCR for the first time. It is notable that, in the meanwhile, a lot of countries that have and still are considered to be tax havens like the Cayman Islands, Malta, Cyprus, and others are part of the game and have signed the MCAA on the Exchange of CbC Reports.

---

7. *Supra* n. 6, para. 5.5.
8. *See* EU, Council Directive 2016/88, *Amending Directive 2011/16/EU as regards mandatory automatic exchange of information in the field of taxation*, Official Journal of the European Union (May 25, 2016).

It can thus be concluded that the overarching goal of the BEPS project to achieve more transparency about a taxpayer's global tax structures has been accomplished.

Regarding the CbC Reports, many countries have also implemented notification requirements for taxpayers. This is an obligation of the taxpayer to notify to the tax authority in its country of residence which related group entity is the UPE and in which country the group will submit its CbC Reports. Notably, some countries have combined such notification requirements with penalties in case of no or late notification. In countries that implemented CbC Reports for fiscal year 2016, the notification deadlines were typically set in 2017. In that respect, it was to be observed that many taxpayers overlooked the notification requirements and, in many cases, no or late notification was provided. In some of the countries, the penalties went beyond pure monetary penalties and could go as far as personal sanctions against the management of the local group entity.[9]

It will be very interesting to see how tax authorities will deal with the CbC Reports and how they approach and examine them. Due to the highly imprecise requirements about the financial data to be included in the CbC Reports that leave a lot of room for interpretation, there is little chance for tax authorities to examine the data as to its correctness. This would also mean that there cannot be any sanctions if it would ever turn out that a CbC Report is wrong or incomplete. As mentioned above, in particular in MNEs consisting of different business units or subgroups, the data included in the CbC Reports is not meaningful anyway and would not even allow tax authorities to do a reasonable risk assessment. Therefore, it will be of utmost importance for taxpayers to comply with the notification requirements and submit the CbC Reports in due time in order to avoid penalties. Once the CbC Reports are submitted, there should be no possibility for tax authorities to assess any further penalties related to them.

---

9. In the respect, e.g., the Netherlands has implemented pretty strict rules. Here, the general penalty regime is applicable for noncompliance with CbCR requirements. This means that, in principle, noncompliance will be regarded as a criminal offence for which a criminal penalty can be imposed. In case the offence was not intentional, the penalty can be a monetary fine of max EUR 8,100 or detention of a maximum of six months. In case of intentional noncompliance, the penalty can be a monetary fine of max EUR 20,500 or imprisonment of max four years. A proposal has been adopted by the Second Chamber on April 18, 2017 to increase the CbCR penalty from up to EUR 20,250 to up to EUR 820,000. The offenders are: (a) the taxpayer (if the Dutch constituent entities are part of a fiscal unity, they are considered together as the taxpayer) and, in addition; (b) the co-perpetrator (the tax advisor can also be considered in this category if there was conscious and close cooperation between the taxpayer and the tax advisor); and (c) the principal or executive (e.g., statutory director, tax manager). The district attorney decides whether to prosecute someone else than the taxpayer.

   In addition to these parties, criminal prosecution may also be imposed on the party causing, inciting, or being an accessory to the infringement. An example of the party causing the infringement is the situation in which a shareholder deliberately has the taxpayer file a false report, while the taxpayer is not to blame.

   When the district attorney does not file criminal charges, an administrative penalty will be imposed when the noncompliance is due to gross negligence or intention.

4 TAXPAYER REACTION TO ACTION 13

4.1 Review of Transfer Pricing Documentation Approach

The vast majority of MNEs had transfer pricing documentation approaches in place for a long time before the BEPS project started. These approaches were typically characterized by some central support usually taken by the group's global or regional headquarters related to the preparation of group transfer pricing policies; the preparation of draft documents that were made available to subsidiaries like, e.g., draft functional analyses; industry analyses; or centrally prepared benchmarking studies. However, the typical attitude toward transfer pricing documentation was that it is a local country compliance exercise where the various individual group entities have to fulfill their local country compliance obligations. Therefore, it was often eventually the responsibility of the local group entities to compile the transfer pricing documentation in their countries of residence. In that respect, centrally prepared documents were used to the extent this was deemed useful or in line with local country requirements but, in the end, each local group entity was allowed to do what it takes to comply with local regulations and requirements. Very few MNEs had transfer pricing documentation approaches in place where the responsibility for the documentation preparation process was in the main responsibility of a central, typically regional, or global headquarters.

When the OECD published its Final Report on Action 13, most MNEs revisited and finally changed their transfer pricing documentation approach. This was, on the one hand, driven by the new three-tiered structure designed by the OECD for transfer pricing documentation. In that respect, it became clear very quickly that at least two components, namely, the master file and the CbC Reports, require preparation at a central place in the MNE because the information required in these two components were either not available for or not accessible by each group entity. This required MNEs to reorganize their documentation process by determining a central place in the organization that would take the responsibility for compiling the necessary information to complete the required master file and the CbC Reports.

Further, it also became obvious that the dramatically increased level of transparency that tax authorities would have once they receive the master file and, in particular, the CbC Reports also triggers the need to establish a process which ensures that any information included in local files is consistent with information in the master file and the CbC Reports. In that respect, MNEs also had to consider that certain information included in the CbC Reports needs to be further explained in the local files. In the end, MNEs realized that the new three-tiered approach to transfer pricing documentation requires an enormous degree of consistency between local files that are presented to local country tax authorities around the globe. This is also due to the fact that information exchange for tax (and transfer pricing) purposes between countries was significantly improved during and after the BEPS project, and MNEs faced the situation that the likelihood that a tax administration in country A gets access to local files presented in countries B and C has increased materially.

The result of the aforementioned considerations was that many MNEs revisited and adjusted their transfer pricing documentation processes and assigned many more responsibilities to a central place in the group, typically the global headquarters. This, as such, created a challenge for many MNEs, in particular for those where there were little or no transfer pricing specialist resources available at a central place. As a consequence, it could be observed that most MNEs extended or built-up in-house transfer pricing departments over the last two to three years.

4.2 Increasing Importance of Technology

Further, many more MNEs than ever before digested to what extent technology could help them in the transfer pricing documentation process. In that respect, IT solutions were required and designed, on the one hand, related to gathering and compiling the data for CbC Reports. As said before, although the OECD tried to keep the requirements rather simple in this regard, many companies ran into numerous challenges because their reporting or consolidation lines were not tied to geographies but rather to business units or subgroups, and the requested reporting by country for CbC Reports purposes had to be established from scratch.

On the other hand, MNEs increasingly started to look into technical solutions that would support them in compiling the transfer pricing documentation, i.e., in particular the master file and the local file. This trend is clearly driven by: (i) the increasing need for consistency of particularly the local files; and (ii) the above-mentioned need to take more responsibility for the contents of transfer pricing documentation in a central place. In the meanwhile, various tools are available in the market that were developed by IT companies, accounting firms, or even in-house by MNEs. The use of technology thereby ensures a high degree of consistency between documents that are prepared. However, the use of technology also necessarily results in a lower degree of detail of the information included in the documentation. Therefore, MNEs had to compromise between consistencies, on the one hand, and level of detail of the documentation, on the other.

4.3 Timing of Implementation

When redesigning their documentation approach, MNEs were also facing the challenge that the local country legislative implementation of BEPS Action 13 does not take place at the same point in time and is also not fully consistently around the world. Still, though, many MNEs changed their approach toward Action 13 compliance documentation the first time for fiscal year 2016. When doing so, they accepted that many countries had not yet implemented Action 13 into local laws and thus detailed analyses were required to determine whether local country documentation prepared in line with Action 13 could trigger local noncompliance risks. Where ever this was the case, the local files had to be adjusted to still comply with local country requirements. Unfortunately, this situation will continue regarding fiscal year 2017 and potentially longer until Action 13 has found its way into local country legislation.

4.4 Changes in Transfer Pricing Principles Affecting Documentation Approach

MNEs also had to deal with the fundamental changes in certain areas of transfer pricing which were laid down in Action 8-10 and resulted in partly fundamental changes in the areas of risk allocation, intangibles (namely, the DEMPE analysis), and value chain analysis. Prior to BEPS, taxpayers mostly applied one-sided transfer pricing methods and structured their factual analyses for documentation purposes accordingly. That is, they documented the "tested party" in detail and left anything out that was not directly relevant in this regard. In that respect, changes to the structure of the transfer pricing documentation were required to reflect the new viewpoints of the OECD. Although this did not result in a change of the transfer pricing method in most cases, it required additional efforts on the documentation front to delineate the functions, risks, and assets of the nontested party in much more detail.

Obviously, the changes to the transfer pricing documentation led to the question of consistency with historical documentations that were prepared and submitted to tax authorities in the past. It is to be expected that this issue in particular will raise a lot of questions of local country tax authorities in the future once they receive the new Action 13 based documentation and compare this with prior documentation that is available to them. This is specifically true because the MNEs' goal to ensure consistency across local files submitted in various countries often results in the new Action 13 compliant local file being significantly shorter and crisper than local country documentation prepared under a more decentralized approach before the BEPS project. As this will be scrutinized in detail by such local tax authorities. MNEs need to prepare for these situations. A trend that can be observed in this regard is that many MNEs start to build up tax audit defense files for group entities based in jurisdictions where, historically, in depth audits of the MNE's transfer pricing took place. Such tax audit defense files do not form part of the Action 13 documentation but are held in the back pocket so that they can be used in an audit situation in a timely manner. Depending on the nature of the critical issues covered in such defense files, the same are prepared either centrally to be available for all group entities or locally if the issue relates only to a particular country.

4.5 Documentation and Tax Audit Management

The point mentioned in the last paragraph also raises the question of the purpose of the transfer pricing documentation as such. Whereas, prior to Action 13, transfer pricing documentation was mainly prepared for defending the group's transfer pricing in a tax audit situation (even in countries with transfer pricing documentation regulations where compliance requirements existed), this perception seems to have changed after the BEPS project. Many MNEs still consider the extremely higher level of transparency for tax authorities as a consequence of the three-tiered documentation approach as a major threat and try to address this with a transfer pricing documentation approach which, on the one hand, fully ensures compliance as to the information to be included in the transfer pricing documentation but, on the other hand, focuses strongly on consistency of information provided across countries and thus avoids including any information which is deemed to be not completely necessary to fulfill the compliance requirements. As a result, transfer pricing documentation seems to be regarded as a compliance exercise more than ever before. MNEs following this direction are thus separating the compliance exercise "transfer pricing documentation" from the controversy exercise "defending the transfer pricing position." This is a very similar development as that with other tax declaration obligations when taxpayers have, e.g., filed a tax return that includes the taxpayer's go-in-position related to a particular issue which is then examined by the tax authorities typically in the scope of a tax audit. At the time of the examination by the tax authorities, the taxpayer is ready to present additional information to sustain and defend his position. Translated to transfer pricing, this means that the transfer pricing documentation lays out and explains the reasons for a certain position the taxpayer takes as to his intra-group allocation of income and, in addition, complies with local country documentation regulations. Once this position is examined or audited by tax authorities, the taxpayer is ready and prepared to present additional information to defend his position. Such an approach seems to be feasible but requires the respective organizational set up in the MNE's tax and transfer pricing department. It can, on the one hand, result in a more efficient global transfer pricing process and, on the other hand, still ensure an appropriate risk management strategy. The result of this approach, though, may come as a surprise to many tax authorities because the volume and level of depth of a post-BEPS transfer pricing documentation can well be lower than what they were used to in the past.

5 OUTLOOK: WHAT COMES NEXT?

5.1 Changes to Conduct Tax Audits

The OECD/G20 BEPS project as a whole and Action 13 together with Action 8-10 on transfer pricing delivered a huge set of new toys to global tax administrations and, as experience shows, it can be expected that tax administrations will play with them. That is, the BEPS project is now entering the enforcement stage where the new set of rules is to be applied particularly to transfer pricing.

One trend that will certainly continue is the ongoing implementation of transfer pricing regulations around the world including documentation obligations. Over the last two years, it could be observed almost on a weekly basis that countries either adjusted their regulations to BEPS Action 13 and Action 8-10 or that countries implemented transfer pricing regulations on the basis of Action 13 as well as Action 8-10 for the very first time. In this regard, many developed countries only had to adjust to the new framework and did so by retaining what they liked in their old regulations while adding the minimum requirements of the new framework. As the vast majority of the intercompany transactions in terms of volume still takes place between developed countries, including China, it is of utmost importance that a consistent implementation, application, and interpretation of the regulations is ensured at least between those countries.

As stated earlier, however, the BEPS project put transfer pricing and the global allocation of income on the top of the agenda on a global scale. As a consequence, numerous developing countries introduced transfer pricing regulations in their local tax laws. Although most of them adhered fully to the new OECD Guidelines, it remains to be seen how such countries will apply the new framework in practice. In that respect, MNEs shall put particular focus on regions like Latin and South America, on Africa where more than 30 countries have enacted Action 13 in the meanwhile, or on smaller countries in South East Asia. These countries' tax administrations are typically not equipped with highly experienced international tax and transfer pricing practitioners and—even worse for taxpayers—in many cases, also do not have a large double tax treaty network that provides at least some protection against double taxation. If double taxation occurs due to local country transfer price adjustments, there is no way to resolve it by means of a mutual agreement procedure. It could be taken from press releases of, e.g., some African countries that they consider their new legislative transfer pricing framework as a major source of future tax revenues.

5.2 Increasing Risk of Double Taxation and Disputes

A major area of dispute to be expected by MNEs is the overarching goal of the transfer pricing related BEPS Actions which is the alignment of value creation and taxation. The major problem arising in this respect results from the fact that all of the hundreds of pages produced within the BEPS project do not include any clear definition of what "value creation" actually means and how taxpayers can document it. Rather, it is to be expected that tax authorities around the world will develop their own interpretation of the term "value creation" on a case by case basis. Taking into consideration that they will have access to an MNE's CbC Reports which allows them to calculate all kinds of ratios to "prove" that value is created in a certain country in particular (e.g., where a lot individuals are employed, assets are held, or sales are made), it is to be expected that many disputes will be grounded on this issue. Therefore, it will be key for taxpayers to address the issue of value creation comprehensively in the transfer pricing documentation and to have additional documentation available to substantiate their position in case of tax audits. Whereas developed countries usually tie value creation with the creation and existence of intangibles, it is to be expected that developing and emerging countries rather focus on items like low cost workforce, natural resources, market potential, and others and use the UN Transfer Pricing Manual as the basis for their argumentation.

In that context, it is also to be expected that more controversy arises around intercompany transactions that, in the past, were less in the focus of MNEs as they were deemed to be of a routine nature. Under the headline of value creation, many of the existing intercompany service agreements about routine types of services in the areas of contract manufacturing, contract research and development, contract marketing, etc. will be areas of challenge by tax authorities in the countries where these functions are located. Therefore, it will be critical for MNEs to document why these relationships are deemed to be of a routine nature and thus why the existing cost plus a rather low mark-up type of arrangements are in line with the arm's length principle. Over the last years and even before the BEPS project started, it could be observed that countries like China or India disagreed with the positions taken by MNEs in this respect and were quite successful to finally get to transfer pricing adjustments.

All in all, it is definitely fair to conclude that, in light of the new regulatory framework and the continuously growing number of countries implementing transfer pricing regulations, MNEs can expect (i) significantly more tax transfer pricing audits than in the past in (ii) many more countries than before. As transfer pricing audits result in a transfer pricing adjustment in the majority of the cases, MNEs will also face more double taxation than before the BEPS project. It needs to be seen whether the envisaged and announced improvements of dispute resolution processes will be able to cope with the increasing number of double taxation cases.

The major change to be expected as to the course of future tax audits is based on the unseen level of transparency that tax authorities will have about MNEs in the future. In that respect, certain information included in the master file like, e.g., the list and description of all unilateral advance pricing arrangements and other transfer pricing rulings will be an area of particular interest. Taxpayers should be aware that tax authorities will get access to such arrangements at the latest by exchange of information with the relevant tax administration and should thus be prepared to explain the nature of these arrangements to avoid adverse consequences. Going forward, MNEs might also have to rethink their unilateral APA strategies and analyze to what extent they could be converted into bi- or multilateral APAs.

5.3 Other International Developments Affecting Success of CbCR

In addition, the CbC Reports will obviously impact the future tax audit landscape. As the misuse of this information was expected during the BEPS project, the OECD provided guidance as to the purpose of the information and how it should be used. However, it would be a big surprise if this unseen level of transparency about the financial performance of taxpayers would not result in detrimental consequences. To a certain extent, it would only be "human" that tax authorities use this data to develop tax audit strategies in order to challenge the MNE's transfer pricing system. Taxpayers, therefore, should be well prepared to be able to explain potential outliers in terms of financial performance, alleged untypical legal structures within the group, or why certain group entities with a rather small number of employees deserve significant portions of the MNE's global income under the arm's length principle. Respective information may partly flow into the master file or local file but will potentially mainly be part of tax audit defense files prepared centrally on a headquarters level and be available in case it is needed on a global basis. In particular in this regard, the role of a central transfer pricing department of the MNE will be absolutely critical in the future as local group entities will typically not be able to respond to questions regarding the

CbC Reports. The first series of CbC Reports was submitted by taxpayers in various jurisdictions at the end of fiscal year 2017 and will be subject to information exchange in the course of 2018. It is to be expected that, from this point in time onwards, the quality, depth, and course of local country tax audits will undergo a dramatic change.

Finally, it needs to be observed how and to what extent two other current megatrends will impact the transfer pricing agenda and the way how MNEs need to document the arm's length nature of their global transfer pricing systems. These megatrends are protectionism and digitalization.

Regarding protectionism, it is very interesting to see that two major developed countries, i.e., the UK and the US, seem to step out and rather drive a political agenda that puts protectionism in the core of political behavior at a time where tremendous effort is put into a stronger global alignment and cooperation of countries in relation to international taxation,. The UK will leave the European Union in March 2019 and, by that time, will have to establish a political agenda that ensures a prospering future for the country. Although, so far, no developments are observable that indicate that the UK will no longer follow the OECD recommendations as to the interpretation of the arm's length principle, it can certainly not be excluded that the UK Government will have to protect UK headquartered companies after the BREXIT. In this respect, it can certainly be expected that the UK will also use its tax law to attract or retain foreign investment as was already done with the UK patent box regime. Historically, the UK has been a country where transfer pricing was not a key focus area of the HMRC to protect UK tax revenues. However, with the introduction of the diverted profits tax, the UK demonstrated that they are willing and able to take rather creative routes to enforce UK taxation. MNEs, therefore, are well advised to monitor the developments in the UK very closely.

Even more important for MNEs are the developments in the US. In the course of the BEPS project, the US took a leading role in regard to many of the actions and led a number of the BEPS working groups. However, in terms of implementing the BEPS framework, at least with regard to transfer pricing, it can be noted that not too much has happened yet. The US did implement CbC Reports but did not change its transfer pricing documentation regulations to be aligned with BEPS Action 13. It also does not seem to be inclined to adjust the 1-482 Regulations in light of BEPS Actions 8-10. Both result in significant challenges for non-US headquartered MNEs striving for a globally consistent transfer pricing documentation approach. In addition to that, the recently enacted US tax reform provides for numerous provisions that could result in transfer pricing controversy or at least in huge challenges for MNEs. Although the long discussed so-called border adjustment tax (BAT) did not find its way into the US tax laws which would have meant, more or less, the end of transfer pricing in the US,[10] other provisions like, e.g., the so-called base erosion anti-abuse tax (BEAT) or the foreign derived intangibles income (FDII) regime, have the potential to have a huge impact on MNEs' global transfer pricing. In this respect, it always has to be noted that

10. The BAT was a cash flow based tax regime that basically considered all intercompany cash flows going out of the US (imports of goods, services, etc.) as nondeductible and all intercompany cash flows into the US (exports of goods, services, etc.) as nontaxable.

the US group entities of a non-US headquartered MNE typically represent 30%-40% of the MNE's global sales revenues. Under the BEAT, even arm's length intercompany (outbound) transactions may end up to be subject to an additional tax and thus be partly nondeductible. The FDII incentivizes the creation of intangibles and the subsequent global exploitation of them out of the US by allowing a lower than usual taxation. Because of their potential magnitude, both new tax regimes will impact the way MNEs design their operating models going forward and thus will impact their transfer pricing systems and documentation approaches.

Even worse, the question arises to what extent protective developments like in the UK or the US will undermine the results achieved in the BEPS project.

Lastly, operating and tax models of MNEs are significantly affected by the largest disruptive development in history, i.e., digitalization. This relates in particular to the impact of digitalization on operating models of MNEs. BEPS Action 8-10 that resulted in significant changes of the transfer pricing guidelines in relation to the allocation of risks and the attribution of intangibles in light of the newly established DEMPE framework put the human being into the core of its considerations. That is, it is assumed that human beings eventually make decisions and thus determine risk assumption or intangible attribution. At the same time, the global digitalization process makes human beings less relevant and changes historical business models fundamentally. Therefore, it seems that many of the principles developed in scope of the BEPS project only in 2015 are already outdated in 2018. This creates a lot of uncertainty and thus risk for MNEs because they have to develop responses to the questions around digitalization today. Tax authorities, however, might only review this in two to five years from now and, at that time, will have a much clearer view and potentially even a regulatory framework to deal with the questions arising out of the changing business environment. This implies the risk for MNEs that tax authorities will use hindsight when examining the conclusions that MNEs draw today. Therefore, MNEs are well advised to prepare comprehensive documentation related to any business decisions that are taken regarding digitalization so that this is available at the time of future tax audits.

CHAPTER 6

Recent Developments on Comparability Analysis in Transfer Pricing

*Stefaan De Baets & Junling Gao**

* The views expressed are the views of the authors and are not necessarily the views of the PwC or any of its member firms.

1 INTRODUCTION

Comparability is at the center of transfer pricing and the application of the arm's length principle (ALP). The authoritative statement or definition of the ALP as expressed in Article 9 of both the OECD Model Tax Convention on Income and on Capital (OECD MTC) and the UN Model Double Taxation Convention between Developed and Developing Countries reads:

> [Where] conditions are made or imposed between the two [associated or related] enterprises in their commercial or financial relations which "differ" [emphasis added] from those which would be made between independent enterprises, then any profits which would, but for those conditions, have accrued to one of the enterprises, but, by reason of those conditions, have not so accrued, may be included in the profits of that enterprise and taxed accordingly.

The importance of a comparability analysis is well described in the 2017 United Nations Practical Manual on Transfer Pricing for Developing Countries (2017 UN Manual). It states that "a good comparability analysis is an essential step in any transfer pricing analysis in order to gain a correct understanding of the economically significant characteristics of the controlled transactions and of the respective roles of the parties to the controlled transaction. This will assist in the selection of the most appropriate transfer pricing method to the circumstances of the case. [...] In most cases, the application of the selected transfer pricing method will then rely on the identification of uncontrolled comparable transactions."[1]

Of note is that the definition of the arm's length principle does not use the term "transactions" but uses the—in the authors' opinion, broader—terms "relations" and "conditions." As the guidance that is published on transfer pricing also uses the term "transactions," the authors will also refer to this term.

In order to determine the differences between the conditions established between associated or related parties (in the so-called controlled transactions) and the conditions that third parties (in the so-called comparable uncontrolled transactions) agree upon—or would agree upon—it is obvious that one can only do so by "comparing"

1. 2017 UN Practical Manual on Transfer Pricing for Developing Countries—paras. B.2.5.2. and B.2.5.3.

those conditions. In other words, one has to define and analyze the following two terms of an equation:

Conditions controlled transactions ≈[2] *conditions comparable uncontrolled transactions*

This equation leads to a two-pronged approach under the so-called comparability analysis: defining the controlled transactions and the search for comparables.

This contribution will explore the recent developments on the comparability analysis in transfer pricing. It will give a brief history of the guidance on comparability since the first OECD transfer pricing guidelines (Transfer Pricing and Multinational Enterprises—Report of the OECD Committee of Fiscal Affairs—1979) were published up to and including the 2017 revision of the OECD Transfer Pricing Guidelines for Multinational Enterprises and Tax Administrations. It will also address the recent comparability issues addressed in guidance published by the United Nations, the Platform for Collaboration on Tax, the World Bank, and the EU Joint Transfer Pricing Forum (JTPF). It will also analyze the comparability aspects as they can be deduced from some recent State aid decisions of the European Union Commission (EC). Finally, it will discuss potential pitfalls and address possible improvements in the different reports as well as probable enhancements.

While the time span between the updates in the guidance was quite long in the past, the development in recent years has been continuous. The timeline shown in Figure 6.1 gives an overview of the recent developments and publications of the international organizations in the area of transfer pricing.

2. The symbol ≈ is used to indicate that it is not necessary to have an absolute match between the controlled and uncontrolled transactions.

Figure 6.1 Timeline: Publications on Transfer Pricing by International Organizations

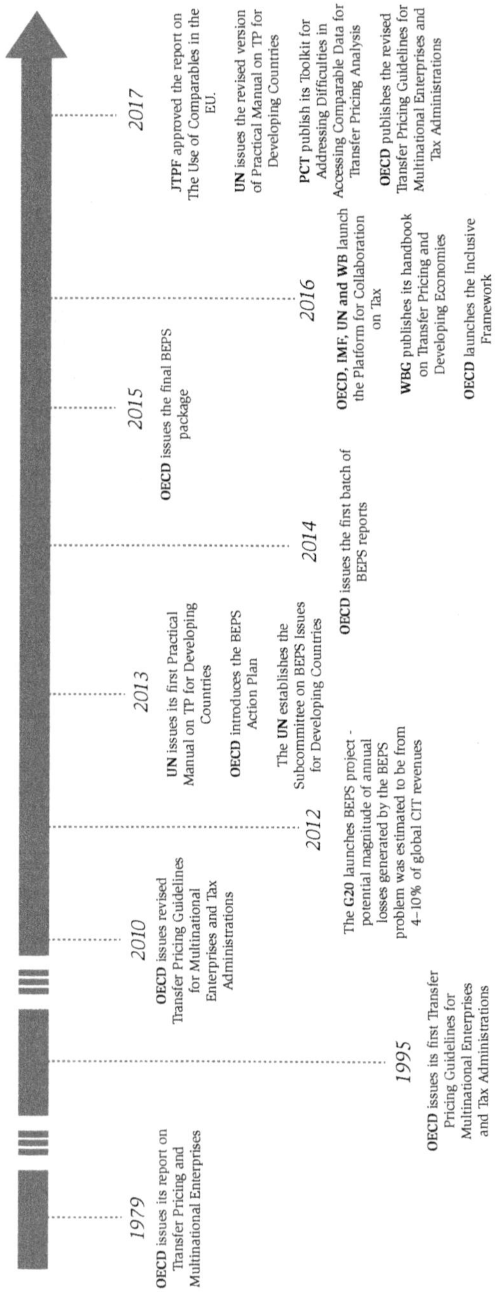

2 OECD HISTORICAL DEVELOPMENTS ON STANDARDS OF COMPARABILITY

Over the past decades, the international authoritative guidance on the ALP and the standards of comparability have mainly emerged from OECD work. The following sections briefly outline the historical development of OECD guidance on comparability from the first OECD transfer pricing report published back in 1979 up to and including the 2017 revision of the OECD Transfer Pricing Guidelines for Multinational Enterprises and Tax Administrations.

2.1 1979 OECD Report: Transfer Pricing and Multinational Enterprises[3]

The 1979 OECD Report of the OECD Committee on Fiscal Affairs—Transfer Pricing and Multinational Enterprises (hereafter, 1979 Report) did not contain detailed guidance on how to perform a comparability analysis except for a short discussion on functional analysis under the General Considerations of the Report.[4] Although the discussion was relatively short, the 1979 Report focused on the importance of analyzing the functions of the various entities in a multinational enterprise (MNE). The 1979 Report already recognized the importance of identifying the first leg of the comparability equation, i.e., defining the controlled transaction.

The concept of "comparability" was, for the first time, cited in the 1979 Report in the context of the application of the ALP. Paragraph 48 of the 1979 Report stated that:

> The comparable uncontrolled price method offers the most direct way of determining an arm's length price. The transfer price is set by reference to comparable transactions between a buyer and a seller who are not associated enterprises [...]. The method requires the uncontrolled transactions to be carefully reviewed for "comparability" [emphasis added] with controlled transactions.[5]

The 1979 Report further cited the need for comparability of: geographic markets,[6] market levels,[7] goods,[8] functions performed and risks assumed by resellers,[9] and other considerations such as product innovativeness, market conditions, custom of the trade, how the MNE is organized, general economic functions, and "all other relevant facts and circumstances of each individual case [...]."[10] Unfortunately, no further guidance was developed at that stage.

3. OECD, *Transfer Pricing and Multinational Enterprises* (Paris: OECD Publishing, 1979).
4. 1979 Report, *supra* n. 3, at para. 17.
5. 1979 Report, *supra* n. 3, at para. 48.
6. 1979 Report, *supra* n. 3, at para. 49.
7. 1979 Report, *supra* n. 3, at para. 50.
8. 1979 Report, *supra* n. 3, at paras. 51–54.
9. 1979 Report, *supra* n. 4, at para. 59.
10. 1979 Report, *supra* n. 4, at para. 55.

2.2 1995 OECD Transfer Pricing Guidelines for Multinational Enterprises and Tax Administrations[11]

The OECD Transfer Pricing Guidelines for Multinational Enterprises and Tax Administrations were first published in their original version in 1995 (1995 OECD TPG). They were intended as a revision and compilation of previous reports by the OECD Committee on Fiscal Affairs. The 1995 OECD TPG already contained detailed provisions on comparability including a discussion of functional analysis that was applicable to all transfer pricing methods and set forth five factors that can influence the comparability of controlled and uncontrolled transactions for purposes of applying the ALP.[12] These are:

- characteristics of property or services;
- functional analysis (functions performed taking into account assets used and risks assumed);
- contractual terms;
- economic circumstances; and
- business strategies.

In this respect, the 1995 OECD TPG made a significant development regarding the factor on business strategies. The 1979 Report barely recognized the possible effects of business strategies on pricing policy as well as the need to adjust for any difference in business strategies between controlled and uncontrolled transactions. The 1979 Report acknowledged two examples of business strategies that might significantly influence price: (1) a supplier waives payment from a customer "in temporary difficulties in order to preserve a potentially valuable outlet for his goods;"[13] and (2) sellers temporarily lower prices as part of a market penetration or start-up strategy.[14]

The 1995 OECD TPG already contained a nonexhaustive list of business strategies that could influence price including elements such as market penetration, innovation and new product development, degree of diversification, risk aversion, assessment of political changes, and input of existing and planned labor laws. [15] The 1995 OECD TPG cited market penetration schemes as one example[16] and specifically acknowledged that market penetration schemes may fail and gave some guidance on how to approach a strategy where profits are lowered temporarily in return for higher profits in the long run.

11. OECD, *Transfer Pricing Guidelines for Multinational Enterprises and Tax Administrations* (Paris: OECD Publishing, 1995).
12. 1995 OECD TPG, *supra* n. 11, at paras. 1.19–1.35.
13. 1979 Report, *supra* n. 3, at para. 40.
14. 1979 Report, *supra* n. 3, at para. 43.
15. 1995 OECD TPG, *supra* n. 11, at paras. 1.31–1.35. Note the phrases "such as" and "could include" when referring to business strategies.
16. 1995 OECD TPG, *supra* n. 11, at paras. 1.32–1.35.

2.3 2010 OECD Transfer Pricing Guidelines for Multinational Enterprises and Tax Administrations

After its publication in 1995, the first significant update of comparability standards of the OECD TPG occurred in 2010.[17] In the 2010 OECD Transfer Pricing Guidelines for Multinational Enterprises and Tax Administrations (2010 OECD TPG),[18] the general guidance on the comparability analysis described in Chapter I of the 1995 OECD TPG is updated, and the TPG are completed with a new Chapter III containing detailed guidance on how to perform a comparability analysis and an illustration of a possible working capital adjustment to improve comparability, when appropriate. The updated standards of comparability provided in the 2010 OECD TPG thoroughly emphasized the importance of aligning the facts and circumstances with an in-depth analysis of the five comparability factors.

The section that discusses the five OECD comparability factors is expanded with a new paragraph that reflects the need for a balanced approach on how the comparability factors should be assessed. The linkage between the applicable transfer pricing methods and comparability factors is made much more explicit. It states:

> Both the nature of the controlled transaction and the transfer pricing method adopted should be taken into account when evaluating the relative importance of any missing piece of information on possible comparables, [...] If it can be reasonably assumed that the unadjusted difference is not likely to have a material effect on the comparability, the uncontrolled transaction at issue should not be rejected as potentially comparable, despite some pieces of information being missing.[19]

This balanced approach (or reasonableness test) towards comparability factors is further specifically addressed in the discussion around the first comparability factor (characteristics of property or services),[20] the third comparability factor (contractual terms),[21] and the fourth comparability factor (economic circumstances).[22] Furthermore, consideration is also given to the notion of local country comparables versus regional comparables, and the 2010 OECD TPG provides support for reliance upon regional approaches if the facts and circumstances of the MNE are consistent within the defined region.[23]

17. A limited update was made in 2009 primarily to reflect the adoption in the 2008 version of the OECD MTC of a new paragraph 5 of Article 25 dealing with arbitration and of changes to the Commentary on Article 25 on Mutual Agreement Procedures. The 2009 update did not contain updated guidance with regard to comparability and, therefore, is not discussed in this contribution.
18. OECD, *Transfer Pricing Guidelines for Multinational Enterprises and Tax Administrations* (Paris: OECD Publishing, 2010).
19. 2010 OECD TPG, *supra* n. 18, at para. 1.38.
20. 2010 OECD TPG, *supra* n. 18, at paras. 1.40–1.41.
21. 2010 OECD TPG, *supra* n. 18, at para. 1.54.
22. 2010 OECD TPG, *supra* n. 18, at para. 1.55.
23. 2010 OECD TPG, *supra* n. 18, at paras. 1.57–1.58.

The 2010 OECD TPG further introduces a new Chapter III dedicated to the analysis of comparability, *inter alia*, with the aim of selecting reliable comparables. Some key changes and items which are, for the first time, endorsed by the OECD are further discussed in the sections below.

2.3.1 *Most Reliable Comparables*

The 2010 OECD TPG introduces the concept of "most reliable comparables" which plays a prominent role in the typical process in performing a comparability analysis established in Chapter III (*see* section 2.3.2). It states that, in principle, the comparability analysis aims at finding the most reliable comparable. The 2010 OECD TPG, however, acknowledges that finding the most reliable comparables does not entail a requirement for an exhaustive search of all possible sources of comparables in view of information limitations and the potentially burdensome nature of a comparables search.[24] This is again an expression that reviewers in transfer pricing must be reasonable in their analysis.

2.3.2 *The Nine-Step Process*

The OECD introduced a nine-step process, as shown in Table 6.1, that could be used when performing a comparability analysis. It explicitly states that such a process is not compulsory as reliability of the outcome is more important than the process itself; and it further continues to clarify that "going through the process does not provide any guarantee that the outcome will be arm's length, and not going through the process does not imply that the outcome will not be arm's length."[25] Most of the steps are relatively straightforward but require thorough factual analysis. The focus of the nine-step process is on finding reliable comparables.

Table 6.1 The Nine-Step Process

1	Determination of years to be covered.
2	Broad-based analysis of the taxpayer's circumstances.
3	Understanding the controlled transaction(s) under examination based in particular on a functional analysis in order to choose the tested party (where needed), the most appropriate transfer pricing method for the circumstances of the case, the financial indicator that will be tested (in the case of a transactional profit method), and to identify the significant comparability factors that should be taken into account.
4	Review of existing internal comparables, if any.

24. 2010 OECD TPG, *supra* n. 18, at para. 3.2.
25. 2010 OECD TPG, *supra* n. 18, at para. 3.4.

5	Determination of available sources of information on external comparables when where such external comparables are needed taking into account their relative reliability.
6	Selection of the most appropriate transfer pricing method and, depending on the method, determination of the relevant financial indicator (e.g., determination of the relevant net profit indicator in case of a transactional net margin method).
7	Identification of potential comparables: determining the key characteristics to be met by any uncontrolled transaction in order to be regarded as potentially comparable based on the relevant factors identified in 3 and in accordance with the five comparability factors (characteristics of property and services, functional analysis, contractual arrangements, economic circumstances, and business strategies).
8	Determination of and making comparability adjustments where appropriate.
9	Interpretation and use of data collected, determination of the arm's length remuneration.

The guidance further indicates that the process is not a linear one, and there might be a need to repeatedly carry out certain steps.

Each of these steps is then discussed in further detail. The guidance states that the broad-based analysis is an essential step in the comparability analysis including analysis of the industry, competition, economic, and regulatory factors.[26] In reviewing the controlled transaction and choice of the tested party, the 2010 OECD TPG continues to state that the ALP should be applied on a transaction-by-transaction basis. However, a portfolio approach is introduced under which certain transactions can be bundled if the portfolio approach is part of the company's business strategy.[27] Furthermore, the term "tested party" is also introduced which should be the party with the less complex functional analysis.[28] Although not as expressly stated as in the 2017 revision of the OECD TPG, the two legs of the comparability equation (defining the controlled transaction and looking for comparable uncontrolled transactions) are already clearly present in the 2010 OECD TPG.

Reviewing of existing internal comparables is considered a significant step in view of the fact that internal comparables are often overlooked in practice. The 2010 OECD TPG, however, recognize that internal comparables may have a more direct and closer relationship to the transaction under review than external comparables but are not always necessarily more reliable.[29] The use of foreign-source or nondomestic comparables and their relative reliability should be assessed on a case-by-case basis by reference to the five comparability factors instead of default or automatic rejections of nondomestic comparables.[30]

26. 2010 OECD TPG, *supra* n. 18, at para. 3.7.
27. 2010 OECD TPG, *supra* n. 18, at paras. 3.9–3.10.
28. 2010 OECD TPG, *supra* n. 18, at para. 3.18.
29. 2010 OECD TPG, *supra* n. 18, at paras. 3.27–3.28.
30. 2010 OECD TPG, *supra* n. 18, at para. 3.35.

2.3.3 *Comparability Adjustments*

The 2010 OECD TPG contained, at that time, newly developed guidance on comparability adjustments. The guidance also indicated that there should be no presumption that comparability adjustments are always needed or will always improve comparability or its reliability. It is a matter of judgment that should be evaluated in light of the costs and compliance burden.[31] The OECD took the safe route by providing only illustrative guidance regarding working capital adjustments in an Annex to Chapter III. The challenges that are often encountered in practice pertaining to differences in, for instance, volume or operational scale, risks or geographic markets, however, are not really addressed with practical guidance, but the discussion remains theoretical.

2.3.4 *Arm's Length Range*

The 2010 OECD TPG also gives guidance on the use of an arm's length range (and the appropriate point within such a range) and provides consideration for the treatment of extreme results (e.g., eliminations of loss-making comparables if the losses do not reflect normal business conditions) to enhance the quality of the range and minimize error due to unknown facts or defects by using measures of central tendency. For the first time, the OECD endorsed the use of an interquartile range, albeit in terms which do not preclude the use of other statistical approaches that may be appropriate in the particular circumstance of a case. [32]

With the publication of the 2010 OECD TPG, the updated guidance confirmed approaches (such as, for example, interquartile ranges or working capital adjustments) that were already used in practice for a long time. Theory met practice again with the 2010 OECD TPG.

2.4 2017 OECD Transfer Pricing Guidelines for Multinational Enterprises and Tax Administrations

On July 10, 2017, the OECD released its 2017 version of the OECD Transfer Pricing Guidelines for Multinational Enterprises and Tax Administrations (2017 OECD TPG)[33] which further aims at clarifying and strengthening the guidance on the application of the ALP and standards of comparability. In this respect, the OECD has fundamentally redrafted Chapter I, Section D ("Guidance for applying the arm's length principle") of the 2010 OECD TPG, in particular, Section D. 1. which is renamed from "Comparability analysis" to "Identifying the commercial or financial relations."

The 2017 OECD TPG expands the discussion on the comparability analysis, the essential part of application of the ALP, with guidance on the important first leg of the comparability analysis that is now referred to as "accurately delineating the actual

31. 2010 OECD TPG, *supra* n. 18, at paras. 3.47 and 3.52.
32. 2010 OECD TPG, *supra* n. 18, at paras. 3.55–3.66.
33. OECD, *Transfer Pricing Guidelines for Multinational Enterprises and Tax Administrations* (OECD Publishing, 2017).

transaction." It requires determining whether a controlled transaction has economic substance and involves a significantly more granular functional and risk analysis. In particular, the granularity and complexity of the analysis may give rise to concerns. In other words, the 2017 OECD TPG expressly indicates the two phases under a comparability analysis:

(1) accurately delineating the actual transaction (or real deal) on the basis of economically relevant characteristics or comparability factors; and
(2) making comparisons between the controlled transaction and uncontrolled transaction on the basis of the economically relevant characteristics or comparability factors in order to determine an appropriate arm's length price or remuneration.

In other words, the first phase determines the real deal between the related parties. The second phase is used to search for comparable uncontrolled transactions or enterprises.

The five-step process outlined below is provided in the guidelines to accurately delineate the transactions. For each transaction, the process involves reviews of:[34]

- the contractual terms of the transactions;
- the functions, assets, and risks of each participant including an assessment of how these relate to the wider generation of value within the group;
- the characteristics of the property transferred or services provided;
- the economic circumstances of the parties and of the market in which the parties operate;
- the business strategies pursued by the parties.

This five-step process corresponds to the five comparability factors set forth in the 1995 and 2010 OECD TPG, albeit the order of the factors being analyzed is slightly adjusted (*see* Table 6.2).

Table 6.2 Comparability Factors

1995–2010 OECD TPG		*2017 OECD TPG*
Characteristics of property or services		Contractual terms
Functional analysis		Functional analysis
Contractual terms		Characteristics of property or services
Economic circumstances		Economic circumstances
Business strategies		Business strategies

34. 2017 OECD TPG, *supra* n. 33, at paras. 1.33–1.118.

The more salient changes that were made to the first two comparability factors ("contractual terms" and "functional analysis") are discussed below. From the order of the comparability factors in the 2017 OECD TPG, it is now made clear that the starting point of the analysis are the contractual terms.

2.4.1 *Contractual Terms*

The 2017 OECD TPG suggests taking written contractual agreements as the starting point for delineation of the transactions between the associated enterprises and the division of responsibilities, risks, and anticipated outcomes.[35] It further states that information from the written contracts should be clarified and supplemented by considering evidence of the commercial or financial relations provided by the other four comparability factors.[36] An analysis of all five comparability factors should provide evidence of the actual conduct of the parties. The 2017 OECD TPG goes further and provides that, when no written contracts or terms exist or the terms of the written contracts are incomplete, delineating a transaction on the basis of the actual conduct of the parties would generally provide results that are more reliable.[37]

2.4.2 *Functional Analysis: In Particular Allocation of Risks*

Newly developed guidance is provided for conducting a functional analysis especially with regard to the allocation of risks to the parties in a transaction.

The guidance of Chapter IX on Business Restructurings of the 2010 OECD TPG already contained a more in-depth discussion on the allocation of risks in an Article 9 context and, in particular, the interpretation and application of the high-level discussion on risks in Chapter I of the 2010 OECD TPG. The authors believe, however, that Chapter I of the OECD TPG is the appropriate place for such in-depth discussion.

Under the new guidance, irrespective of the contractual allocation of risks (and associated expected return), the risks need to be allocated to the parties that have the control over such risks and have the financial capacity to assume such risks. Control over risk is defined as[38]

(1) The capability to make decisions to take on, lay off, or decline a risk-bearing opportunity together *"with the actual performance"* [emphasis added] of that decision-making function (i.e., who makes the decisions and performs the function to take on, lay off or decline risk); and
(2) The capability to make decisions on whether and how to respond to the risk-bearing opportunity together *"with the actual performance"* [emphasis added] of that decision-making function (i.e., who makes the decisions and performs the related functions responding to risk).

35. 2017 OECD TPG, *supra* n. 33, at para. 1.42.
36. 2017 OECD TPG, *supra* n. 33, at para. 1.43.
37. 2017 OECD TPG, *supra* n. 33, at para. 1.49.
38. 2017 OECD TPG, *supra* n. 33, at para. 1.65.

Performance of risk mitigation functions (or day-to-day risk mitigation) is not necessary to have control over the risk, and these functions can be outsourced. When these risk mitigation functions are outsourced, it is still required to have the "end-control" over those functions, for example, hiring, adapting, or terminating the contract with the risk provider or objective setting and control on whether the objectives of risk mitigation are met.[39]

It is needless to say that the analysis of risks and of the functional control of the risks and the financial capacity to assume the risks thus become pivotal elements of the expanded functional analysis.

The 2017 OECD TPG points out the importance of understanding how value is generated by the groups as a whole, the interdependencies of the functions performed, and the contributions that the parties make to that value creation.[40] However, the guidance goes further and states that a functional analysis is incomplete unless the material risks assumed by the parties are identified and considered in the analysis. The new guidance emphasizes the significance of risk allocation in transfer pricing and its interrelation with "human interaction" (i.e., "functions") and presents a six-step process for the arm's length pricing of risks on a transaction-by-transaction basis as illustrated in Figures 6.2 and 6.3.[41]

39. 2017 OECD TPG, *supra* n. 33, at para. 1.64.
40. 2017 OECD TPG, *supra* n. 33, at para. 1.51.
41. 2017 OECD TPG, *supra* n. 33, at paras. 1.56–1.70.

Figure 6.2 Six-Step Risk Analysis Approach

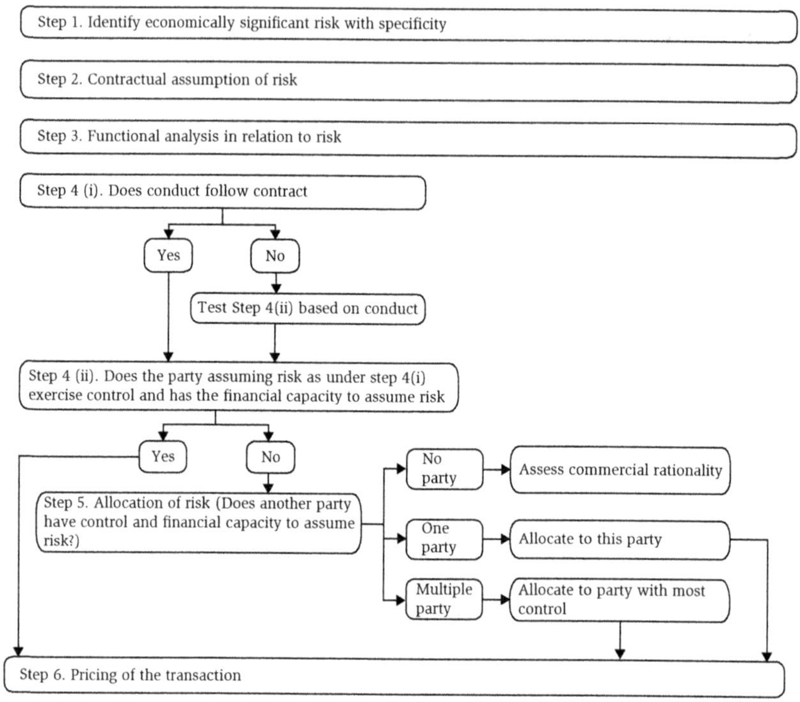

Figure 6.3 Risk Management Functions

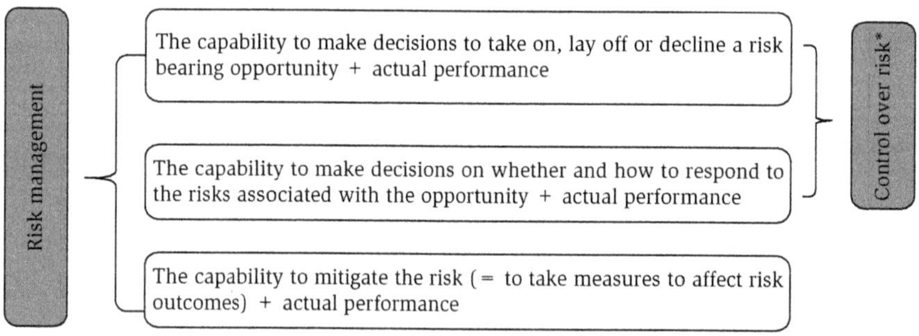

* Including control over outsourced day-to-day risk mitigations functions

Step 1: Identify economically significant risks with specificity

The first step advocated by the OECD aims at identifying the risks that should be considered in the course of a transfer pricing analysis. A materiality threshold is introduced by focusing on identifying only economically *significant* risks with specificity. The 2017 OECD TPG broadly define risk as "the effect of uncertainty on the objective of business."[42] The sources of risk may include but are not limited to: (1) strategic risk or marketplace risks; (2) infrastructure or operational risks; (3) financial risks; (4) transactional risks; and (5) hazard risks.[43]

Under the new guidance, determining the economic significance of risk and how risk may affect the pricing of a controlled transaction is part of the functional analysis on how value is created by the group and the activities that allow the group to sustain profits.[44]

Step 2: Contractual assumption of risk

The second step consists of determining the group entities which contractually assume the risks identified under Step 1. Written contracts between the parties to a transaction typically describe the party or parties assuming the specific risks. The 2017 OECD TPG states that it should not be concluded that the pricing arrangements adopted in the contractual agreement alone determine which party assumes risk (conduct test).[45]

Step 3: Functional analysis in relation to risk

This step analyzes the functions in relation to risk of the associated enterprises that are parties to the transaction. Under such an analysis, it is paramount to determine which enterprise(s): [46]

- perform(s) risk management functions. This function covers two types of activities being control over risk functions and risk mitigation functions;
- bear(s) the upside or downside consequences of risk outcomes; and
- has/have the financial capacity to assume the risk.

As already indicated, under the new guidance, control over risk[47] requires: (1) the capacity to make decisions to take on, lay off, or decline a risk-bearing opportunity together with the actual performance of that decision-making function; and (2) the capacity to make decisions on whether and how to respond to the risks associated with the opportunity together with the actual performance of that decision-making function. This implies that these functions are executed by the persons who, in practice, decide whether or not to pursue an opportunity and decide on the risks to take on board. Performing the day-to-day risk mitigation is not required in order for a party to have control over the risk. It is possible to outsource the day-to-day risk mitigation but not the functions associated with the control over risk.

The financial capacity[48] to assume a risk is defined in the 2017 OECD TPG as access to funding to take on the risk or to lay off the risk, to pay for the risk mitigation functions, and to bear the consequence of risk materialization.

42. 2017 OECD TPG, *supra* n. 33, at para. 1.71.
43. 2017 OECD TPG, *supra* n. 33, at para. 1.72.
44. 2017 OECD TPG, *supra* n. 33, at para. 1.73.
45. 2017 OECD TPG, *supra* n. 33, at para. 1.81.
46. 2017 OECD TPG, *supra* n. 33, at para. 1.82.
47. 2017 OECD TPG, *supra* n. 33, at para. 1.65.
48. 2017 OECD TPG, *supra* n. 33, at para. 1.64.

With regard to which party should be allocated the risk in a transaction on the basis of the guidance on control over risk and the financial capacity to assume the risk, the authors want to point out a significant change in approach between the 2010 and 2017 OECD TPG. The 2010 OECD TPG indicates that control over risk or the financial capacity to assume the risk are relevant, although not determinative factors that can assist in the determination of whether a risk allocation in a controlled transaction is one which could be found between independent parties.[49] Under the 2017 OECD TPG, both conditions (i.e., having control over the risk and having the financial capacity to assume the risk) must be fulfilled before it is determined which party assumes the risks. This can be considered to be a more stringent approach than under the 2010 OECD TPG.

Step 4: Interpreting Steps 1–3

Based on the information collected in Steps 1–3 regarding the assumption and management of risks, Step 4 is to analyze:[50]

(1) *whether the parties follow the contractual terms in terms of the assumption of risk*. In case the contractual assumption of risk is not aligned with the conduct of the parties, the latter will prevail and will be considered as best evidence of the intentions of the parties and be subject to further transfer pricing analysis;
(2) *whether the party controls the risk and has the financial capacity to assume the risk*. If it does, the analysis can directly jump to Step 6. If it does not, the analysis continues with Step 5.

The 2017 OECD TPG also provides guidance as to which entity a risk should be allocated to in the case when more than one entity is capable of exercising control over a risk. The guiding principle remains unchanged. If the entity either does not exercise control over the risk or does not possess the financial capacity to assume the risk, the analysis under Step 5 needs to be performed.[51]

Step 5: Allocation of risk

If the entity (contractually) assuming the risk does not exercise control over the risk or does not have the financial capacity to assume the risk, then the risk should be allocated to the entity exercising control and having the financial capacity to assume the risk. The 2017 OECD TPG also states that, in case multiple parties exercise control over risk and have the financial capacity to assume the risk, then the risk should be allocated to the party exercising the most control.[52] The other parties should, nevertheless, be appropriately compensated according to the significance of the control they exerted over the risk. It is unclear, however, how exercising the most control should be evaluated or analyzed.

49. 2010 OECD TPG, *supra* n. 33, at paras. 9.22–9.32.
50. 2017 OECD TPG, *supra* n. 33, at para. 1.86.
51. 2017 OECD TPG, *supra* n. 33, at paras. 1.93–1.97.
52. 2017 OECD TPG, *supra* n. 33, at paras. 1.98.

Step 6: Pricing of the transaction, taking account of the consequences of risk allocation

The last step is to price the accurately delineated transaction in accordance with the tools and methods set out in Chapters II (transfer pricing methods) and III (comparability analysis) of the 2017 OECD TPG. The financial and other consequences of risk-assumption and the remuneration for risk management should also be taken into account.

2.4.3 *Evaluation on the Guidance on the Accurate Delineation of the Actual Transaction*

The revised guidance in the 2017 OECD TPG stresses the importance of looking beyond the contracts to the actual conduct of the parties in order to establish the "real deal." The guidance now seems to indicate that the conduct of the parties "effectively controls the definition of the taxpayer's transactions regardless of the content of related party contracts."[53] This actually replaces the substance-over-form approach that was embedded in the guidance since 1995 and allowed tax authorities to recharacterize the transaction. Also, the commercial rationality factor is still vague, in particular as a transaction should not be disregarded just because no comparables exist. The accurate delineation of the transactions may give rise to different interpretations of the same facts leading to disputes and controversies between taxpayer(s) and tax authorities and also between the different tax authorities.

2.4.4 *Evaluation of the Guidance on Risk*

In order to be assigned the assumption of the risk and to receive premium returns from that assumption, a party must actually fulfill the following conditions:

- the party must be assigned the contractual allocation of the risk;[54]
- the party must bear the financial consequences of the realization of the risk;[55]
- some, but not all, decisions with regard to the risk (take on, lay off, respond to, and mitigate) must be taken by the party's staff;[56]
- supervision of the outsourced risk mitigation function by the party's staff.[57]

It is not clear, however, how these conditions will work out in practice.

It may seem from the 2017 OECD TPG that two or more parties may jointly assume a risk and jointly control the risk.[58] This would seemingly still allow cost contribution arrangement (CCA) structures, although each participant should exercise

53. Richard S Collier, Joseph L Andrus, 2017, Transfer Pricing and the Arm's Length Principle after BEPS, Oxford University Press 2017, Oxford, at para. 6.11.
54. 2017 OECD TPG, *supra* n. 33, at paras. 1.77–1.81.
55. 2017 OECD TPG, *supra* n. 33, at paras. 1.88–1.89.
56. 2017 OECD TPG, *supra* n. 33, at paras. 1.94–1.95.
57. 2017 OECD TPG, *supra* n. 33, at para. 1.65.
58. 2017 OECD TPG, *supra* n. 33, at para. 1.95.

control over the risk. Another point of uncertainty is that, between unrelated parties, sharing of risk is certainly not an exception. This may contrast with the guidance that, in case more than one enterprise in the multinational controls a risk and has the financial capacity to control it, the risk should be allocated to the party that exercises most control. This approach would seem to go against practice between third parties and one could, therefore, wonder whether the approach is at arm's length. [59]

Looking at the six-step approach and the guidance on risks, one can only conclude that the guidance is very complex—as is the result of all BEPS outcomes. In the case of the risk analysis between related parties, one should, in principle—be it with an extended burden or more red tape—be able to analyze the risk functions. When performing the same analysis between unrelated parties, the risk analysis will become very burdensome, if possible at all. The million dollar question is how to retrieve that information that is needed in the absence of internal comparables. Some conformity changes have been introduced in Chapter III on comparability analysis but, in particular with regard to the nine-step process and the selection of reliable comparables, no guidance has been developed on how the six-step risk analysis could be married with the nine-step process.

Throughout the 2017 OECD TPG, different expressions with regard to risk are used. For example, the 2017 OECD TPG uses the terms "important risks,"[60] "relevant risks,"[61] and more predominantly "economically significant risk."[62] It is unclear whether these terms should be read as having the same meaning or whether they should be interpreted as having a different meaning.

Tax authorities will undoubtedly focus their attention dynamically on the risk discussion, giving rise to uncertainty, controversy, and disputes. In view of the lukewarm reception of mandatory arbitration under BEPS Action 14 and the multilateral instrument, an increase in double taxation and a spike in resulting disputes may be expected.

2.4.5 *Revised Guidance on Safe Harbors*

The revised guidance in the 2017 OECD TPG on safe harbors actually predates the BEPS project. In early 2012, the OECD embarked on a project on simplification of transfer pricing. One outcome of that project was the 2013 Report on the Revised Section E on safe harbors of Chapter IV of the OECD TPG.[63]

Safe harbors are defined as a provision that applies to a defined category of taxpayers or transactions and that relieves qualifying taxpayers from certain

59. 2017 OECD TPG, *supra* n. 33, at para. 1.98.
60. 2017 OECD TPG, *supra* n. 33, at paras. 1.34; 6.59 and Annex I to Chapter V: Transfer Pricing Documentation—Master File.
61. 2017 OECD TPG, *supra* n. 33, at paras. 1.59; 6.42; 6.45; 6.68; 6.152; and 62—Annex to Chapter VI: Examples on Intangibles.
62. 2017 OECD TPG, *supra* n. 33, at paras. 1.60; 1.82; 1.83; 1.84; 1.85; 1.88; 1.103; 2.39; 6.4; 6.34; 6.61; 6.70; 6.72; 9.19; 9.22; 9.23; 9.90; 9.108; 9.112; and section 1.2.1.1.
63. 2013 OECD Report, Revised Section E on Safe Harbours in Chapter IV of the Transfer Pricing Guidelines.

obligations under the general transfer pricing rules of a jurisdiction. In other words, it introduces simpler obligations for the qualifying taxpayers or may even exempt them (for example, small taxpayers) from certain obligations. They allow for simplified compliance and reduction in compliance costs, provide certainty to both taxpayers and tax authorities when the qualifying conditions of the safe harbors are met, and allow tax authorities to redirect resources to other—more risky—taxpayers or transactions. In particular, safe harbors can be useful for developing economies.

The negative recommendations on safe harbors in the 1995 and 2010 OECD TPG were departed from and turned into positive guidance, in particular for bilateral or multilateral safe harbors. The new guidance stresses the significant relief from compliance burden and complexity without creating double (non-)taxation.[64] The inclusion of three sample Memoranda of Understanding to conclude bilateral safe harbors on low-risk distribution services, low-risk contract manufacturing services, and low-risk R&D services[65] should help particularly developing economies in concluding bilateral safe harbors.

The use of bilateral safe harbors may overcome the complexity under the appropriate circumstances of a comparability analysis. Unfortunately, to date, there is very little experience with bilateral or multilateral safe harbors.

From all of the above, it may be concluded that, even though the 2017 Update was supposed to give more guidance and clarification on the application of ALP and the comparability analysis, in fact, it added even more complexity to the latter issue.

3 INTERNATIONAL GUIDANCE ON STANDARDS OF COMPARABILITY FROM OTHER INTERNATIONAL ORGANIZATIONS

Over the past few years, international guidance on standards of comparability in applying the ALP have also emerged from other sources including the United Nations, the World Bank Group, the EU JTPF, and the Platform for Collaboration on Tax. Most of the work on standards of comparability from those organizations are broadly consistent with the OECD approach (*see* Section 2).

3.1 The United Nations

In 2013, the United Nations published the first edition of the Practical Manual on Transfer Pricing for Developing Countries (2013 UN Manual).[66] In this Manual the United Nations acknowledge the ALP as the international standard. Consistency with the OECD TPG was sought when drafting the 2013 UN Manual. On April 7, 2017, the United Nations released the second edition of the UN Manual (2017 UN Manual)[67] which provides revised guidance on, amongst others, the comparability analysis. The

64. 2017 OECD TPG, *supra* n. 33, at para. 4.130.
65. 2017 OECD TPG, *supra* n. 33, Annex I to Chapter IV: Sample Memoranda of Understanding for Safe Harbours.
66. United Nations, *Practical Manual on Transfer Pricing for Developing Countries* (2013).
67. United Nations, *Practical Manual on Transfer Pricing for Developing Countries* (2017).

2017 UN Manual incorporates aspects of the changes to the OECD TPG following the final papers of the OECD/G20 Base Erosion and Profit Shifting (BEPS) Project released in 2015.

The standards of comparability contained in the 2017 UN Manual are mainly based on the same principles as in the OECD TPG.[68] The framework of the comparability analysis is based on the comparability factors defined in the OECD TPG including the characteristics of the property or service transferred; the functions performed by the parties, taking into account the new six-step risk analysis process provided in the updated OECD guidance; contractual terms; economic circumstances; and business strategies that are pursued.[69] The comparability analysis process provided in the 2017 UN Manual details a similar, although slightly different, process compared to the typical nine-step process provided for in the OECD TPG (*see* Table 6.3).

Table 6.3 The OECD Nine-Step Process and Its Equivalent in the 2017 UN Manual

	Typical Process in Chapter III on Comparability Analysis of the 2017 OECD Transfer Pricing Guidelines	*Equivalent in the Discussion on Comparability Analysis in the 2017 UN Practical Manual on Transfer Pricing for Developing Countries*
Broad-based analysis	Step 1 on determination of the years to be covered Step 2 on broad-based analysis of the taxpayer's circumstances—analysis of the industry, competition, economic and regulatory factors as well as other factors affecting the taxpayer and its environment (but not yet at a transactional level)	Section B.2.3.1 on understanding the significant characteristics of the industry, business, and controlled transactions
Accurate delineation of the transaction	Step 3 on understanding the controlled transaction or transactions under review based in particular on a functional analysis, in order to choose the tested party (when needed), the most appropriate transfer pricing method, the financial indicator (when needed under a transactional profit method), and the significant comparability factors that should be considered	Section B.2.3.1.4 on identification of the accurately delineated transaction Section B.2.3.2 on examination of the comparability factors of the controlled transaction Section B.2.3.3 on selection of the tested party

68. 2017 OECD TPG, *supra* n. 33. *Chapter III, Comparability Analysis*.
69. United Nations, *supra* n. 67, section B.2.3.2.

	Typical Process in Chapter III on Comparability Analysis of the 2017 OECD Transfer Pricing Guidelines	*Equivalent in the Discussion on Comparability Analysis in the 2017 UN Practical Manual on Transfer Pricing for Developing Countries*
Initial review of possible sources of information on comparables	Step 4 on review of existing internal comparables, if any Step 5 on determining the available sources of information on external comparables when such comparables are needed taking into account their relative reliability	Section B.2.3.4 on identifying potentially comparable transactions or companies
Select the most appropriate transfer pricing method	Step 6 on selecting the most appropriate transfer pricing method and, depending on the method, determining the relevant financial indicator (for example, in the case of a TNMM)	Section B.2.3.6 on comparability considerations in the selection of transfer pricing methods
Identification of potential comparables	Step 7 on identifying potential comparables including determining the key characteristics to be met by any uncontrolled transaction in order to be potentially comparable	Section B.2.3.4 on identifying potentially comparable transactions or companies
Comparability adjustments where appropriate	Step 8 on determining of and making comparability adjustments, where appropriate	Section B.2.3.5 on adjustment to comparables
Interpretation of the analysis	Step 9 on interpreting and using the data collected and determining the arm's length remuneration	Section B.2.3.7 on determining an arm's length price or profit (or a range of arm's length prices or profits)

Some BEPS revisions to the OECD TPG are not considered in the 2017 UN Manual. For instance, the 2017 OECD TPG advocates taking contractual terms as the starting point for comparability analysis. The respective process provided in the 2017 UN Manual, however, apparently remains unchanged compared with those of the 2013 version. There is also further guidance that is applicable specifically to issues in relation to developing countries including, amongst others, the dearth of comparable information and reasoning and issues pertaining to the use of secret comparables.

The 2017 UN Manual also endorses the use of safe harbors.

One major advantage of the 2017 UN Manual is that the language used therein is more accessible than the language used in the OECD TPG. Further, the principles are illustrated not only by way of examples but also through (simplified) case studies. A downside of the UN Manual is that it does not represent a consensus document and, therefore, one may question its authoritative powers in applying the principles that it illustrates.

3.2 The World Bank Group

On December 23, 2016, the World Bank Group published a transfer pricing handbook "Transfer Pricing and Developing Economies: A Handbook for Policy Makers and Practitioners" (WBG Handbook). The WBG Handbook does not give additional or other guidance on the ALP and comparability than what is already available under the OECD TPG or the UN Manual. Rather, it gives guidance on how to design and implement transfer pricing legislation.

Comparability is mainly discussed in Chapter 4 (Applying the Arm's-Length Principle) of the WBG Handbook and is based predominately on the guidance found in the OECD TPG and its amendment from 2015 with references to the UN Manual, other international and regional guidance, and country-specific examples. The two steps of a comparability analysis (delineating the transaction and comparables search) as endorsed in the 2017 OECD TPG, however, are not specifically mentioned in the WBG Handbook. An update of the WBG Handbook to reflect the changes in the 2017 OECD TPG and 2017 UN Manual would be welcomed.

The dearth of comparable information even for day-to-day transactions in developing countries is highlighted. Some potential alternative approaches (e.g., using foreign comparables, use of secret comparables, safe harbors with fixed margins) are further elaborated with advantages and disadvantages associated thereof (*see* Table 6.4).[70] The WBG Handbook does not comment, however, on how to arrive to the lasting solution (e.g., reporting requirements, regional access to databases).

Table 6.4 Potential Alternative Approaches

Solution or Alternative Approaches	*Advantages*	*Disadvantages*
Use of foreign comparables (i.e., use of comparables from other geographic markets)	- Widens the pool of potential comparables	- Access to databases containing foreign comparables may not be available or can be expensive - Complex (and somewhat arbitrary) comparability adjustments may be required

70. World Bank Group, *Transfer Pricing and Developing Economies: A Handbook for Policy Makers and Practitioners*, at pp. 143–151.

Solution or Alternative Approaches	*Advantages*	*Disadvantages*
Use of comparables from other industries or with different functional profiles	– Widens the pool of potential comparables	– Requires that comparables exist for which differences that materially affect the condition being examined can be appropriately adjusted for – Complex (and somewhat arbitrary) comparability adjustments may be required
Safe harbors (with fixed margins)	– Safe harbors can increase certainty for both taxpayers and the tax administration and can increase administrative efficiency – No reliance on comparables information required—Design can draw on administrative data that is readily available	– Where safe harbors are unilateral, there is a risk of economic double taxation (if not optional) or foregone revenues – Scope for safe harbors may be limited (i.e., generally used for low-value adding services, small loans, etc.)
Rebuttable fixed margins	– Simple to administer – No reliance on comparables (except for initial determination of margins) – Certainty	– Similar to safe harbors: Risk of double taxation; limited scope – Complacent tax administration may ignore arguments for rebuttal
Advance pricing arrangements	– Can provide a solution where no comparables are available – Provides certainty for the taxpayer and the tax administration – Bilateral or multilateral advance pricing arrangements can limit instances of economic double taxation	– Arrangement should be based on the arm's length principle which generally requires comparables – Can be resource-intensive for the tax administration – Unilateral advance pricing agreements do not prevent economic double taxation – Needs capacity and skilled staff
Use of internal rates of return	– Provides a solution when no comparables are available	– Relies upon subjective assumptions – Rate of return can be influenced by a range of different factors other than transfer prices

Solution or Alternative Approaches	*Advantages*	*Disadvantages*
Lower independence requirements for uncontrolled transactions	- Widens the pool of potential comparables	- Transactions between associated parties may be influenced by those parties' transfer pricing policies
Use of secret comparables	- Greater availability of information for the tax administration	- Not equitable as information cannot generally be disclosed to taxpayers, hence, the taxpayer is unable to defend its position - Information cannot generally be disclosed in mutual agreement procedures, hence, may lead to cases of unrelieved economic double taxation
Use of customs valuations	- Access to vast amounts of transactional data	- Generally, information required to conduct a comparability analysis is unavailable - Customs valuation methods and transfer pricing operate differently and have different objectives - Only limited transactions types are dutiable
Use of industry average returns	- Greater availability of information	- Limited information as to composition of industry average, hence, cannot assess comparability - Industry averages generally include data from controlled transactions

3.3 European Union JTPF

In March 2017, the European Union JTPF[71] approved the *Report on the Use of Comparables in the EU* (the Comparability Report). The JTPF recognizes the two

71. The European Union JTPF is an expert group that assists and advises the European Commission on TP matters. It provides a platform to develop practical solutions that are compatible with the OECD TPG. The twenty-eight EU Member States are joined by eighteen Non-Government Members (representatives from the business community, consultancy, academia, and civil society). Representatives from candidate countries (Albania, FYR Macedonia, Iceland,

separate steps of the comparability analysis outlined in the 2017 OECD TPG (delineating the actual transaction and looking for reliable comparables). Although the Comparability Report recognizes the two steps are interlinked, it also states clearly that the comparables search should follow the delineation of the real deal and not conversely. The better the first step has been conducted, the more accurate the comparables search will be.

The Comparability Report establishes best practices and pragmatic solutions by issuing various recommendations for both taxpayers and tax administrations in the EU and aims at increasing the objectivity and transparency of comparable searches for transfer pricing in practice. The Comparability Report relies on the OECD TPG to issue recommendations relating to the application of the transparency (documentation) and proportionality principle (administrative burden), internal vs. external comparables, and comparability adjustments, etc.

The JTPF indicates that transparency can be achieved through documenting the steps of the comparables search keeping in mind that the search should still be proportionate but with a focus on quality, transparency, and consistency.[72]

The JTPF further recommends to increase transparency by:[73]

- documenting the search and screening criteria, rejection criteria, and adjustments made;
- a broad range of sources is useful and add value in refining the comparables search;
- transparency and proportionality when judgment is used;
- explaining the choice of deductive approach or additive approach and why the approach is appropriate;
- mentioning the financial data of the comparables and its sources;
- maintaining the document supporting the search.

Within the EU, there seems to be a preference for using internal comparables, although they are often dismissed by lack of data or material differences. It might sound rather strange that lack of data is mentioned as a reason for dismissal by tax authorities as one of the parties to the controlled transaction is also taking part in the uncontrolled transaction. Hence, information within the group on the uncontrolled transaction should be readily available. However, because more information is available on internal comparables, there may also be more opportunity to dismiss them. Internal comparables are, of course, readily available to the MNE and hence meet the criterion of proportionality.

Montenegro, Serbia, and Turkey) and from the OECD and UN may be invited to the JTPF as observers. The JTPF works within the framework of the OECD TPG—as they may be amended from time to time—and operates on the basis of consensus to propose to the Commission pragmatic, nonlegislative solutions to practical problems posed by transfer pricing practices in the EU.

72. EU Joint Transfer Pricing Forum (JTPF), *Report on the Use of Comparables in the EU* (2016), at para. 8 (Recommendation 1).
73. EU Joint Transfer Pricing Forum (JTPF), *Report on the Use of Comparables in the EU* (2016), at para. 11 (Recommendation 2).

The JTPF has prepared a useful selection flow chart as an example for selecting external quality comparables (*see* Figure 6.4). It is composed of three main parts: (1) setting of the analysis/scope; (2) quantitative analysis; and (3) qualitative analysis.

However, like the OECD, the JTPF has no preference for using internal and external comparables. The key aspect is comparability, and one may perhaps add the quality of the comparable. With respect to comparability adjustments, the JTPF mentions only working capital adjustments as being encountered frequently.

Figure 6.4 Selecting External Comparables

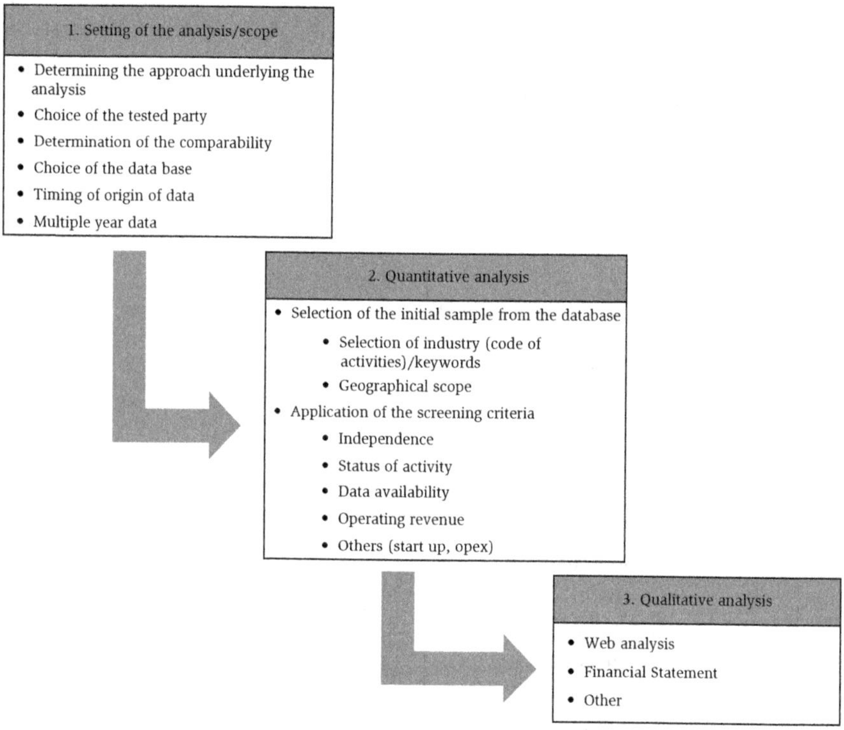

3.4 Platform for Collaboration on Tax

On June 22, 2017, the Platform for Collaboration on Tax (PCT)[74] published its *Toolkit for Addressing Difficulties in Accessing Comparable Data for Transfer Pricing Analyses*

74. The Platform for Collaboration on Tax (PCT) is a joint effort launched in April 2016 by the International Monetary Fund, the OECD, the United Nations, and the World Bank Group. The Platform is designed to intensify the cooperation between these international organizations on tax issues. A major aim of the PCT is to better frame technical advice to developing countries as they seek both more capacity-building support and greater influence in designing international standards.

(the Toolkit). The Toolkit addresses practical ways that emerging economies can help overcome comparability issues, e.g., in particular due to the lack of comparable data that is required for a benchmarking study when conducting transfer pricing analysis. A number of key elements on standards of comparability are discussed below.[75]

3.4.1 *Accurate Delineation of the Transaction*

The Toolkit reiterates the importance of accurately delineating the transaction, which is the first phase of the two-phase comparability analysis approach as set out in the revised Chapter I of the 2017 OECD TPG. It emphasizes that inaccuracies in delineating the actual transaction may lead to inappropriate selection of the method (and when relevant, inappropriate selection of the tested party). The inappropriate selection of the method is likely to have a far greater impact on the outcome than the accuracy of the comparable data used in the method's application.[76] The Toolkit also refers to the five comparability factors described in the OECD TPG and the UN Manual that are usually considered to perform the accurate delineation of the control transaction.[77]

3.4.2 *Comparables Search Process*

In terms of the comparables search process provided in the Toolkit, there are two elements worth noting: (1) the Toolkit advocates to prioritize the search criteria that are the most economically relevant; and (2) the Toolkit tends to abolish or demote the impact of geographic differences where appropriate and promotes a diagnostic (financial) ratio to achieve functional comparability.

---

75. The Toolkit outlines various country risk adjustments that have been implemented to add a premium or discount to the comparables' result (e.g., use of weighted average cost of capital, bond yields, etc.) (*see* Section 5.5.2 of the Toolkit). However, it further points out that "there is little empirical evidence on the reliability of the proposed approaches. Careful consideration should be given as to whether such approaches can account for differences in risks and thus in expected profitability for commercial ventures in different countries." Given the skeptical attitude of the Toolkit towards the approaches presented in conducting country risk adjustments, no further discussion is included in the present work in this respect.
76. The Platform for Collaboration on Tax (PCT), *A Toolkit for Addressing Difficulties in Accessing Comparables Data for Transfer Pricing Analyses (2017) (The Toolkit)*, p. 34, specifies that "the accurate delineation of the transaction, and from it, the selection of the most appropriate method (and the selection of the correct tested party where relevant), is so important to a reliable transfer pricing analysis: if this foundation is incorrect, irrelevant and inappropriate comparables may be used [...] Data quality and availability also matter, of course: imperfect or imprecise comparables applied to the correct tested party or using the most appropriate method will obviously lead to less accurate outcomes. A key point, nonetheless, is that it is essential to consider the functional analysis (taking into account the assets used and risks assumed) of the parties to the transaction to determine which transfer pricing method is the most appropriate to the actual transaction, and how it should be applied, including—critically—what kind of comparables should be sought. Neither taxpayers nor tax administrations can choose a method at will: the selection of the most appropriate method is a matter of fact and application of principle."
77. The Toolkit, *supra* n. 76, at p. 19.

The Toolkit provides that the screening criteria selected and the ordering of those criteria should be considered carefully based on the identification of the most economically relevant characteristics of the transactions to be tested.[78] It further states that search criteria should be widened or reordered to prioritize the features of the transaction that are the most economically relevant and by using other means such as carefully selected financial or diagnostic ratios to refine the search.[79]

As indicated above, when comparables that are geographically local to the transaction under review ("local comparables") are scarce or unavailable, the Toolkit advocates demoting or even abolishing the geographic screening criterion so that comparables that show high comparability in other respects can be used.[80] It states:

> *In such cases, it will be important to examine whether differences in markets are likely to make a material difference to the condition being examined. Where the transaction occurs in a truly global market, geography may not make a material difference. [...] an independent entity from a foreign market with highly comparable functions, assets, and risks may provide a more reliable comparison for transfer pricing purpose than an uncontrolled entity from the local market with a lower degree of comparability in terms of its functional analysis*[81]

The Toolkit also suggests, in some cases, using a diagnostic ratio to improve the reliability of a potential set of comparables and to use them as an alternative to industry classification codes.[82] The underlying logic is that industry codes are broad and do not attempt to align functions, assets, and risks whereas certain diagnostic ratios are likely to better align functional similarities. The Toolkit refers the example below:

> *A distributor of pharmaceutical goods with a large sales force which outsources logistics and goods handling to a third party provider (and thus has no warehouses, logistics infrastructure or inventory risk) is unlikely to be comparable to entities falling within the industry classification of "pharmaceutical goods importer, wholesale" if typical companies within that classification in fact have significant warehousing and logistics functions, assets and risks, and smaller sales forces.*[83]

Following the above proposed usage of financial ratios as sector diagnostic, one may, however, reasonably question whether this can indeed enhance the comparability or whether it is rather the other way around—i.e., reduce the comparability. In the above cited example, screening financial ratios such as fixed assets to sales, inventory to sales, and employee costs to total operating costs may identify potential comparables (with low fixed assets, low/nil inventory, and large sales) in, for instance, the IT sector. Would a pharmaceutical distributor be comparable with a software distributor?

78. The Toolkit, *supra* n. 76, at p. 42.
79. The Toolkit, *supra* n. 76, at p. 43.
80. The Toolkit, *supra* n. 76, at p. 43.
81. The Toolkit, *supra* n. 76, at p. 42.
82. The Toolkit, *supra* n. 76, at pp. 42–43.
83. The Toolkit, *supra* n. 76, at pp. 42–43.

In terms of the use of "foreign comparables," the Toolkit indicates that, while the use of foreign data is fairly extensive in practice, there are no sufficient studies available to draw a final conclusion about the reliability of the use of foreign data. This critical attitude of the Toolkit towards foreign comparables is inconsistent with the positions set forth in the OECD TPG[84] and the UN Manual.[85] The latter do support the use of foreign comparables (possibly adjusted) under certain circumstances. In this respect, the authors share the view as elaborated in some other recent publications.[86] The critical attitude of the Toolkit towards the use of foreign comparables contradicts the general tone of it in seeking pragmatic solutions. Further discussion and guidance on the use of foreign comparables are definitely welcome.

3.4.3 Safe Harbors

Another main focus of the Toolkit is on safe harbors. In the context of a comparability analysis aligned with the revised Chapter I of the OECD TPG, safe harbors are promoted as a useful tool to increase transparency and compliance while, at the same time, reducing resources and costs. The safe harbor provisions contained in the Toolkit are similar to those provided in the OECD TPG. The Toolkit in particular notes merit of bilateral safe harbors and regional cooperation in establishing unilateral safe harbors.

The Toolkit suggests that developing countries use safe harbor approaches with an "opt-out"[87] mechanism to help overcome the data sufficiency problems that are encountered. For the purpose of identifying data on comparables suitable for setting a safe harbor margin, if data is otherwise scarce or unavailable, the Toolkit refers to the use of data already in the hands of the tax administration that is sourced primarily from tax return information.[88] It further suggests that countries as well as regional and international organizations assess the potential for building up an international or regional set of data based on data already in the hands of tax administrations, presented in an aggregated format that retains taxpayer confidentiality, and subject to the process of selecting, and updating the data set is conducted in a transparent way.

84. 2017 OECD TPG, *supra* n. 33, at paras. 1.113 and 3.35.
85. 2017 UN Manual, *supra* n. 67, at paras. B.2.3.4.13, B.2.4.3.3.-B.2.4.3.5., D.2.4.3.4., D.2.4.7.1.
86. *See* O. Treidler, B. Grothe and A. Paprotny, *Comparability—Moving to the Top of the EU's Transfer Pricing Agenda*, Tax Notes International (March 6, 2017).
87. The Toolkit, *supra* n. 76, p. 70 specifies that "'opt-in' refers to a safe harbor in which the taxpayer is able to choose to 'opt-in' in order to benefit from it. In this type of region, a taxpayer that chooses not to opt-in must apply the transfer pricing rules and document their application. Under 'opt-out' safe harbor, the taxpayer is required to apply the method specified in the safe harbor to any transactions that fall within its scope unless it opts not to."
88. The Toolkit, *supra* n. 76, at p. 72.

4 EC STATE AID INVESTIGATIONS AND COMPARABILITY[89]

Over the past couple of years, the EC has investigated certain transfer pricing approaches under article 107(1) [90] of the Treaty on the Functioning of the European Union (TFEU).[91] Several of these investigations are discussed in more detail in Chapter II on the Transfer Pricing Developments in the European Union.

From those investigations and decisions, it is clear that the EC in the State aid analysis does not use the OECD TPG as binding guidance but as "a framework to provide useful guidance to tax administrations and multinational enterprises on how to ensure that transfer pricing and profit allocation arrangements produce outcomes in line with market conditions."[92] The EC is, of course, correct in stating that the OECD TPG are only soft law but, nevertheless, it also recognizes that the outcomes must be in line with market conditions. It is not clear, however, whether the EC interprets outcomes in line with market conditions as in line with the ALP under the OECD TPG. It would seem that these two approaches may overlap to some degree, but there can also be differences.

Although the EC recognizes the value of the OECD TPG in establishing arm's length transactions or, in their wording, in line with market conditions, the EC does not seem to perform a full comparability analysis in accordance with the guidance provided. Very likely for discretionary reasons, the EC always states that the analysis is performed consistent with Art. 107 TFEU.

Based upon the explicit recognition of the value of the OECD TPG, one could wonder why the EC does not perform a full comparability analysis in analyzing the State aid cases. Indeed, the EC analyses the conditions of the controlled transactions, i.e., the first leg of the equation (identifying the real deal) but limits itself to that part. Although references to market conditions are made in the decisions, the EC falls short in demonstrating that the conditions of the controlled transactions are or are not similar to uncontrolled transactions. It does not indicate what the normal market conditions

89. This section on EC State aid investigations and comparability contains a brief discussion of some findings in recent EC decisions with regard to the use of comparability analysis in State aid transfer pricing cases. It does not, however, contain a discussion on the appropriateness of the State aid investigations itself or its outcomes.
90. *See* Article 107, para. 1 of Treaty of the Functioning of the European Union. It specifies: "Save as otherwise provided in the Treaties, any aid granted by a Member State or through State resources in any form whatsoever which distorts or threatens to distort competition by favouring certain undertakings or the production of certain goods shall, in so far as it affects trade between Member States, be incompatible with the internal market."
91. EC Decision SA.38373, State aid implemented by Ireland to Apple (August 30, 2016), not published on O.J. L 187, 1-110, July 19, 2017. EC Decision SA.38375, State aid which Luxembourg granted to Fiat (October 21, 2015), O.J. L 351, 1–67 (December 22, 2016). EC Decision SA.38944, State aid which Luxembourg granted to Amazon (October 4, 2017), not yet published on O.J. EC Decision SA.38374, State aid implemented by the Netherlands to Starbucks (October 21, 2015), O.J., L 83, 38–115 (March 29, 2017). EC Decision SA.37667, Excess profit exemption in Belgium—Art. 185§2 b) CIR92 (January 11, 2016), O.J. L 260, 61–103 (September 27, 2016).
92. EC Decision SA 38373, State aid implemented by Ireland to Apple (August 30, 2016), OJ L 187, 1-110, July 19, 2017, recital 255.

would be for a particular kind of transaction which is, of course, the purpose of the second leg of the comparability analysis. In particular in that respect, the EC does not recognize the—albeit nonbinding—guidance of paragraph 1.11 of the OECD TPG indicating that related parties may engage in transactions that would not be undertaken by third parties. This in and of itself does not indicate that the transactions are motivated for tax reasons and can be genuinely commercially rational transactions. As indicated in the OECD TPG, paragraph 1.11,[93] "The mere fact that a transaction may not be found between independent parties does not of itself mean that it is not arm's length."

The EC is not aiming at establishing whether the amount of profit that would have been taxed if the same transactions had been executed by independent companies negotiating under comparable circumstances is in accordance with the OECD arm's length principle. Rather, the EC compares the effective tax outcomes based upon the first leg of the comparability analysis with what the EC assumes should have been taxed under the general corporate tax system of the country concerned. What is missing in the analysis of the EC, however, is the second leg of the comparability analysis, namely, the determination of the conditions of the uncontrolled transactions, i.e., determining the market conditions.

As mentioned under Chapter II on Transfer Pricing Developments in the European Union, the EC applies a strictly legalistic approach based upon Article 107 TFEU to lead to a conclusion that double nontaxation may exist.

Recital 172 of the Commission Notice on the notion of State aid as referred to in Article 107(1) of the Treaty on the Functioning of the European Union [94] adds to the confusing by stating that "'This' [emphasis added] arm's length principle necessarily forms part of the Commission's assessment of tax measures granted to group companies under Article 107(1) of the Treaty, independently of whether a Member State has incorporated this principle into its national legal system and in what form."

The Commission Notice paper does not make any reference to double taxation agreements or the European Arbitration Convention, which should also be considered as being part of a country's domestic tax system. Although the State aid analysis performed by the EC at multiple occasions refers to the OECD TPG, the Commission Notice further explains in the same recital that "'The arm's length principle the Commission applies in assessing transfer pricing rulings under the State aid rules is therefore an application of Article 107(1) of the Treaty' [emphasis added], which prohibits unequal treatment in taxation of undertakings in a similar factual and legal situation. This principle binds the Member States and the national tax rules are not excluded from its scope."

The EC recognizes in recital 173 of the Commission Notice that, in the State aid examination, regard may be had to the OECD guidance and OECD TPG. The EC states that "Those guidelines do not deal with matters of State aid per se, but they capture the

93. The text of para. 1.11 of the 2010 OECD TPG is identical to the text of para. 1.11 of the 2017 OECD TPG.
94. Commission Notice on the notion of State aid as referred to in Article 107(1) of the Treaty on the Functioning of the European Union (2016/C 262/01)—OJ C 262, 1–50, July 19, 2016.

international consensus on transfer pricing and provide useful guidance to tax administrations and multinational enterprises on how to ensure that a transfer pricing methodology produces an outcome in line with market conditions. Consequently, if a transfer pricing arrangement complies with the guidance provided by the OECD Transfer Pricing Guidelines, including the guidance on the choice of the most appropriate method and leading to a reliable approximation of a market based outcome, a tax ruling endorsing that arrangement is 'unlikely' [emphasis added] to give rise to State aid." It is, of course, the word "unlikely" in the last sentence that gives rise to uncertainty.

Could this go as far as indicating that Article 107 TFEU leads to a different arm's length principle than under the OECD TPG? Certainly the limited—one leg—comparability analysis performed in the State aid analysis and comparing the outcome with taxation under the national corporate tax system seems to indicate so. Another indication that the EC might be thinking about their own arm's length standard lies in the hallmark on transfer pricing in the Annex of the Proposal of June 21, 2017 for a Council Directive amending Directive 2011/16/EU regarding mandatory automatic exchange of information in the field of taxation in relation to reportable cross-border arrangements. This hallmark indicates *inter alia*, "an arrangement or series of arrangements 'which does not conform with the arm's length principle or with the OECD transfer pricing guidelines' [emphasis added] including the allocation of profit between different members of the same corporate group."[95] Is the reference to the arm's length principle a reference to the arm's length principle under Article 107 TFEU or as defined under Article 9 of the OECD MTC. The use of the conjunction "or" in the hallmark seems to indicate—or at least can be interpreted in a manner—that the arm's length principle is not one of the OECD TPG. After a meeting of the High Level Working Party, a second Presidency Compromise was achieved.[96] The wording is now redrafted into "An arrangement which benefits from simplified determination of arm's length price." According to the Presidency Compromise, this new wording is based upon Section B.2 of Chapter VII on Intra-Group Services of the OECD TPG which reads "Simplified determination of arm's length charges for low value-adding intra-group services." It is not clear to the authors, however, how a generic hallmark under the Directive proposal can be derived from a very specific discussion on low value-adding intra-group services in the 2017 OECD TPG aiming at very specific services that is even assorted with specific documentation requirements and is supposed to enhance transparency and compliance.

Paragraph 1.51 of the 2017 OECD TPG indicates that, in performing a functional analysis "it is important to understand how value is generated by the group as a whole, the interdependencies of the functions performed by the associated enterprises with the rest of the group, and the contribution that the associated enterprises make to that value creation." A functional analysis is an inherent part—and may be the most

95. A discussion of the hallmark lies outside the scope of this contribution.
96. Proposal for a Council Directive amending Directive 2011/16/EU as regards mandatory automatic exchange of information in the field of taxation in relation to reportable cross-border arrangements—Presidency compromise, WK 12400/2017 INIT, October 31, 2017.

important part—in a comparability analysis. Now let this part be an element that is not thoroughly examined in the State aid analysis, including how value is created. In other words, the EC may disregard the actual transaction and value creation it brings to the different parts of the MNE. Also, one could wonder whether, in the State aid examinations, the EC is speculating about what independent parties (or market conditions defined as independent parties negotiating at arm's length) might or might not have done. However, such speculation is generally not permitted under the OECD TPG.[97] Related parties remain free to structure transactions that are never seen in uncontrolled transactions.[98] This indeed is a sharp contradiction with the State aid arm's length speculation that strictly refers to "market conditions."

As stated by R Goulder, "There's a lingering issue about whether the Commission is properly interpreting transfer pricing concepts. It's no stretch to say that the Commission's view of the arm's-length standard is out of sync with how the OECD's transfer pricing guidelines are applied in practice."[99]

What can be learned from the EC approach is that their comparability analysis is:

- a one-sided approach linked to the national corporate tax system;
- separate and distinct from the comparability analysis under the OECD TPG;
- increasing uncertainty.

5 CONCLUSIONS

Several international organizations—if not all—are in favor of using safe harbors under the appropriate circumstances, in particular for developing economies.

The revised OECD guidance on accurately delineating the transaction has the benefit of being clearer on the issue that the analysis to be performed is a two-sided analysis. At the same time, the revised OECD guidance on risk is complex and may[100] lead to uncertainty and increased disputes. It is not clear how developing economies will approach and apply the complex guidance.

The comparability analysis under the State aid discussions will decrease the certainty of taxpayers even more. Even if the transaction is arm's length, the EC may still claim under its discretionary powers that the transaction is not in accordance with market conditions and the domestic corporate tax rules.

Several international organizations have each now published their own set of guidance on the arm's length principle including comparability but with a somewhat different focus, content, message, and purpose or degree of authority. This could be understood from the point of view of the international organizations for profiling themselves but, in particular where the views diverge, this leads to confusion with the

97. Transfer Pricing and the Arm's Length Principle after BEPS—Richard S Collier and Joseph L Andrus, Oxford University Press, p. 200—para. 6.14.
98. *Ibid.*, para. 6.14.
99. Robert Goulder, Ikea's Royalty Conduit—Some Assembly Required, Tax Notes International, p. 198, January 8, 2018.
100. Or should we say "will?"

tax practitioners, be it at the level of the tax administrations or at the level of businesses and their advisors/consultants. In the end, it should be clear that only one authoritative guidance should prevail, and the other publications should be interpreted in light of that authoritative guidance. That authoritative guidance should preferably be the OECD TPG as it will be updated regularly in light of its drafting through the Inclusive Framework[101] that is installed under BEPS and its status as a consensus document.

101. The Inclusive Framework on BEPS brings together over 100 countries and jurisdictions to collaborate on the implementation of the OECD/ G20 Base Erosion and Profit Shifting (BEPS) Package.

CHAPTER 7

Recent Developments on the Profit Split Method

*Sébastien Gonnet**

The Transactional Profit Split Method ("TPSM") is described in Chapter II.C (§2.114–§2.155) of the OECD Transfer Pricing Guidelines. On June 22, 2017, the OECD

* The author would like to thank Emilie Feyler, Economic Analysist at NERA, for her contribution to this chapter. The views expressed in this chapter are solely those of the author and are not necessarily the opinions of NERA Economic Consulting.

published a public discussion draft on the application of the TPSM[1] (the "TPSM Draft"). The final guidelines were published on June 20, 2018.

This chapter focuses on the application of the TPSM. This chapter purposely does not address the circumstances under which the TPSM applies, which has been covered in the previous edition.[2]

This chapter provides an economic view on the application of the TPSM, and refers to the final guidelines by the OECD on the profit split method from 20 June 2018.

The latest discussions among the Transfer Pricing stakeholders[3] confirm that the TPSM still causes some anxiety, particularly in the business community.[4] The main concerns relate to the circumstances of the application of the TPSM, which these stakeholders wish to see as sufficiently well-defined in order to avoid the opening of a proverbial "Pandora's box."

This has been expressed by a number of stakeholders in transfer pricing praising the OECD to reiterate that the TPSM is applicable only in very limited circumstances.

The fears expressed by transfer pricing stakeholders relate primarily to the perceived subjectivity and/or complexity of the application of the method. Andrew Hickman, a former Head of the Transfer Pricing Unit at the OECD also commented that "[TPSM] is often not an easy method to apply." Some academics also commented on the perceived complexity highlighted by the OECD: "The OECD states that difficulties in application are a major drawback of the PSM."[5]

This perception is also due to the comparison with the now well-known Transactional Net Margin Method (TNMM) that has been widely (almost exclusively) applied by MNEs in developed economies for a number of years and reviewed by tax administrations.

However, the TPSM should be a strong candidate for application in cases when: (1) the controlled parties have highly integrated operations; (2) the controlled parties jointly assume economically significant risks; and (3) the remuneration of unique and valuable contributions by each of the controlled parties cannot be reliably benchmarked in other ways, e.g., by means of independent comparable transactions using one-sided methods.

This chapter aims at illustrating the application of the TPSM and is structured around two case studies that demonstrate its application. Each case study has been selected to highlight some of the major challenges that practitioners face in relation to the TPSM:

---

1. Base Erosion and Profit Shifting (BEPS), Public Discussion Draft, Revised Guidance on Profit Split, June 22, 2017.
2. Sébastien Gonnet, "Recent Developments on the Profit Split Method," in *Transfer Pricing Developments Around the World 2017*, edited by Michael Lang, Alfred Storck & Raffaele Petruzzi.
3. Public Consultation on Transfer Pricing Matters, November 6-7, 2017, as well as written comments to the Public Draft.
4. Note that some NGOs, notably The BEPS Monitoring Group, are defenders of the method and suggest that the PSM "should be designated the default method."
5. Olbert & Spengel, 'International Taxation in the Digital Economy: Challenge Accepted?', *World Tax Journal*, February 2017.

- Case Study #1 covers the evaluation of the arm's length nature of trademark license royalty rates in an intra-group context in the luxury industry using a contribution analysis based on comparable data. This case study will illustrate that comparable data can be used to apply the Contribution Profit Split Method ("Contribution PSM").
- Case Study #2 covers the determination of prices of products and services for a multinational enterprise involved in performing and managing projects using the Residual PSM. This case study illustrates the detailed process of the application of a Residual PSM, which is the most common PSM used. It will show that the Residual PSM can be used to set prices of products and services on a budget basis and may allow managing deviations from the budget and allocating such deviations between entities of the MNE.

Each of the case study chapters is structured in the same manner:

- The first section provides the description of the background of the case as well as the rationale for selecting the PSM and the key parameters of its application.
- The second section provides the theoretical basis for the application of the TPSM: what OECD references help for the application the TPSM in the context at hand? What non-OECD references may help (such as U.S. regulations or other regulations)?
- The third section provides the detailed application of the TPSM with stylized numerical examples.

The author presents the case studies below under the assumption that the facts and circumstances of each case have led to selection of the PSM as the most appropriate method after the applicability of other transfer pricing methods has been carefully evaluated. The readers should not assume that the PSM will always be the best method to analyze transactions that appear to be similar to those discussed in this chapter. Rather, the most appropriate method has to be selected after an analysis of facts and circumstances of the specific transaction at hand which will necessarily be more complex than the stylized cases presented in this chapter. Therefore, other transfer pricing methods may be more reliable than the PSM under different circumstances despite the transactions taking place in the same industries as described in the case studies below.

1 CASE STUDY #1: ARM'S LENGTH TRADEMARK LICENSES USING THE CONTRIBUTION PSM BASED ON COMPARABLE DATA

1.1 Background

An MNE ("Lux Distrib Co") operates in the luxury retail industry. Its business consists of negotiating and signing license agreements for distributing licensed products in Europe and the U.S. As a licensee, Lux Distrib Co manufactures (or has manufactured) the products and distributes the products through its own retail stores or using franchised stores. The unrelated (luxury) brand owner receives royalty licenses as a remuneration for access to the licensed trademark as well as some marketing support, investment, and services.

From time to time, Lux Distrib Co purchases a trademark as opposed to licensing it. For one of the purchased trademarks, Lux Distrib Co has structured an intra-group license and wishes to establish an arm's length level of royalties between the group licensor (owner of the trademark) and the group licensee (user of the trademark).

The primary approach used is the Comparable Uncontrolled Price (CUP) method. It consists of establishing the universe of available trademark license agreements concluded by Lux Distrib Co and unrelated parties. Selected agreements need to be the ones that are the closest to the tested intra-group transaction. The nominal royalty rates for trademarks found in such contracts can represent valid external references to the extent they are considered as sufficiently comparable (or, if they are not, adjustments need to be performed to cope with differences that may affect the price agreed between parties). If there are no transactions with unrelated parties whose terms are sufficiently comparable to the controlled transaction at hand, the arm's length nature of the nominal royalty rates selected from such uncontrolled transactions may need to be verified using the Contribution PSM.

The Contribution PSM, based on comparable data, aims at confirming the arm's length nature of the nominal royalty rates. This method does have the same starting points, i.e., a set of similar transactions concluded between third parties (in this case, Lux Distrib Co and the third-party luxury brand owners). The difference between the two methods is the following:

- The CUP method relies on the royalty rates themselves.
- The Comparable Profit Split Method (Comparable PSM) uses the information about the split of profits between the licensor and the licensee that results from the application of the royalty rates agreed between the parties.

The benefits of using the Contribution PSM are the following:

- It sheds light on the profit potential of license agreements.
- It uses a two-sided perspective both from the licensor and from the licensee.
- It assumes that a negotiation between unrelated parties for similar assets would result, on average, in a similar distribution of profits.

The following section provides the theoretical foundation and guidance that is available for the application of such a method (both OECD and non-OECD).

1.2 PSM "Theory" Relevant to the Case

The Contribution PSM, based on comparable data is described by the OECD:

> Under a contribution analysis, the relevant profits […] are divided between the associated enterprises in order to arrive at a reasonable approximation of the division that independent enterprises would have achieved from engaging in

> comparable transactions. This division can be supported by comparables data where available. (paragraph 2.150 of the OECD Guidelines[6])

With respect to the use of comparable data for the split factor, the OECD indicates:

> Profits should be split on an economically valid basis, that reflects the relative contributions of the parties to the transaction and thus approximate the division of profits that would have obtained at arm's length. (paragraph 2.166)
> One possible approach is to split the relevant profits based on the division of profits that actually is observed in comparable uncontrolled transactions. (paragraph 2.167)
>
> External market data can be relevant in the profit split analysis to assess the value. (paragraph 2.168)

The Contribution PSM, based on the comparable market data, therefore, is endorsed by the OECD.

The OECD also advocates the reference to the profit potential of an intangible asset as a comparability factor in Chapter VI of the OECD Guidelines covering intangibles:

> it is important to consider the actual and potential profitability of products or potential products that are based on the intangible. (paragraph 6.127).

The UN also refers to the Contribution Analysis in the UN Manual:

> B.3.3.14.2. Under the contribution analysis the combined profits from the controlled transactions are allocated between the associated enterprises on the basis of the relative value of functions performed by those associated enterprises engaged in the controlled transactions. External market data that reflect how independent enterprises allocate the profits in similar circumstances should complement the analysis to the extent possible.

However, the Manual does not make a specific reference to the Contribution Analysis based on comparable data.

Outside of the OECD, the U.S. regulations[7] have a reference to the "Comparable PSM" which is the equivalent to the OECD Contribution PSM based on comparable data.

Finally, some practitioners have formalized and commented on the use of the Comparable PSM. Rozek[8] has demonstrated the relevance of the Comparable PSM in the case of pricing royalty licenses for blockbusters in the pharma industry:

> A taxpayer's own transactions with third parties are often the most reliable data available for determining transfer prices for intangible property, even for products with profit potential either substantially above or below that of the taxpayer's own

6. OECD: *Revised Guidance on the Application of the Transactional Profit Split Method, Inclusive Framework on BEPS: Action 10*, June 21, 2018 (OECD, Paris)
7. U.S. Treasury Regs. 1.482-6(c)(2).
8. R.P. Rozek & G.G. Korenko, "Transfer Prices for Intangible Property Embodied in Products with Extraordinary Profit Potential," *BNA Tax Notes International*, October 1999.

> transactions with third parties. When detailed financial data on the taxpayer's transactions with third parties exist, the Comparable Profit Split Method is the best method for establishing an arm's-length transfer price consistent with the section 482 regulations.

Neither the OECD nor the US Regulations are very explicit with respect to the actual application of the method. Only Rozek introduces the two conditions of the application of the methodology:

- Financial data on the comparable unrelated agreements suggest that the licensor's share of the profits does not fluctuate too drastically over time (a maximum ratio of 1 to 3).
- There is no statistical relationship between the portion of the profits attributable to the licensor and the profits themselves. The reason for this assumption is that Rozek suggests using a relatively large sample of unrelated comparable transactions for the purpose of the application of the CPSM and not only agreements with the same profit potential of the tested transaction. He can do so only to the extent that the level of profits that the licensor and licensee jointly generate does not affect their sharing of profits. Rozek suggests using a regression analysis to confirm the assumption.

Apart from these, the application of the Contribution PSM based on comparable data is not detailed which necessitates MNEs and tax administrations to make decisions with respect to the key criteria of the application of the method including the ones below:

(1) **The selection of comparable uncontrolled transactions** that will serve as a basis for the application of the Method: the comparability factors as set out by the OECD should be respected, notably, the five comparability factors including the contractual terms of the transaction, the functional analysis, characteristics of property and services, economic circumstances, and business strategy as well as the specific criteria added in Chapter VI. As discussed above, the profit potential is one of those suggesting that two intangibles contracts with highly dissimilar profit potential cannot be compared or would necessitate adjustments.

(2) **The determination of the profits to be split**: the Contribution PSM based on comparable data starts with the profitability of transactions with third parties; in the case at hand, the license transactions between Lux Distrib Co and the luxury brand owner. The application of the method necessitates making choices with respect to what profits should constitute the starting point of the analysis:

 (a) **Gross or net profits**: gross profits include the joint profits that the licensee (Lux Distrib Co) and the licensor (luxury brand owner) jointly make including the accounting of their respective operating expenses (costs of operating the business for Luxury Distrib Co; some costs of brand protection (legal) and possibly some brand-building costs for the licensor).

(i) The OECD discusses this issue in Section C.4.2 of the revised Guidelines.

(b) **Anticipated (budget) profits or actual profits**: using anticipated budget profits suggests that the arm's length division of profits between the licensor and the licensee is the one resulting from the negotiation at the conclusion of the contract. When such negotiation takes place, parties bargain based on their expectation in terms of profit of the contract. In arm's length negotiations between unrelated parties, the anticipated profits are generally used, and some adjustments to the licensing royalty rates may be included in the agreements, notably if certain thresholds are reached. The author also observes various royalty set-ups such as up-front payments, guaranteed minimum payments, and stepped royalties in license agreements.

Using actual profits (the profits actually realized by each party in the course of the application of the contract) also has some merits: it starts with the actual financial performance of the licensor and licensee's relationship; using a multiple-year approach allows mitigating risks of results biased by extraordinary situations (such as a particularly poor performance of the licensee in a specific year).

(i) The OECD discusses this issue in Section C.4.1 of the revised Guidelines.

(3) **The determination of the split factor:** the split factor is directly impacted by the choices in relation to the above items. In practice, one split factor by contract/relationship is the preferred option suggesting one arm's length equilibrium per relationship/contract. Assuming more than one comparable transaction, the question of the accounting of the various data points is typical in transfer pricing. The OECD recommends the use of a "range"; an interquartile range is typically used by transfer pricing practitioners.

Final adjustments may be performed in cases when certain transactions are outliers for specific reasons. For instance, such license contracts sometimes include certain clauses that may distort the overall arm's length equilibrium and reflect a specific situation.

1.3 Application of the PSM in the Case at Hand

The sections below provide an illustration of the typical application for the Contribution PSM based on comparable data for the Luxury Distrib Co case.

The application of the method starts with the selection of uncontrolled license agreements. Then the combined profits are computed, and the arm's length split factor is derived. Finally, a comparison between the intra-group split of profit and the arm's length range is performed in order to conclude.

1.3.1 *Selection of Uncontrolled License Agreements*

In order to apply the Contribution PSM based on comparable data, Luxury Distrib Co's license agreements are reviewed in line with the OECD comparability factors. The table below provides the list of contracts concluded by Luxury Distrib Co and the rationale for their selection or exclusion from the set of comparable agreements. Five agreements were selected.

Licensing Agreement	*Comments*
Contract 1	**Selected**
Contract 2	**Selected**
Contract 3	**Selected**
Contract 4	**Selected**
Contract 5	**Selected**
Contract 6 **(illustration of reasons for rejection)**	**Rejected** The only available year is the first year of exploitation of Contract 6, provided that Luxury Distrib Co invested for the launch of the license and bears losses during that year. In order to avoid biasing the economic equilibrium between the Licensor and the Licensee, one should only select the agreements that reached commercial maturity and in absence of exceptional circumstances.
Contract 7 **(illustration of reasons for rejection)**	**Rejected** There is a gap between the expected potential on the date of signature of the license and the realization of this potential. Luxury Distrib Co bears losses regarding this contract. In order to avoid bias in the economic equilibrium between the Licensor and the Licensee, one should only select the agreements that reached commercial maturity and those absent of exceptional circumstances.

1.3.2 *Computation of Combined Profits*

Once the most comparable agreements are selected, the Contribution PSM based on comparable data requires: (i) the identification of combined profits for each comparable transaction; and (ii) the computation of the split of these profits between the Luxury Distrib Co (Licensee) and the third-party Licensor.

1.3.2.1 Identification of Combined Profits Related to the License Agreements

For each brand, Luxury Distrib Co can identify the revenues generated under this license as well as the sales costs, the royalty costs, and other operating costs (such as advertising costs, wages, etc.). The Luxury Distrib Co Group thus has a segmented Profit & Loss statement allowing for the computation of an operating profit for each license it owns in its portfolio.

In order to compute the combined profits related to a license, one should also take into account the generated sales and costs borne by the Licensor for this license. The Licensor's revenues for the license are the royalties paid by Luxury Distrib Co. The author assumes that the Licensor does not bear any operating costs to manage the license after signature of the contract with Luxury Distrib Co. Therefore, the profit of the Licensor is equal to the royalties received for the license.

For each selected contract, the combined profit is computed taking into account the revenues and operating costs of the Licensee as well as the operating costs of the Licensor (assumed to be null) but excluding the royalties (i.e., royalties correspond to a cost for the Licensee and to revenues for the Licensor so they do not affect the combined profit).

1.3.2.2 Computation of the Allocation of Combined Profits Between the Licensor and the Licensee

The computation of profits allocated to the Licensor and the Licensee follows three steps:

(1) Step A: Computation of the combined profits (*see* Section a).
(2) Step B: Computation of operating profits made by the Licensor. These profits equal the royalties received for the Licensee (costs are assumed to be null).
(3) Step C: Computation of operating profits made by the Licensee. These profits are computed as the difference between the combined profits computed in Step A and the profit made by the Licensor computed in Step B.

For each selected agreement, the identification of the operating profits made by the Licensor and the Licensee allows the computation of the profit split between the third-party Licensor and Luxury Distrib Co (the Licensee) for the license.

1.3.3 Results

The results of the analysis determining the split of the combined profits between the Licensor and the Licensee for multiple years for each selected comparable agreement are presented below:

	Multi-Year Average (in Thousands of Euros)	*Contract 1*	*Contract 2*	*Contract 3*	*Contract 4*	*Contract 5*
(A)	Licensee's Revenues*	XXX	XXX	XXX	XXX	XXX
(B)	Licensee's costs (including royalties)	XXX	XXX	XXX	XXX	XXX
(C) = (A)-(B)	**Profit (before royalty)**	XXX	XXX	XXX	XXX	XXX
(D)	Licensor's Revenues (Royalty)	XXX	XXX	XXX	XXX	XXX
(E) = (D)	**Licensor's Profit**	XXX	XXX	XXX	XXX	XXX
(F) = (C)-(D)	**Licensee's Profit**	XXX	XXX	XXX	XXX	XXX
(G) = (E)/[(E) + (F)]	*% Licensor's Profit*	*V1%*	*W1%*	*X1%*	*Y1%*	*Z1%*
(H) = (F)/[(E) + (F)]	*% Licensee's Profit*	*V2%*	*W2%*	*X2%*	*Y2%*	*Z2%*

* The Licensee's revenues correspond to the sales generated in the context of the license.

The interquartile range of the share of profits for multiple years earned by the third-party Licensor for the selected comparable agreements is presented in the table below:

IQR (Multiple Year) 5 Observations
Minimum
1st quartile
Median
3rd quartile
Maximum

The intra-group share of profits between the Licensor (Luxury Distrib Co Entity A) and the Licensee (Luxury Distrib Co Entity B) can be benchmarked according to the average share of profits observed in comparable transactions.

The computation of the share of profits between Luxury Distrib Co Entity A and Luxury Distrib Co Entity B is made in the same way as the computation of the profit shares between Luxury Distrib Co and third-party Licensors that is described in section 1.3.2:

Multi-Year Average (in Thousands of Euros)		*Luxury Distrib Co*
(A)	Licensee's Revenues*	XXX
(B)	Licensee's costs (excluding royalties)	XXX
(C) = (A)-(B)	**Profit (before royalty)**	XXX
(D)	Licensor's Revenues (Royalty)	XXX
(E) = (D)	**Licensor's Profit**	XXX
(F) = (C)-(E)	**Licensee's Profit**	XXX
(G) = (E)/[(E) + (F)]	*% Licensor's Profit*	Entity A %
(H) = (F)/[(E) + (F)]	*% Licensee's Profit*	Entity B %

* The Licensee's revenues correspond to the sales generated in the context of the license.

The Luxury Distrib Co's split resulting from the application of an intra-group license agreement can then be compared with the interquartile range of profit shares observed in uncontrolled transaction.

Case Study #1 illustrates that comparable data can be used conveniently in the context of the PSM to determine the likely outcome of an arm's length negotiation within an intra-group context. In a number of cases, information with respect to the respective profitability of the parties to a transaction in which the group is involved is not available. For instance, when an MNE licenses IP outside the group, the third party rarely provides information of the profits that it makes in relation to the licensed IP.

Still, it is good practice to try to leverage as much as possible from the external contracts that the MNE has with third parties as it sheds light on 'real life' arm's length equilibrium. In practice, this third-party evidence necessitates analyses to confirm their relevance and, in some circumstances, the application of economic adjustments.

2 CASE STUDY #2: DETERMINATION OF PRICES OF PRODUCTS AND SERVICES, USING THE RESIDUAL PSM

2.1 Background

An MNE ("Project Co") is an engineering and equipment manufacturing company operating in project management in an industrial sector. More specifically, it designs, manufactures, and installs equipment in manufacturing plants. The MNE responds to tenders, and, if selected, designs, engineers, manufactures, and installs the equipment. Know-how is needed at each stage of the process from the design to the installation, and the MNE is recognized for the high-end quality of its equipment. Not only the MNE needs to ensure the best quality products, but it also needs to manage the various risks involved in project management: resource allocation, optimal costing and pricing, management of deviation from tender specifications, and/or coordination of the various teams leading to delays and penalties. In addition to these contractual risks, the Company faces reputational risks in a small niche market in the case of lower end-product quality or poor management of the contract.

Within Project Co, a "project manager" is responsible for internal project management (coordination of the various functions within the Company), and a "client owner" is responsible for the client relationship. Both are appointed at the inception of the tender process. They manage the process, internally (project manager) and externally (client manager), and coordinate the inputs from the various parts of the Company. All teams (Design, Engineering, Manufacturing, and Assembly) provide their input with respect to the equipment (end-product) and an estimation of the cost and time they will require to execute the project based on each team's standard rates (set every year on a budget basis and accounting for a certain level of under-utilization). A company's process and proprietary tools are used to combine the inputs of the various parts of the Company. The project manager consolidates the inputs and submits the proposal which is then defended by the whole team.

Within Project Co, the various functions such as Design, Engineering, Manufacturing, and Installation are split in the various legal entities. Below is an example of a project ("Project ABC") where two group entities, Affiliate A and Affiliate B, are involved and make functional contributions:

Project ABC involves the following costs, as presented in the table below:

Project Co costs	*Project Co's Functions Involved*
1	Design/Engineering
7	Production
1	Installation
1	Project Management
10	**Total**

With 10 million ("M") of costs, Project Co has won the contract with a price to the client of 14 million, i.e., a mark-up of 40% = 4 million.

Project ABC P&L	
Project Costs	**10**
Project Profit	**4**
Project Price	**14**

Affiliate A is involved in the design and engineering and hosts the project management team (project manager and client owner).

Affiliate B is involved in the production and installation as well as books sales to the client.

Both Affiliates A and B have been key contributors to the tender process. They have provided their respective inputs both in terms of costs and time and have worked jointly to define the best solution for the client, also taking into account the minimum gross margin that Project Co, as a company, has set as a target for accepting a new project.

The project costs are borne by Affiliate A and Affiliate B respectively:

Affiliate A Costs	*Affiliate B Costs*	*Total Costs (A and B)*	*Function*
1		1	Design/Engineering
	7	7	Production
	1	1	Installation
1		1	Project Management
2	**8**	**10**	**Total**

Project Co applies a Profit Split Method for setting and adjusting the intra-group price of services from Affiliate A to Affiliate B in which the two affiliates share anticipated and actual profits of the project.

The Company applies the PSM initially for operational reasons:

(a) Within the Project Co Group, each subsidiary is treated as a profit center, and the entity's performance is reviewed after application of the intra-group pricing among group entities.

(b) Both Affiliates A and B:

- have contributed to the tender process and securing the project for Project Co and, therefore, should get a portion of the total project profits;
- have developed unique know-how in relation to their respective functions and activities (design/engineering and project management for Affiliate A, production/installation for Affiliate B) in a niche sector; this know-how as well as the as the ability of the Project Manager supported by appropriate tools to merge all of the inputs and of the client owner to negotiate the conclusion of the contract have been instrumental in the retention of Project Co;
- should be incentivized to produce the quantity/quality offered to the client within the proposed time in order to avoid cost deviations on the side of Project Co as well as possible additional contractual costs (such as penalties for delays, penalties for defaults in the conception/ execution);
- should be held jointly responsible for deviations/issues which cannot be specifically attributed to one entity. In the sector that Project Co is in, the execution of projects entails a significant number of risks, some of them relating to errors that do not exclusively tie to only one function. Responsibilities are often widespread: for instance, delays in the installation may be due to some product features related to either the assembly/production of the products or to a misconception possibly due to the original design phase; extra hours spent on the project by the design team might be related to poor communication by the client owner or project managers not having communicated all of the requirements made by the client; production may appear to be more costly than expected due to a design of the products different from expected; and, finally, a number of external events such as delays from suppliers to Project Co or the quality of the goods that are supplied being different from that required in the project specifications may negatively impact the project.With the sharing of responsibilities within the company, coordination and communication between (intra-group) parties are improved: this is particularly important in a sector where projects tend to be late and appear to cost more than anticipated as well as when contracts are generally complex and litigious. For this company, the sharing of anticipated and actual project results allow operating more optimally:

During the tender phase, affiliates are incentivized to work jointly in an optimal manner (notably, from a timing and cost perspective). As affiliates share the anticipated and actual profits, they have no incentives to show higher costs than needed as they face the risks of not being (price) competitive vis-à-vis the client and of suffering from large cost deviations when the project is executed.

During the execution phase of the project, affiliates are incentivized to work together to identify optimal solutions to problems that are faced during the project. For instance, if the client asks for further/new specifications (without an addition to the budget), the design and production teams are incentivized to work together on the optimal solutions to answer the client's request with minimal additional internal resources.

This sharing of anticipated and actual profits comes with internal rules on the allocation of risks and deviations to an individual entity in case the responsibility can clearly be traced to a specific entity. For instance, only the production unit will be made responsible (financially) if it is less efficient than anticipated due to specific issues relating to productivity of the plant that cannot be related to the design or engineering specifications of the product. The resulting "loss" will then be carved out from the profits to be shared.

It is recognized that the PSM should apply in cases when related parties share the assumption of the same economically significant risks or separately assume closely related economically significant risks.[9] A detailed discussion on the conditions of the application of the PSM is available in a prior publication.[10] As previously indicated, the selection of the method requires careful consideration and should be based on specific facts and circumstances. For the purpose of illustrating the case study, the RPSM has been selected here as the primary method for price setting. Other transfer pricing methods may be more reliable than the PSM under different circumstances despite the transactions taking place in the same industry.

The PSM applied by the Company is a Residual Profit Split Method (RPSM):[11]

(a) Some of the activities performed by Project Co' s members are benchmarkable; and players in the market may perform some or all of the activities provided by Project Co's members. For instance, independent design houses exist, and they could take on some of the design work that Affiliate A is performing. It is the same for the manufacturing activity; some independent assembly companies can be found in the market. The main difference, though, is the ability of Project Co's members to work jointly in responding to tenders and in executing projects successfully. Smaller independent design houses or assembly companies may provide some references for the prices or margins that Project Co could obtain for the performance of specific

9. OECD Revised Guidance (June 2018), para. 2.121.
10. Sébastien Gonnet, "Recent Developments on the Profit Split Method," in *Transfer Pricing Developments Around the World 2017*, edited by Michael Lang, Alfred Storck & Raffaele Petruzzi.
11. The contribution is also an available method (which tends to have the same "dynamic" than the RPSM): the method is viable to the extent that the contribution split can be reliably determined.

tasks but not for the remuneration of the contribution of the function. These external references, though, can provide an indication for the benchmarkable part of the RPSM.

(b) The split of the residual profits (or losses) needs to be done in light of the economic contribution of the various functions and the extent to which they can be held responsible for risks during the contract execution. The more expertise a function entails, the more risks it faces, and the higher share of residual it should get.

The following section provides the theoretical foundation and guidance that is available (both from the OECD and other sources) for the application of such a method.

2.2 PSM "Theory" Relevant to the Case

The Residual PSM is described in the revised Guidelines:

> A residual analysis divides the relevant profits from the controlled transactions under examination into two categories. In the first category are profits attributable to contributions which can be reliably benchmarked: typically less complex contributions for which reliable comparables can be found. Ordinarily this initial remuneration would be determined by applying one of the traditional transaction methods or a transactional net margin method to identify the remuneration of comparable transactions between independent enterprises. [...] Typically, the allocation of the residual profit among the parties will be based on the relative value of the second category of contributions of the parties in the same way as in the application of the contribution analysis outlined above [...]. (paragraph 2.152)

In the revised Guidelines, the OECD provides more elaborations on the determination of the profits to be split (C.4, paragraphs 2.154 et seq.) and on profit split factors (C.5; paragraphs 2.166 et seq.).

The UN Manual provides the following description of the RPSM:

> B.3.3.14.4. Under the residual analysis the combined profits from the controlled transactions are allocated between the associated enterprises based on a two-step approach:
>
> > Step 1: allocation of sufficient profit to each enterprise to provide basic arm's length compensation for routine contributions. This basic compensation does not include a return for possible valuable intangible assets owned by the associated enterprises. The basic compensation is determined based on the returns earned by comparable independent enterprises for comparable transactions or, more frequently, functions. In practice TNMM is used to determine the appropriate return in Step 1 of the residual analysis; and
> >
> > Step 2: allocation of residual profit (i.e. profit remaining after Step 1) between the associated enterprises based on the facts and circumstances. If the residual profit is attributable to intangible property then the allocation of this profit should be based on the relative value of each enterprise's contributions of intangible property.

The U.S. Regulations also provide references to the RPSM (U.S. Treasury Regs. 1.482-6(c)(3)).

The application of the RPSM has been formalized in economic literature, notably by transfer pricing economists. Harlow Higinbotham, in the article, *The Profit Split Method: Effective Application for Precision and Administrability*,[12] provides a general review of the PSM that is consistent with the IRS regulations and the OECD Guidelines. It defines the general economic conditions under which the profit split may be an appropriate method and presents an overview of three profit split methods (Overall PSM, Residual PSM, and Comparable PSM). The article focuses on the computational aspects of the application of the RPSM and describes two particular techniques to value non-routine intangibles: (i) the DCF approach; and (ii) the Economic Operating Profit approach. Other transfer pricing economists have commented on the use and application of the RPSM.

Outside of the Transfer Pricing field, the closest financial valuation method to the RPSM is the Excess Operating Profits method which is used in Intellectual Property Valuation. It consists of capitalizing the additional profits generated by the company owning the property over and above those generated by similar businesses that do not benefit from the IP. These excess profits may be computed in various ways (e.g., comparing the ROCE earned by the business owning the property with other companies' ROCE). The computed excess operating profits expected to be earned over the life of the intangible asset are then discounted to the present day.

Apart from the above guidance, the application of the RPSM is not detailed which necessitate MNEs and tax administrations to make decisions with respect to key criteria of the application of the method, including those below:

(1) **The determination of the profits to be split**: the RPSM starts with the joint profits that two (or more) parties realize together; in the case at hand, Affiliates A and B. The application of the method necessitates making choices with respect to what profits should constitute the starting point of the analysis:

(a) **Segmented profits**: the RPSM applies on a transaction basis and, therefore, the application of the method necessitates the delineation of a transaction and the revenues and costs related to such a transaction. In the case at hand, this involves preparation of the segmented P&L of Project ABC including all of the revenues and expenses related to the project as well as other provisions/liability that can negatively impact the segmented P&L. Management P&Ls are generally available in project companies to track the performance of individual projects, but these management P&L do not necessarily:

– include all costs related to the project (for instance, overhead costs or costs not allocated, for instance, HQ costs); and

12. Tax Management Transfer Pricing Special Report, Vol. 5, no. 11, Report No. 24, October 2, 1996.

- account for items at their arm's length value (for instance, if the project benefits from access to technology, arm's length intra-group royalties may not be accounted for in the Project P&L).

(b) Additional challenges of the application of the RPSM include the decision on whether to use **gross or net profits** (i.e., profits before or after the investments in creating the intangibles) as well as using anticipated (budget) profits or actual profits.

(2) **The determination of benchmarkable returns**

(a) Contrary to the Contribution Analysis, the RPSM involves the identification of **benchmarkable returns**, thus the question of the determination of such profits. In the view of the author, not only the TNMM can be used to set the remuneration of benchmarkable functions within the RPSM. Other methods are also available as well to do so. In the view of the author, as an illustration, the CUP Method can be used to determine prices of transactions considered as benchmarkable if comparable uncontrolled transactions can be identified.

(b) The account for **synergies and economies of scale** under a typical RPSM model: generally, the method implies that the residual profits remunerate only the intangible(s). In case synergies and economies of scale are present, a fact-based analysis is necessary to establish how these synergies/economies of scale should be accounted for.

(c) **The Split factor** is generally the major source of challenges and difficulties in the RPSM. The split factor should rely on solid economic analysis. The OECD has recently expressed a strong preference in the latest draft for "asset-based and cost-based factors." This raises a number of interesting questions:

- To what extent does the asset/cost-based split factors allow for an allocation of profits that third parties would arrive at under arm's length conditions?
- Can alternative approaches allow achieving this arm's length allocation in certain circumstances more reliably than cost-based approaches?

In this respect, the OECD does not prohibit the use of split factors different from assets or costs. On the contrary, the reference to the contributions to value creation is clearly made by the OECD:

> Arm's length parties can be assumed to split profits on the basis of their relative contributions to the creation of those profits. The division of the relevant profits under the transactional profit split method is generally achieved using one or more profit splitting factors. The determination of appropriate profit splitting factor(s) should, therefore, reflect the key contributions to value in relation to the transaction. (paragraph 2.169)

In practice, the evaluation of the respective contribution to value creation requires a broad understanding of:

- the industry in which the company operates, notably, the critical success factors of companies in the sector and the major risks to which the companies are exposed;
- how a specific company creates value within the sector, notably, its value drivers;
- the company's internal organization and how functions, risks, and assets link with each individual value driver;
- the identification of the responsibilities of individual parties and entities;
- the assessment of the relative bargaining position of individual entities in regard to the contributions to value creation and risks that are carried.

The above process is a Value Chain Analysis (VCA) process that is described in former publications of the same author.[13] The VCA process is essential as it provides the economically sound understanding that is needed to map the bargaining power of the parties in a transaction and to subsequently form a view of the split factor:

- Critical success factors (CSFs) and risks vary by sector and, even for firms within the same sector, the emphasis on certain CSFs and risks may vary drastically.
- Value drivers are not homogeneous across industries and, even if certain industries may display relatively close value chains, the relative weight of each individual value driver may vary.
- Some industries are very (tangible) asset-intensive while others rely significantly more on intangibles, including intellectual property (as emphasized by the OECD report on the Digital Economy[14]). In some industries, marketing intangibles play a greater role than technical intangibles while, in others, technical intangibles are predominant and feed the (value of) marketing intangibles.
- One can also observe variations among companies in terms of where the control over major decisions underlying each value driver is exercised. Some companies have a highly centralized process for decision making while others have a high degree of decentralization.
- It is also worth noting that the history of the company and the various legal entities matters significantly in the VCA: value creation cannot be evaluated on a contemporaneous basis and needs a historical perspective, notably when long-lived intangibles are involved. This is what the author has referred to when commenting on the OECD new risk framework:[15]

13. Sébastien Gonnet, "Risks Redefined in Transfer Pricing Post-BEPS," in *Transfer Pricing in a Post-BEPS World*, edited by Michael Lang, Alfred Storck & Raffaele Petruzzi, pp. 43 et seq.; and Sébastien Gonnet, "Recent Developments on the Profit Split Method," in *Transfer Pricing Developments Around the World 2017*, edited by Michael Lang, Alfred Storck & Raffaele Petruzzi, pp. 155 et seq.
14. OECD/G20 BEPS Project. Tax Challenges Arising from Digitalisation—Interim report 2018.
15. Sébastien Gonnet, "Risks Redefined in Transfer Pricing Post-BEPS," in *Transfer Pricing in a Post-BEPS World*, edited by Michael Lang, Alfred Storck & Raffaele Petruzzi, pp. 43 et seq.

> The new OECD risk framework indeed appears to focus on only people and control on a contemporaneous basis while the arm's length principle refers to commercial and financial relationships between entities within a group. In order to design an arm's length transfer pricing system, it is necessary to map the relative position of group entities involved in the process of jointly creating value by taking into account functions (with people as a key element) as well as risks and assets. Such an analysis cannot be focused exclusively on people and made on only a contemporaneous basis:
> - History of an entity matters (for instance, its history in terms of cost assumption, assumption of capital expenditures investments, start-up losses).
> - Legal rights of an entity should also be taken into account.
> - Intangibles should not be disregarded. They generally result from a long process that an MNE has been establishing for years or even decades and have a long lifetime.

The above, in the view of the author, pertains to the bargaining power of the respective parties to a transaction. It does not provide the split factor, per se, but provides a qualitative assessment.

The quantification itself should, as reiterated by the OECD, be grounded in the VCA discussed above and should leverage from available external and internal information that can help to quantify the contribution of the transacting parties to value creation.

Before commenting on the methods that are available to split profits, it is worth reiterating that, in the application of the RPSM, what needs to be split is the residual and not the total profits. In the RPSM, all of the benchmarkable profits are remunerated in the first step of the analysis: what remains is what the parties achieve jointly in addition to the sum of the benchmarkable profits; it is the synergistic, the above market value, that the company generates which is, by definition, difficult to delineate, to qualify, and to apportion among the contributing group entities.

The benefit of using cost-based approaches as a basis for the split factor is that it objectivizes the split factor by referring to the underlying investments made by each party that is entitled to a share of residual profits.

Yearly accounting expenses that are incurred by parties identified with the value drivers that give rise to the residual profit will rarely provide an estimation of an arm's length split; however, the review of the costs respectively incurred by the transacting parties over a longer (relevant) period of time and the computation of the economic capital formed by these investments for each party provide information that is more relevant. When the split factor is based on the respective economic capital of each transacting party, it provides an equalization of the return of each transacting party relative to its weighted (by significance/importance) investments. When expenses for intangible-creating activities are capitalized and amortized over the useful lives of the respective intangibles, this cost method allows for reliably accounting for contributions of the value drivers that may have different useful lives (e.g., R&D and marketing).

Economic literature[16] provides elaborations on the relevance of using economic capital in the context of PSM.

In this respect, the OECD revised Guidelines refer to:

- "risk-weighting" (paragraph 2.181);
- the "timing of expenditure" (paragraph 2.182);
- the "relevant period of time from which the elements of determination of the profit splitting factor(s) (e.g., assets, costs, or others) should be taken into account" (paragraph 2.183).

The OECD, therefore, acknowledges the need to adjust yearly investments in the context of the determination of the split factor. Economic literature that covers the economics of transfer pricing provides a good complement to the OECD concepts.

If the costs/investments do not constitute good proxies, alternative measures can be used:

(1) The OECD refers to other profit splitting factors, such as "incremental sales, or employee compensation (relating to the individuals involved in the key functions that generate value to the transaction, for example in relation to the global trading of financial instruments). In other situations it is possible that headcount or time spent by a certain group of similarly skilled employees with similar responsibilities could be used if there is a strong and relatively consistent correlation between this and the creation of value represented by the relevant profits." (paragraph 2.172)

(2) Economic literature had also introduced:

   (a) The bargaining theory approach: "Bargaining theory can be a powerful tool for assessing the contribution of the entities, as it allows evaluating the role and so the contribution, of each actor collaborating and creating a gain or an added value."[17]

   (b) The survey approach. "Survey approaches can be applied in certain circumstances, where it is not possible to identify external or internal data, to be used as the basis for the contribution analyses. One of the main advantages of applying a survey approach is to avoid (or substantiate) rule-of-thumb approaches for assessing the respective contributions of the parties. The survey approach identifies observers both inside and outside the company who can provide expert opinions regarding the assumptions for the split. With this approach, the reliability of valuing intellectual property can be increased. A representative (i.e. statistically significant) panel of industry experts provide information for the assessment of valuation assumptions. In general, personal interviews provide the most reliable results. The main challenge lies in identifying internal

16. Harlow Higinbotham (2006), "Profit Split Method", Chapter 10, in *Practical Guide to U.S. Transfer Pricing*, William H. Byrnes (principal author), Release no. 8 (December 2014).

17. Sébastien Gonnet and Pim Fris, "Contribution Analyses Under the Profit Split Method," in *International Tax Review's Intellectual Property*, 6th edition (December 2007).

and external experts (although not necessarily used in the same context) and compiling relevant questions. Statistical tools are applied to convert the aggregated expertise into quantitative measures that can be used for numerical valuation."[18] "The survey approaches also necessitate excellent documentation of the options retained, the survey design, and the survey answers."[19]

(c) The **Management of deviations** and the need for adjusting the allocation of profits between group members based on the actual profits.
This is an important area of application of the PSM: to which extent the application of the PSM necessarily involves yearly adjustments to ensure that the "actual" split of profits between the parties equate the anticipated one. If the application of the PSM on an ex-ante basis provides that the arm's length split of the residual profit is 50/50, it is likely that the residual profit split will not be achieved based on actual figures in light of deviations between budget and actual financials. This may not necessarily be an issue in a number of circumstances if:
   - it can be shown that, in similar circumstances, parties would not have renegotiated the terms of their contract, and/or
   - the reasons for deviations relate to responsibilities of only one party which then would not be shared at arm's length, and/or
   - if the actual profit sharing lies within a reasonable range of the anticipated split of margins. It is common that the application of the PSM leads to an arm's length range of outcomes in terms of split as opposed to only one number.

Still, one can also argue that the very essence of the application of a PSM is a sharing of profits like in a joint venture where parties are not sharing anticipated results but rather actual results from their cooperation—positive and negative. It is, therefore, common to set parameters of products, services, and intangibles based on the application of a PSM on an anticipated basis and to then adjust these pricing parameters on a yearly basis in order to obtain an actual basis and the desired outcome in terms of profit sharing. The use of the PSM in the case of pricing IP licensing contracts is specific and is discussed, like the difference between the application of a PSM on an anticipated or actual basis, in a prior publication.[20]

18. Alexander Voegele, Wolf Witt & Stuart Harshbarger, *"IP Valuation Puts New Theories into Practice". International Tax Review*, 10th Edition (December 1, 2006).
19. Sébastien Gonnet & Pim Fris, "Contribution Analyses under the Profit Split Method," *International Tax Review's Intellectual Property*, International Tax Review, 6th edition (December 1, 2007).
20. Sébastien Gonnet, "Recent Developments on the Profit Split Method," in *Transfer Pricing Developments Around the World 2017*, edited by Michael Lang, Alfred Storck & Raffaele Petruzzi, pp. 160 et seq.

2.3 Application of the PSM to the Case at Hand

The application of the PSM to the case at hand for the Project Company involves the following steps.

The first step consists of determining the expected joint profits of Affiliates A and B in relationship to Project ABC. Figure 7.1 shows this joint profit. The application of the PSM aims at determining transfer prices to be charged by A to B in relation to design and project management services. As a reminder to the facts of the case, Affiliate A in the project provides design and project management services while Affiliate B performs manufacturing and installation.

Figure 7.1 Identification of Profit Split

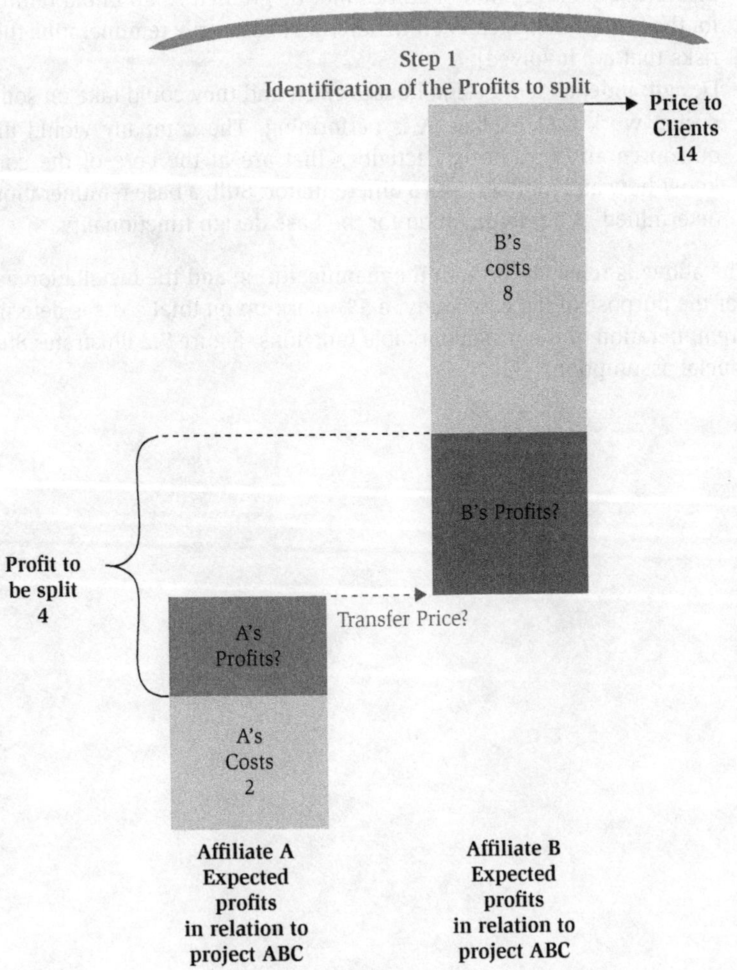

The second step consists of determining the expected remuneration for the benchmarkable functions by benchmarking them with functionally comparable and independent companies. In the case at hand, all of the functions in the value chain can be benchmarked:

- Project Management: consulting companies may provide similar services, and the return earned by such companies may provide a base for the functional remuneration of the teams involved. In practice, this activity is likely to not be outsourced by the company as it is at the heart of the success of the project (both internal organization and client communication). In addition, it can be tied to / held responsible for a number of risks that may significantly positively impact the project financials and potentially the company's reputation (or provide an uplift if they do not materialize). Still, in the view of the author, the fact that the company would not outsource this function does not necessarily mean that a base remuneration cannot be granted as an initial remuneration for the project management function (not necessarily remunerating the related risks that are involved).
- Design: independent design houses exist, and they could take on some of the design work that Affiliate A is performing. The company would likely not outsource all of its design activities that are at the core of the company's know-how and may serve as a differentiator. Still, a base remuneration can be determined as a remuneration for the base design functionality.

The above is relevant for both the manufacturing and the installation activities.

For the purpose of the case study, a 5% mark-up on total costs is determined as a base remuneration of the benchmarkable functions. Figure 7.2 illustrates Step 2 and the financial assumption.

Figure 7.2 Determination of "Benchmarkable" Profits

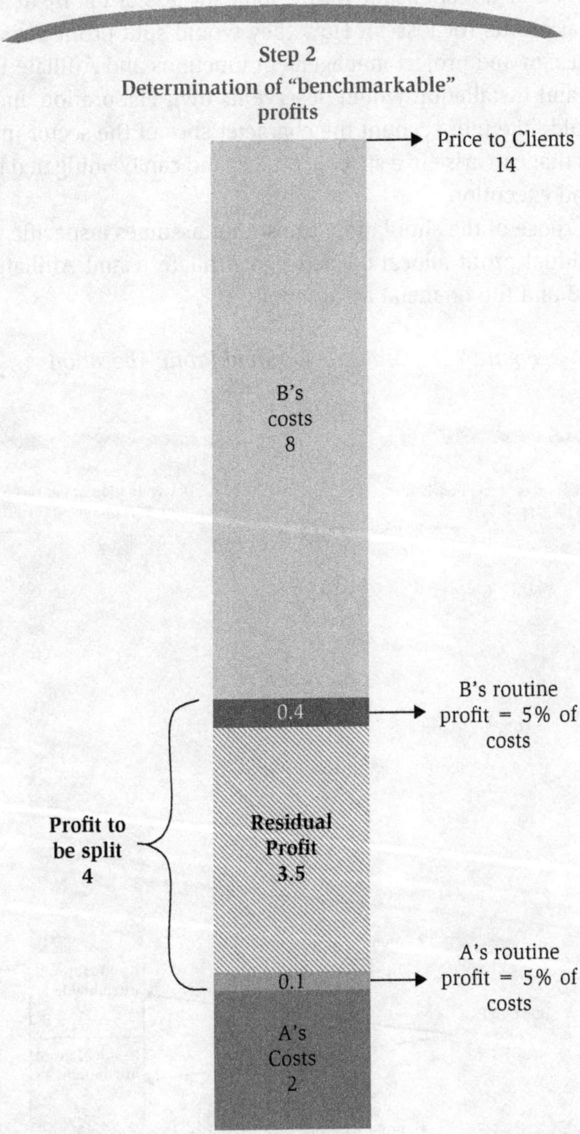

The third step would consist of determining the transfer price on the basis of an arm's length expected split of profits. The residual profit (or loss) is allocated between the related parties based on an arm's length split factor.

The determination of the split factor is very fact-specific, and the above sections provide an overview of the various options that allow estimating the contribution to value creation of the transacting parties that are entitled to residual profits. In the case at hand, it has been identified that the assumption of risks is such that all of the functions can be held responsible for the major risks that are involved and, therefore, that they should be held responsible for the joint success or failure at arm's length, in terms of residual profits (or losses). How they would split profit between Affiliate A that performs design and project management functions and Affiliate B that performs manufacturing and installation would deserve its own elaboration and analysis. The split factor should take into account the characteristics of the sector involving a large number of risks that can arise in a specific project and can be mitigated by good project management and execution.

For the purpose of the simulation, the author assumes a specific split factor that equates the residual profit allocation between Affiliate A and Affiliate B. Figure 7.3 illustrates Step 3 and the financial assumption.

Figure 7.3 Equating Residual Profit Allocation

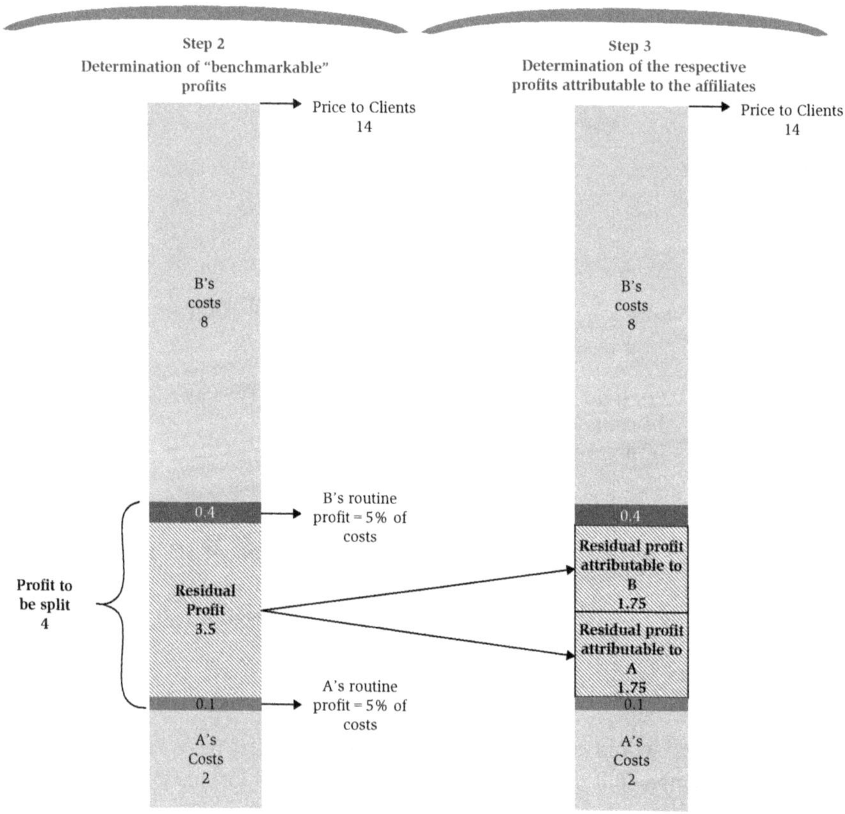

The above process allows the determination of the transfer price between Affiliate A and Affiliate B:

- Services for design/engineering and project management related to Project ABC will be charged by Affiliate A to Affiliate B at 3.85.
- Total services charged to the client by Affiliate B are charged at 14.
- This implies that the arm's length 'value' of production and installation services of Affiliate B is 10.15.

Figure 7.4 Resulting Transfer Price

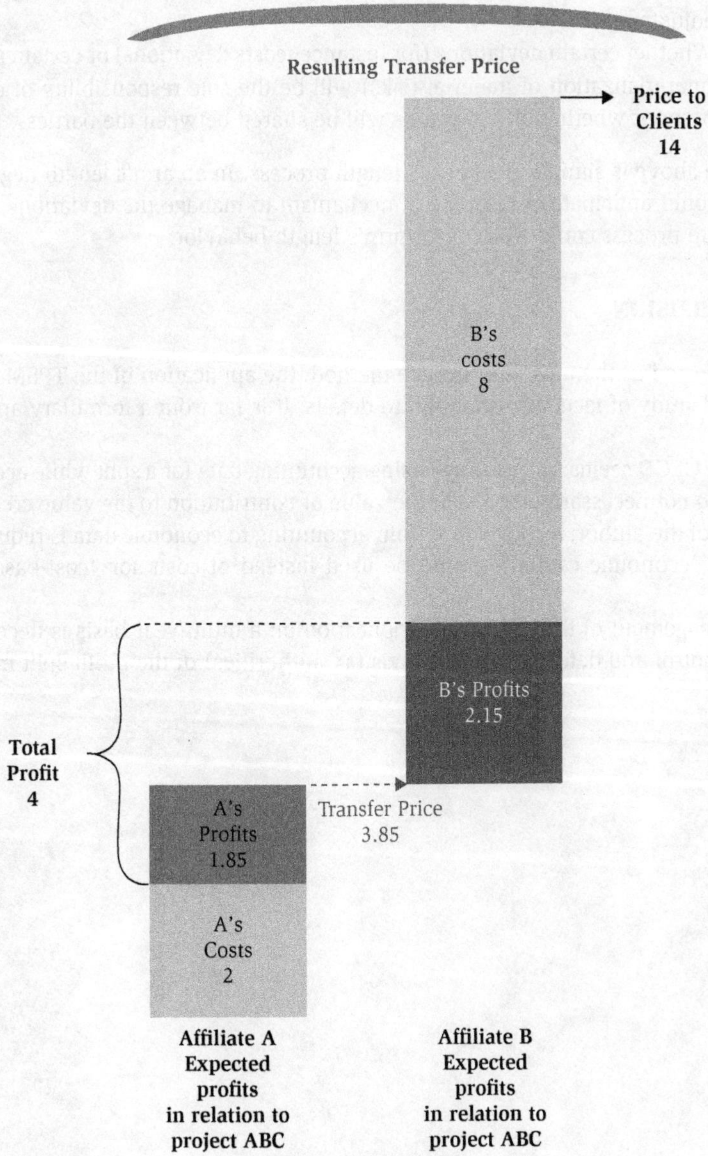

Based on the results of the above step illustrated in Figure 7.4, contracts can be formalized between Affiliate A and Affiliate B including the determination of the above pricing method or price (3.85 in the above example). It is recommended that these contracts that formalize the financial and commercial relationships between Affiliate A and Affiliate B provide an elaboration on the management of deviations. Such a contract should shed light on:

- Whether the prices are fixed prices or if they will be adjusted.
- In case of adjustment, what will be the parameters for the determination of the adjustments.
- Whether certain deviations (for instance, costs deviations) or certain penalties (materialization of material risks) will be the sole responsibility of only one party or whether all deviations will be shared between the parties.

The above is similar to an arm's length process. In an arm's length negotiation, parties would anticipate developing a mechanism to manage the deviations, and the intra-group process could well mirror arm's length behavior.

3 CONCLUSION

When selected as the most appropriate method, the application of the TPSM requires a detailed study of facts and attention to details. It is far from a formulary apportionment.

The OECD seems to encourage using accounting data for a split while accounting metrics do not necessarily represent the value or contribution to the value creation. In the view of the author, a conversion from accounting to economic data is required, for instance, "economic capital" should be used instead of costs for "cost-based" split factors.

Management of the profit split application on a multi-year basis is necessary to ensure control and defensibility (vis-à-vis tax authorities) of the profit split model.

Index